THE HORSE IN
MAGIC AND MYTH

Frontispiece.

Per Aspera ad Astra.

THE HORSE IN MAGIC AND MYTH

M. Oldfield Howey

DOVER PUBLICATIONS, INC.
Mineola, New York

Bibliographical Note

This Dover edition, first published in 2002, is an unabridged reprint of the edition originally published by William Rider & Son, Ltd., London, in 1923.

Library of Congress Cataloging-in-Publication Data

Howey, M. Oldfield.
    The horse in magic and myth / M. Oldfield Howey.
        p. cm.
    Originally published: London : W. Rider, 1923.
    Includes bibliographical references and index.
    ISBN 0-486-42117-1 (pbk.)
        1. Horses—Folklore. 2. Horses—Mythology. I. Title.

GR715 .H6 2002
398'.36996655—dc21
[B]

2001047927

Manufactured in the United States of America
Dover Publications, Inc., 31 East 2nd Street, Mineola, N.Y. 11501

INTRODUCTION

TO-DAY a renewal of interest in spiritual matters has replaced the wave of materialism that so nearly engulfed us some years ago. We are bravely searching for the hidden meaning of the phenomena surrounding us, and are endeavouring to unlock the stores of knowledge which sages of ancient days hid from their own and succeeding generations—but preserved whilst they hid—in a symbolism of which we are discovering the keys.

The author of this work has here brought together the facts about one of the most widely diffused of these sacred and magical symbols—The Horse. This subject has a special appeal to the English people, for as Emerson said, we, as a nation, love horses, and understand them " better than any other people in the world." A perusal of this book will show why the bond of sympathy is so strong.

The information here collected touches little more than the fringe of the subject, but it is hoped that the reader may be sufficiently interested to make further inquiries and new discoveries on his own account.

The author thanks all those who have aided in the compilation of this book, and especially Mr. Ralph Shirley for his kind assistance in revision and other practical help.

CONTENTS

CONTENTS

CONTENTS

ILLUSTRATIONS

M. *Oldfield Howey.*

CHAPTER I

Fairy Horses

INTRODUCTORY

FAMILIAR as we have all been from early childhood with some of the equine marvels which inhabit Fairyland, many people may be surprised to discover what a large amount of tradition is to be found in regard to the existence of such an order of beings. I have endeavoured to collect certain instances that are fairly representative, and it will be seen that a number of these are singularly arresting and dramatic in character.

This visible, physical world in which we live is interpenetrated by more than one unseen world, just as perfect and complete in itself as the material planet, which is the only one most human beings are conscious of. All around us is the great crowd of witnesses, themselves, except upon rare occasions, invisible. The fairy realm in which we are now about to wander in search of fairy steeds is remarkably like our own in many respects. Even the denizens of the ghostly realm, consisting of the earthbound spirits of former mortal creatures, cannot draw quite so close to us, for they are nearly always living over and over some regrettable event of their past life, or are obsessed by some one dominant desire which allows them to think only of the means by which they hope to fulfil it ; but the fairies, if tradition is to be credited, eat and drink, and marry, and have children and homes and horses and cattle, and even assume the human form so perfectly for the purpose of associating with man, that mortals talk and trade with them totally unaware of their true nature. The "Good People" are often extremely "horsey" in their tastes and fond of acquiring mortal horses for their purposes, though why, it is hard to say, since fairy horses exist as certainly as fairies. Apparently the supply does not equal the demand, however, and fairies seem to have the power of bestowing some of their own gifts upon the mortal steeds they take over, including that of immortality, or at least of comparative immortality.

The following story concerning a fairy horse and its rider may be found in the *Minstrelsy of the Scottish Border* :

"Osbert, a bold and powerful baron, visited a noble family in the vicinity of Wandlebury, in the bishopric of Ely. Among other stories related in the social circle of his friends, who amused each other by repeating ancient tales and traditions, he was informed that if any knight, unattended, entered an adjacent plain by moonlight, and challenged an adversary to appear, he would be immediately encountered by a spirit in the form of a knight.

"Osbert resolved to make the experiment, and set out attended by a single squire, whom he ordered to remain without the limits of the plain, which was surrounded by an ancient entrenchment.

"On repeating the challenge, he was instantly assailed by an adversary, whom he quickly unhorsed, and seized the reins of his steed. During this operation, his ghostly opponent sprang up, and darting his spear like a javelin at Osbert, wounded him in the thigh. Osbert returned in triumph with the horse, which he committed to the care of his servants. The horse was of a sable colour, as well as his whole accoutrements, and apparently of great beauty and vigour. He remained with his keeper till cock-crowing, when, with eyes flashing fire, he reared, spurned the ground, and vanished.

"On disarming himself, Osbert perceived that he was wounded, and that one of his steel boots was full of blood. . . . As long as he lived the scar of his wound opened afresh on the anniversary of the eve on which he encountered the spirit."

Another story of a similar case is related in the *Hierarchy of Blessed Angels*, but has a tragic ending. A Bohemian knight was travelling on horseback at night accompanied only by a single friend, when they came suddenly upon a fairy host arrayed under displayed banners.

The knight, in spite of all his companion could say to deter him, spurred forward to combat with a champion who came from out the ranks of the fairies apparently in challenge. The knight and his steed were quickly vanquished by their fairy adversaries. The companion fled, but next morning returned to the place, only to find the mangled bodies of the knight and his horse lying on the ground.

It is interesting to note here how fairy customs and fashions keep pace with those of human beings. A completely modern fairy scene might show them using aeroplanes!

The ancient Highland family of Maclean of Lochbury are forewarned of death by the spirit of an ancestor who was slain in battle. Mounted on his steed, he is heard to gallop along a stony bank, and then to ride three times round the family residence, ringing his fairy bridle. Thus he presages the approaching peril. Probably his faithful steed bore him in his last fight and perished beside him on the battlefield, though the fairy bridle which is so expressly mentioned seems to connect his charger with elf-land, and we have therefore decided to include the legend in this category, rather than among the stories of ghostly horses. Perhaps horse and rider were admitted into Fairyland at death.

There are many legends of such admissions even before death. The doorway between the two worlds is not always closed, though those mortals who pass its portals seldom have any wish to return. For them time ceases to exist and life is one long joy. There, at least, existence justifies itself. Yet those who have loved do not entirely forget, and the peril of the loved ones has often proved to be a spell of such potent power that it has recalled mortals even from Fairyland. This would seem to be the case of our Highland rider.

The following story is related by Dr. Grahame :

"A young man, one day roaming through the forest, observed a number of persons all dressed in green, issuing from one of those round eminences which are commonly accounted fairy-hills. Each of them in succession called upon a person by name *to fetch his horse*. A caparisoned steed instantly appeared ; they all mounted and sallied forth into the regions of the air. The young man ventured to pronounce the same name, and called for his horse. The steed immediately appeared ; he mounted and was soon joined to the fairy choir. He remained with them for a year, going about with them to fairs and weddings. On one of these occasions the bridegroom sneezed, and the young man, according to the usual custom, said 'God bless you.' The fairies were angry at the pronunciation of the sacred name, and when he repeated the offence on a third occasion they hurled him down a precipice. He found himself unhurt and restored to mortal society."

Here, indeed, is an instance of the open door to which we have just referred. The story also illustrates the equestrian tastes of the Good People and the power of aerial flight possessed by the fairy steed.

Nearly two centuries ago the mountain known as Southerfel, in Cumberland, was haunted by spectral horses and their riders. Apparently the first human beings to note these uncanny apparitions were a shepherd of the name of John Wren, of Wilton Hill, and his servant, Daniel Stricket. These two were sitting at the door together one summer evening after supper, in 1743, when they saw a man and dog chasing some horses on the steep and slippery sides of Southerfel. Although it would have been most difficult for a horse to keep its footing there at all, these creatures fled at an extraordinary speed, and seemed to disappear at the lower end of the hill. Their wonderment thoroughly aroused, Wren and Stricket went next morning expecting to find the dead body of the venturous man and the cast shoes of the fleeing horses. But not a trace of either man or horse having passed that way could they discover. Fearing to arouse the ridicule of their neighbours, they refrained from telling their story for a long time, but when they did venture to relate it, they were much laughed at, and no one believed them. Nothing further happened until the

23rd of June (the eve of St. John's Day) in the following year. Stricket had changed his master and now served a Mr. Lancaster, of Blake-hills, the next house to Wilton Hill. He was taking an evening stroll a little way above Blakehills about 7.30 when, chancing to look over to Southerfel, he saw a company of mounted men riding along the mountain side in fairly close formation, at a brisk walk. He gazed on the strange sight for some time before he could bring himself to tell anyone else what he saw, fearing further ridicule, but at last, satisfied of the reality of his vision, he asked his master to come out as he had something to show him. Mr. Lancaster came, expecting to see a bonfire, as it was the custom for shepherds to light these on St. John's Eve, but to his amazement saw what we have just described. Finding they both saw alike, the two men called the other members of the household, and all saw the phenomena. The troops of horsemen appeared to come from the lower part of the fell, and first to become visible at a place called Knot. From thence they rode in regular order along the side of the hill in a curving line until they were opposite to Blakehills. Then they disappeared over the mountain. The last but one in every troop galloped to the front, and then walked at the same quick speed as his comrades. The spectators found on comparing notes that one and all saw these changes of relative position alike and at the same time, and not only the witnesses we have followed saw the phenomena, but every person within a mile saw it also. The procession lasted two hours and a half from the time when Stricket first observed it, and then night shut out any further view. Blakehills was half a mile from where the troops were seen. The account in Mr. Lancaster's own words, signed, and declared to be true by himself and Daniel Stricket, is given in Clarke's *Survey of the Lakes* (1789).

Mr. Clarke suggests that the vision might have been prophetic of the rebellion which took place the year after its occurrence.

The date on which it was observed was the 23rd of June, 1744, and it appeared on the side of the mountain between Penrith and Keswick.

To take another parallel case to that we have just recited : Lord Lindsay has described how his friend and companion, Mr. William

Wardlaw Ramsay, when crossing the valley of the Wady Arabia, saw, to his own complete conviction, a party of horses and riders moving along the sandhills, though accurate information obtained after the vision proved that no horseman could have been in the neighbourhood. Lord Lindsay speaks of the experience of his friend as affording an example " of that spiritualised tone the imagination naturally assumes in scenes presenting so little sympathy with the ordinary feelings of humanity," but this does not give us much of a clue. He seems to imply that he thought his friend had imagined the horsemen. He goes on to describe Mr. Ramsay as " a man of remarkably strong sight, and by no means disposed to superstitious credulity," adding that he was never able to divest himself of the impression that he had distinctly seen the horsemen. To the Arabian, no such apology and explaining away of phenomena is necessary. To those who spend their lives in the vast loneliness of the desert such glimpses of the inhabitants of another world are almost commonplace. But they are not regarded lightly, but with awe, as foretelling that death is nigh for the seer. Thus it proved in this case, for a few weeks after the vision Mr. Ramsay died at Damascus.

It is probable that the reason why these strange horsemen are seen by those about to cross over is not that they have any intention of giving a warning of the approach of death, but that those who are nearing the crossing have their spiritual senses sharpened, and get glimpses of the inhabitants of other worlds—the interpenetrating astral regions, which normally are invisible.

Whether the desert horsemen seen by Mr. Ramsay were fairies or not, I cannot say. They may have been the ghosts of men and horses whose lives had been spent in these lonely fastnesses. Or they may have belonged to some celestial order.

Many are the legends that a hero of bygone days has never died, but sleeps along with his warriors and horses in some hidden cave awaiting the call of his country's need to lead them forth to victorious combat on her behalf.

The Moors, for instance, who were left in the Valentia mountains, expected that their hero, Alfatimi, would one day return from his hiding-place in the Sierra de Aguar to avenge their wrongs and destroy their tyrants. The point to be noted here is that he was to be mounted upon a *green* horse when he fulfilled the prophecy. This, being the special colour of the little people, is certainly a clue to its origin, and justifies us in classifying it as a fairy steed (see Malory's *Morte d'Arthur*).

The horse of Vishnu, on the other hand, I have included among the angel horses, as it is obviously of a celestial nature.

Cheshire furnishes the following curious and interesting tradition of the adventures into which the ownership of a white horse drew a local farmer. According to the legend, about the twelfth or thirteenth century a certain farmer who lived at Mobberley had a beautiful white horse which he decided to put up for sale at Macclesfield Fair. On the morning of the fair, therefore, he set off riding his horse. His road led along the heath that skirts Alderley Edge. As he went, he stooped over his steed to arrange its mane to the best advantage. Suddenly he felt the animal start beneath him, and, looking quickly up, he found himself confronted by an exceedingly tall and commanding figure dressed as a monk, which barred his further progress by holding a staff of black wood across his path. The apparition informed him that he was on a fruitless errand, since Destiny had decreed a far nobler mission for his horse. It then proceeded to bid the farmer meet it again with the steed on the same spot that evening when the sun had set. The message given, it disappeared.

The farmer decided to test the truth of the strange monk's words and hurried on to the fair. But his efforts to sell his horse were in vain. He reduced his price to half, but no one could be found to buy, though the beauty of the steed provoked much admiration. At last he resolved that he must brave the worst and meet again the strange monk at the appointed place, so, summoning all his courage, he rode back to the heath. The monk met him there punctually, and commanding the farmer to follow, led the way by the Golden Stone, Stormy Point, to Saddle Bole. When they reached this spot the neighing of horses was heard, the sound apparently proceeding from under their feet, and on the monk waving his black staff the earth opened, and a pair of heavy iron gates were disclosed to view. The farmer's horse was naturally terrified and in his fright plunged and threw his rider, who, scarcely less alarmed, knelt at the feet of his spectral companion and earnestly prayed for mercy. The monk bade him be of good courage and enter the cavern, where he should see what no mortal had ever beheld. Passing the portals, the farmer found he was within a roomy cavern, on each side of which stood horses that in size and colour were the counterparts of his own. Beside them lay soldiers wearing armour of a by-gone period, and in the recesses of the rock were arms and heaps of gold and silver in ancient coin. Taking the price of the horse from one of these piles, the monk gave it to the farmer, and in reply to his question as to the meaning of the strange spectacle replied as follows :

"These are caverned warriors preserved by the good genius of England, until that eventful day when, distracted by intestine broils, England shall be thrice won and lost between sunrise and sunset. Then we, awakening from our sleep, shall rise to turn the fate of Britain. This shall be when George, the son of George, shall reign, when the forests of Delamere shall wave their arms over the slaughtered sons of Albion. Then shall the eagle drink the blood of princes from the headless cross [query *corse*]. Now haste thee home, for it is not in thy time these things shall be. A Cestrian shall speak of it and be believed."

The farmer left his horse with the monk, and the iron gates closed behind him, but though often sought for, the scene of his strange adventure has never been discovered.

The sign of a small inn on Monk's Heath, near Macclesfield, known as "The Iron Gates" commemorates the event, and represents a pair of heavy gates opening at the bidding of a cowled figure, before whom kneels a yeoman, whilst behind is a white horse rearing, and in the distance a view of Alderley Edge.

A very similar legend is related by Sir Walter Scott in his *Letters on Demonology and Witchcraft*. He writes :

"Thomas of Ercildowne, during his retirement, has been supposed from time to time to be levying forces to take the field in some crisis of his country's fate. The story has often been told of a daring horse-jockey having sold a black horse to a man of venerable and antique appearance, who appointed the remarkable hillock upon Eildon hills called the Lucken-hare as the place where, at 12 o'clock at night, he should receive his price. He came, his money was paid in ancient coin, and he was invited by his customer to view his residence. The trader in horses followed his guide in the deepest astonishment through several long ranges of stalls, in each of which a horse stood motionless, while an armed warrior lay equally still at the charger's feet. 'All these men,' said the wizard in a whisper, ' will awaken at the battle of Sheriffmuir.' At the extremity of this extraordinary depot hung a sword and a horn, which the prophet pointed out to the horse-dealer as containing the means of dissolving the spell. The man in confusion took the horn and attempted to wind it. The horses instantly started in their stalls, stamped, and shook their bridles, the men arose and clashed their armour, and the mortal, terrified at the tumult he had excited, dropped the horn from his hand. A voice like that of a giant, louder even than the tumult around, pronounced these words :

> Woe to the coward that ever he was born,
> That did not draw the sword before he blew the horn.

A whirlwind expelled the horse-dealer from the cavern, the entrance to which he could never again find."

There is an Irish leader of whom a similar tale is told. Earl Gerald of Mullaghmast sleeps with his soldiers and horses in a cavern under the castle of Mullaghmast. The Earl reposes seated at the head of a long table which runs down the middle of the cave. On each side of it sit his warriors, completely armed, their heads resting upon the table. Their horses, fully caparisoned, stand behind the soldiers in stalls on either hand. Once every seven years the Earl and his charger awake and ride around the Curragh of Kildare. When the horse was first immured in the cave his silver shoes were half an inch in thickness. When these septennial rides have worn them as thin as a cat's ear, then a miller's son, born with six fingers on each hand, will blow his trumpet. Earl, warriors, and horses will awake and go forth together to battle with the English and drive them from Erin, after which the Earl will reign as king of Ireland for two-score years.

It is said that a horse-dealer once found the cavern open and illuminated on a night when the Earl was taking his septennial ride. He was so amazed at what he saw that he let the bridle he was carrying fall to the ground, and its sound, echoing through the hollow cave, awakened one of the soldiers nearest to him, who raised his head and said, " Is it time yet ? " The intruder was quick enough to answer, " Not yet, but soon will be." The warrior laid his head on the table once more, and all was still, whilst the horse-dealer lost no time in making good his escape.

According to the old *chanson de geste* entitled *Ogier le Danois*, or *Ogier the Dane*, this famous Prince of Denmark was specially favoured by the fairies all his life. Six fairies brought him gifts whilst he was yet in his cradle. Five of these promised him that all earthly joys should be his, and the sixth, Morgana, said that he should never die, but live for ever with her in the mystic land of Avalon. His life was a most adventurous one, and when voyaging towards France after successful military exploits in the East, his ship was wrecked on the famous lodestone rock, and all his companions were lost. Wandering along the shore, he came to a magic castle, invisible by day, but shining brightly at night. Here his host was the fairy horse Papillon, far famed for wisdom and magic powers, and next day whilst walking over a flowery meadow Morgana herself appeared to him. She gave him a magic ring which renewed his lost youth, and he put on the crown of oblivion which blotted out for him the past. And so for two hundred years he lived in Fairyland with King Arthur, Lancelot, Oberon, and Tristan in perpetual enjoyment, until one day his crown fell from his head and his memory of the past returned. His instant wish was to go to France, and his host, the beautiful Papillon, soon bore him thither. There he was able to assist Paris against the Norman invaders. His mission accomplished, Morgana took him back to the Isle of Avalon, where he will remain with the fairy steed and his other friends until his country needs him.

In Serbia, King Marko and his horse, Sharatz, are believed to slumber in a cavern of Mount Urvina. All the while, as they rest, the king's sword is slowly rising from out the mountain's summit, as from a sheath in which it is held. When it is fully visible, Marko will ride forth on Sharatz and deliver his beloved country from her foes. From time to time the king awakens and looks at his sword to see if the time has yet arrived. Sharatz occupies the waiting-hours by munching hay, but his portion is nearly finished, so the time must be close at hand.

But even during this long wait it would appear that Marko and Sharatz occasionally come forth from their quiet retreat to help their country when she is in difficulty. A most remarkable instance of their doing so was given in *The International Psychic Gazette* for May 1913, entitled "How a Fourteenth-century Serbian Prince achieved a Miraculous Victory in the Late War." The writer of the article was at a banquet where General Mishitch related the incident a few days after its occurrence. The Serbian infantry had received orders that they were to wait at the foot of Mount Prilip (near which the castle of Marko still stands) for their artillery—which was much superior to the Turkish—to take effect. They were specially cautioned against storming the fort before they received orders to do so. The infantry kept quiet during the early part of the morning, but when the first cannon shots were fired, those in command noticed an " effervescence " among the troops, and soon after heard them shouting frantically and saw them " running like wolves " straight to the castle of Marko. General Mishitch could hear the voice of the captain commanding them to stop and await the order, and when discipline proved useless, other leaders endeavoured to appeal to their reason, telling the soldiers they were going to certain death by not awaiting the effect of the artillery. In vain! the men rushed straight into the hostile fire and appeared to fall in dozens. The General closed his eyes. His blood froze. It was too horrible! A disastrous defeat, involving certain degradation for himself! The Serbian artillery ceased firing so as not to kill their own comrades, who were now at grips with the Turks. A few minutes later the Serbian colours were fluttering on the donjon of Marko's castle, and the Turks fleeing in wild disorder! The Serbian victory was complete!

When General Mishitch arrived on the scene and called a parade he found his losses were comparatively insignificant. Whilst praising his soldiers' bravery, he bitterly reproved them for their disobedience. But as he concluded, "from thousands of soldiers in majestic unison came this reply : 'Kralyevitch Marko commanded us all the time : FORWARD ! Did you not see him on his Sharatz ? ' "

The General knew his soldiers were as honest as they were brave, and he dismissed them, ordering that each man should have a double portion of food and wine for a week. Every tenth man was also awarded a medal for courage.

Although Marko and Sharatz are semi-historical figures, occupying in Serbian history much the same position as King Arthur does in our own, yet according to some traditions they were both of fairy origin. Marko was said to be the son of a *veela*, or fairy queen, and a *zmay*, or dragon. Sharatz, the wonderful piebald steed, was a gift to Marko from the same veela who endowed him with his extraordinary powers. But according to another legend, Marko bought Sharatz as a foal suffering from leprosy, and by his loving care and attention healed him, then taught him to drink wine, and finally made him the marvellous steed he became. Still another story says that Marko served a master three years for the privilege of choosing a horse from among those who grazed in a certain meadow. His method of deciding his choice points to his fairy origin, for it was to lift each one by the tail and swing it round and round. At last he came to a piebald foal, and seized it also by the tail, but this time his enormous strength was insufficient even to stir it. Needless to say this was the horse of his choice. He named it Sharatz which means "piebald," and for 160 years it was his closest friend and companion. Marko used often to be described as "a dragon mounted on a dragon." The Prince loved his steed more dearly than a brother, and would feed him from his own plate and drinking-cup with the bread and wine that formed his own food. And Sharatz was worthy of all his master's love. He was so swift that he could overtake even the flying *veela*. Sparks of fire flashed from his hoofs, and from his nostrils he breathed forth a blue flame. The very earth cracked beneath his feet, the stones were scattered in all directions. Yet so careful was he of his master that Marko could peacefully sleep whilst traversing the mountains on his back, knowing the faithful steed would keep him safe. On the battlefield, too, Sharatz knew the exact moment when he must kneel down to save his master from the thrust of the enemy's lance, and how to rear so as to strike the foe's charger with his front feet.   He would trample the Turkish soldiers beneath his hoofs and bite off the ears of their horses.   He could bound into the air to the height of three lance-lengths, and forward as far as four lance-lengths.

The Bohemians believe that their hero, the pious King Wenzel, together with a band of chosen knights and their steeds, sleep in lofty caverns of rock-crystal which are hollowed out beneath Mount Blanik in their beloved land.   Legend says that their slumber will continue until their country by her dire need shall summon them to her aid. There are several traditions relating how mortals have entered the fastness and seen the dormant warriors.

According to one of these, a smith who lived in the neighbourhood was engaged in mowing his hayfield, when a stranger arrived and bid him leave his work and follow him.   The smith complied with the request, and his guide led him into the mountain.   There, to his amazement, he saw the sleeping knights, each one seated on a horse, with his head bent forwards and resting on the steed's neck.   The stranger bid him shoe the horses and provided him with the necessary tools, but warned him to be careful not to knock any of the slumbering riders as he worked.   The smith skilfully carried out the task entrusted to him, but as he was shoeing the last horse he accidentally touched the knight, who sprang up and inquired, " Is it time ? "   The guide, with a sign to the smith to be silent, replied, " Not yet," and all was calm again. The shoeing being completed, the old shoes were bestowed on the smith as his reward.   When he reached home he was amazed to find he had been absent a year, and on looking into his bag he found the old horse-shoes were of solid gold.

Another tradition tells how a serving-man was driving two horses over the Blanik when he heard the trampling of steeds and the sound of martial music.   It was the knights of King Wenzel returning from a mimic battle.   The horses he was driving became uncontrollable, and he was obliged to follow them into the mountain, which closed upon him.   When at last he got back to his home, he found that ten years had passed, though he thought he had been away but the same number of days. This curious lapse of time, or loss of the sense of time, which we have noted in this and the preceding case, is a common experience of those who have been among the fairies, if we may trust their narratives. The transmutation into gold of an apparently worthless gift, after the recipient has returned to mortal life, is also very characteristic of fairy methods, and helped to decide the author to include these stories in this chapter.

Grohmann has preserved for us a different version of the legend of Mount Blanik. According to this, the Knight Stoymir is the hero enchained by spell until the appointed day of deliverance. The mountain was the scene of his last battle, in which he and all his band of horsemen perished. After the battle, when the foe had departed, the knight's friends came to search the scene of the struggle, to bury the dead and succour the wounded, but not a trace could they find of the bodies, and they thought the enemy must have carried them off to be ransomed. But when night came, those who lived in the neighbourhood were awakened from sleep by the sound of a moving army, and looking forth, saw the slain warriors exercising their horses, and afterwards taking them to water at the stream, before returning into the mountain.

The herdsman who told the story declared, moreover, that he had entered the mountain and had himself seen the knight and his soldiers in their sleep.

The Valkyries, or Valkyrs—those dazzlingly beautiful maidens of Scandinavian mythology—are mounted on equally beautiful white horses of extraordinary swiftness. Their mission was to choose the slain in battle for transportation to Valhalla, where Odin reigns supreme and the heroes meet together in joyful feasting, Odin's maidens pouring out the mead for them and waiting upon them.

Mr. J. C. Dollman has given us a wonderful idea of the weird horses and their maiden riders rushing across the stormy sky in his painting entitled *The Ride of the Valkyries*, and another beautiful representation of the same subject is *The Chosen Slain*, by K. Dielitz, depicting one of these maidens on her glorious mount rising skyward with the body of a warrior across her saddle-bow. One half of the dead were thus selected by the Valkyries and borne on their fleet steeds over the rainbow bridge, Bifröst, into Valhalla. There they were welcomed by Odin's sons, Hermod and Bragi, and led to the foot of Odin's throne. According to some authorities, the Valkyries are nine in number, but others name from three to sixteen. Their mission was not only to those who died on the battlefields of the land, but also to those who perished in fight on the sea, and they used to ride over the waves and snatch dying Vikings from their sinking ships. Or sometimes they would stand upon the shore and beckon the Vikings to join them. This was an infallible sign that the coming battle would be the last that those who saw them were destined to take part in, and great were the rejoicings of the seers.

Mrs. Hemans has beautifully pictured the scene :

Slowly they moved to the billow side ;
And the forms, as they grew more clear,
Seem'd each on a tall pale steed to ride,
And a shadowy crest to rear,
And to beckon with faint hand
From the dark and rocky strand,
And to point a gleaming spear.

Then a stillness on his spirit fell,
Before th' unearthly train ;
For he knew Valhalla's daughters well,
The choosers of the slain !

(*Valkyriur Song.*)

The steeds of the Valkyries are supposed to be impersonations of the clouds ; and hoarfrost and dew are said to have dropped from their glistening manes as they rushed hither and thither through the air. Because of this important function they were held in very high honour, for to their activity was ascribed the fruitfulness of the earth. Their maiden riders were looked upon as divinities of the air, and were sometimes called Norns or Wish Maidens. They often visited the earth arrayed in swan plumage. They were eternally young and beautiful, and had flowing golden hair and arms of dazzling whiteness. When they visited the battlefields they wore blood-red corselets and helmets of gold or silver.

Matthew Arnold describes their appearance :

> There through some battlefield where men fall fast,
> Their horses, fetlock-deep in blood, they ride,
> And pick the bravest warriors out for death,
> Whom they bring back with them at night to Heaven
> To glad the gods and feast in Odin's hall.

Wagner does not follow the usual tradition that the horses of the Valkyrs were always white, but mentions a grey and a chestnut. " Gladly my grey will graze near thy chestnut," says one of the maiden riders to her sister, in his play of *The Valkyrie*.

BIBLIOGRAPHY

Sagen aus Böhmen gesammelt und herausgegeben, von Dr. Josef Virgil Grohmann. (Prag. 1883.)

Volkssagen aus Pommern und Rügen. Gesammelt und herausgegeben, von Dr. Ulrich Jahn.

Dr. Grahame's Sketches, pp. 255-7. Second edition.

The Hierarchy of Blessed Angels, p. 554.

Letters on Demonology and Witchcraft, by Sir Walter Scott. (1830.)

Hero Tales and Legends of the Serbians, by Woislav M. Petrovitch. (Geo. G. Harrap & Co., London, 1914.)

The Century Dictionary, 1899 edition ; article " Kelpie." (*The Times*, London.)

Myths and Legends of the Middle Ages, by H. A. Guerber. (Geo. G. Harrap & Co., London, 1910.)

Survey of the Lakes, by Clarke. (1789.)

Occult Review, December 1916 : " Phantoms of the Desert."

The Valkyrie, by Richard Wagner, translated by Frederick Jameson. (Schott & Co., London.)

CHAPTER II

Angel Horses

WE will select our first instances of the presence of this order of the spiritual world becoming known to beings on earth from that rich treasure-house of occult lore, the Bible; though, as we shall see, the evidence of the existence of angel horses is not confined to these Scriptures, but is confirmed by similar phenomena in comparatively recent European history and well attested by contemporary historians. In fact, if human evidence is credible, we must admit that angel horses do exist, though in some cases the records may be spurious.

Our first example is to be found in 2 Kings vii, where the deliverance of the Israelites from the Syrian hosts who were camped against them is described as being due to a miraculous sound of horses. "For the Lord had made the host of the Syrians to hear a noise of chariots, and a noise of horses, even the noise of a great host : and they said one to another, Lo, the king of Israel hath hired against us the kings of the Hittites, and the kings of the Egyptians, to come upon us. Wherefore they arose and fled in the twilight, and left their tents, and their horses, and their asses, . . . and fled for their life." In this instance the horses heard by the panic-stricken foe were invisible, and it may therefore be argued that the noise was of an hypnotic or suggested nature, and had no existence otherwise ; or, granted that it did have a concrete existence, that the horses heard may have belonged to the ghostly world, and have been, when in mortal form, the equine friends of the Israelites they still loved and served. We will admit this is an obscure case and pass on to less disputable ground.

The Jewish scriptures and legends afford so many stories of heavenly horses with angel riders taking sides in battle, and by their aid turning the fortunes of the day and winning apparently lost causes, that we feel no surprise when we find Isaiah warning the Israelites (chap. xxxi. 3): "Now the Egyptians are men, and not God; and their horses flesh, and not spirits." It was but natural that the Jews of that age of miracles should consider the all-conquering Egyptian war-horses were probably spiritual steeds, impervious to merely human weapons.

Let us now take some of the instances in which horses of this heavenly breed are said to have been seen upon earth, and even to have taken an active part in human affairs.

Usually these angel horses are white, with golden harness, though sometimes they appear to be of fiery aspect. They give the same services to angels as their mortal counterparts do to men—that is, they draw chariots and bear riders upon their backs.

If we again open the second book of Kings, this time at chapter ii, we find a remarkable narration of heavenly or angelic horses described as being "of fire," drawing a chariot, and descending to earth that they might take God's prophet to the skies at the close of his earthly career. The story is vividly dramatic and told with the simplicity of absolute truth.

"And it came to pass, as they [i.e. Elijah and Elisha] still went on, and talked, that, behold, there appeared a chariot of fire, and horses of fire, and parted them both asunder; and Elijah went up by a whirlwind into heaven. And Elisha saw it, and he cried, My father, my father, the chariot of Israel, and the horsemen thereof. And he saw him no more."

I cannot agree with those commentators who say that Elisha's exclamation referred to Elijah himself, for it was so entirely appropriate to the vision before his eyes that no other explanation is necessary. But to those who accept this view it may be pointed out that as no mention (except the words of Elisha) is made of horsemen or charioteer, they would be justified in further supposing that the angel horses in this instance were acting as the intelligent messengers of Jehovah—a thought that almost reconciles the author to their view. It may further be noted that the same exclamation, word for word, was made by Joash, the King of Israel, when Elisha died. At least we can gather how important a position horses occupied in Jewish esteem at that period. Indeed, their speed and endurance caused them to be regarded as almost supernatural, and early prophets complained that the Hebrews thought more of them than of Jehovah. (See chapters on Sun-horses and Sacred Horses.)

Zechariah records two visions of horses which seem to be guardian angels of the world. These visions strongly resemble each other, and both represent our earth as traversed by multitudes of unseen presences in equine form, directed in one case by an angel in human shape, who reported to the Lord on the state of the sleeping world, and in the other acting on their own initiative.

" The word of the Lord unto Zechariah . . . saying, I saw by night, and behold a man riding upon a red horse, and he stood among the myrtle trees that were in the bottom ; and behind him there were red horses, speckled, and white. Then said I, O my Lord, what are these ? . . . And the man that stood among the myrtle trees answered and said, These are they whom the Lord hath sent to walk to and fro through the earth. And they answered the angel of the Lord that stood among the myrtle trees, and said, We have walked to and fro through the earth, and, behold, all the earth sitteth still, and is at rest " (Zech. i. 7–11).

The second vision runs :

" Behold, there came four chariots out from between two mountains ; and the mountains were mountains of brass. In the first chariot were red horses ; and in the second chariot black horses ; and in the third chariot white horses ; and in the fourth chariot grisled and bay horses. Then I answered and said unto the angel that talked with me, What are these, my lord ? And the angel answered and said unto me, These are the four spirits of the heavens, which go forth from standing before the Lord of all the earth. The black horses which are therein go forth into the north country ; and the white go forth after them ; and the grisled go forth toward the south country. And the bay went forth, and sought to go that they might walk to and fro through the earth : and he said, Get you hence, walk to and fro through the earth. So they walked to and fro through the earth.

Then cried he upon me, and spake unto me, saying, Behold, these that go toward the north country have quieted my spirit in the north country " (Zech. vi. 1–8).

Here the writer abruptly turns to another subject, leaving us wondering what mission the other equine messengers accomplished, and why the bay horses were so anxious to choose their own path, and many other things which he leaves untold.

Turning to the (apocryphal) second book of Maccabees, we find three instances given of angel horses being seen on earth.

About the year 176 B.C. a dispute arose between the Jewish high priest, Onias III, and the governor of the temple, Simon, probably as to who should have command over the treasury. The latter got the worst of the argument and fled to Apollonius, who governed Cælesyria, under King Seleucus. To him he gave an account of incalculable treasure laid up in the Jewish temple. The king's finances being exhausted by the exactions of the Romans, the royal treasurer, Heliodorus, was immediately dispatched to seize this accumulated treasure. The Jews were plunged into an agony of apprehension, so that " it would have pitied a man to see the falling down of the multitude of all sorts, and the fear of the high priest " when the royal officer came to pillage and profane their holy temple. But as Heliodorus, with his guard, arrived at the treasury, " the Lord of Spirits, and the Prince of all power, caused a great apparition, so that all that presumed to come in with him were astonished at the power of God, and fainted, and were sore afraid. For there appeared unto them an horse with a terrible rider upon him, and adorned with a very fair covering, and he ran fiercely, and smote at Heliodorus with his fore-feet, and it seemed that he that sat upon the horse had complete harness of gold. Moreover two other young men appeared before him, notable in strength, excellent in beauty, and comely in apparel, who stood by him on either side, and scourged him continually, and gave him many sore stripes. And Heliodorus fell suddenly unto the ground, and was compassed with great darkness : but they that were with him took him up, and put him into a litter. Thus him, that lately came with a great train and with all his guard into the said treasury, they carried out, being unable to help himself with his weapons :

and manifestly they acknowledged the power of God : for he by the hand of God was cast down, and lay speechless without all hope of life. But they praised the Lord, that had miraculously honoured His own place : for the temple, which a little afore was full of fear and trouble, when the Almighty Lord appeared, was filled with joy and gladness " (2 Macc. iii. 24-30).

We need only add that the treasurer revived, when the high priest consented to intercede for him with the offended Deity, and that the miracle left the Jews delighted and the Syrians terrified ; though it is but fair to say that Simon was a doubter, and even accused the high priest of imposture !

It is clear that the writer from whose vivid narrative we have quoted believed the " terrible rider " of the horse to be none other than Jehovah. Heliodorus also took this view, for when, after his escape, King Seleucus asked him " who might be a fit man to be sent yet once again to Jerusalem, he said, If thou hast any enemy or traitor, send him thither, and thou shalt receive him well scourged, if indeed he escape with his life. . . . For He that dwelleth in heaven, . . . He beateth and destroyeth them that come to hurt it."

Therefore this angel horse had great honour. If, like Simon, my readers are doubters, they can compare this story with that of the Trojan horse, and must admit that as a ruse it was equally useful.

The second instance our historian gives of angel horses and riders appearing at the critical moment to assist human beings is recorded in 2 Macc. x. 24-32. The date assigned to the happening is about 165 B.C. We will give the account in the writer's own words :

" Now Timotheus . . . when he had gathered a great multitude of foreign forces, and horses out of Asia not a few, came as though he would take Jewry by force of arms. But when he drew near, they that were with Maccabeus turned themselves to pray unto God. . . . And when they drew near to their enemies, they kept by themselves. Now the sun being newly risen, they joined both together ; the one part having together with their virtue their refuge also unto the Lord for a pledge of their success and victory : the other side making their rage leader of their battle. But when the battle waxed strong, there appeared unto the enemies from heaven five comely men upon horses, with bridles of gold, and two of them led the Jews, and took Maccabeus betwixt them, and covered him on every side with their weapons, and kept him safe, but shot arrows and lightnings against the enemies : so that being confounded with blindness, and full of trouble, they were killed. And there were slain of footmen twenty thousand and five hundred, and six hundred horsemen."

Timotheus fled to a fortress, but was captured and slain by the victorious army. " When this was done, they praised the Lord with psalms and thanksgivings, who had done so great things for Israel, and given them the victory."

The third occasion of a heavenly horse and rider coming to the assistance of the hard-pressed Jews is thus narrated by Maccabeus (2 Macc. xi. 1–11) :

" Not long after this, Lysias, the king's protector and cousin . . . when he had gathered about fourscore thousand with all the horsemen, came against the Jews, thinking to make the city an habitation of the Gentiles, . . . not at all considering the power of God, but puffed up with his ten thousands of footmen, and his thousands of horsemen, and his fourscore elephants. So he came to Judea, and drew near to Bethsura, which was a strong town, but distant from Jerusalem about five furlongs, and he laid sore siege unto it. Now when they that were with Maccabeus heard that he besieged the holds, they and all the people with lamentations and tears besought the Lord that He would send a good angel to deliver Israel. Then Maccabeus himself first of all took weapons, exhorting the other that they would jeopard themselves together with him to help their brethren : so they went forth together with a willing mind. And as they were at Jerusalem, there appeared before them on horseback one in white clothing, shaking his armour of gold. Then they praised the merciful God all together, and took heart, insomuch that they were ready not only to fight with men, but with most cruel beasts, and to pierce through walls of iron. Thus they marched forward in their armour, having a helper from heaven : for the Lord was merciful unto them. And giving a charge upon their enemies like lions, they slew eleven thousand footmen, and sixteen hundred horsemen, and put all the other to flight."

The date of this event is said to be 163 B.C.

According to the Revelation of St. John, the Beloved, on the occasion when heaven was opened to his gaze, the glorified Christ appeared before his wondering eyes, mounted on a white horse—the emblem of conquest. " Behold a white horse : and He that sat on him had a bow ; and a crown was given unto Him : and He went forth conquering and to conquer " (Rev. vi. 2).

Again, he says : " And I saw heaven opened, and behold a white horse ; and He that sat upon him was called Faithful and True. . . . And the armies which were in heaven followed Him upon white horses " (Rev. xix. 11, 14).

Here the word " white " in the original signifies pure brightness rather than whiteness, and would be better translated as shining, being intended to typify the holy and spiritual nature of these beings. Thus, if we accept the vision of St. John, in heaven, as on earth, horses serve the Christ.

It was said to be owing to the assistance of Castor and Pollux, the twin equestrian gods, that the Romans overcame the Latins in the battle of Lake Regillus. Mounted on two milk-white steeds, the heavenly champions fought at the head of the legions of the commonwealth, and immediately afterwards carried the news of the victory with incredible speed to the city, and there watered their foaming steeds in the Roman Forum at the fountain of Inturna. A temple was consecrated to the celestial deliverers, close to this hallowed spot on July 15, 269 B.C., and a great annual festival was instituted in their honour on the Ides of Quintilis, the anniversary of the battle, when sumptuous sacrifices were offered to them at the public expense. After the battle there was found on the margin of Lake Regillus a mark in the volcanic rock which resembled in shape a horse's hoof-print, and this was believed to have been made by one of the celestial chargers, and was regarded with awe and reverence accordingly.

Macaulay has given us a fine poetical description of the battle and its sequel. The poem is supposed to be " A lay sung at the feast of Castor and Pollux, on the Ides of Quintilis, in the year of the city CCCCLI." It is too long to quote in full, so we must content ourselves with one or two extracts :

But, Roman, when thou standest
  Upon that holy ground,
Look thou with heed on the dark rock
  That girds the dark lake round,
So shalt thou see a hoof-mark
  Stamped deep into the flint :
It was no hoof of mortal steed
  That made so strange a dint :
There to the Great Twin Brethren
  Vow thou thy vows, and pray
That they in tempest and in fight,
  Will keep thy head alway.

A vivid description of how the Twins appeared and secured the victory to the Romans follows, and then we are introduced to those in the city anxiously awaiting news of the battle :

Since the first gleam of day,
  Sempronius had not ceased
To listen for the rushing
  Of horse-hoofs from the east.
The mist of eve was rising,
  The sun was hastening down,
When he was aware of a princely pair
  Fast pricking towards the town.
So like they were, man never
  Saw twins so like before ;
Red with gore their armour was,
  Their steeds were red with gore.

" Hail to the great Asylum !
  Hail to the hill-tops seven !
Hail to the fire that burns for aye,
  And the shield that fell from heaven !
This day by Lake Regillus,
  Under the Porcian height,
All in the lands of Tusculum
  Was fought a glorious fight.
To-morrow your Dictator
  Shall bring in triumph home
The spoils of thirty cities
  To deck the shrines of Rome ! "

Then burst from that great concourse
   A shout that shook the towers,
And some ran north, and some ran south,
   Crying, " The day is ours ! "
But on rode these strange horsemen,
   With slow and lordly pace ;
And none who saw their bearing
   Durst ask their name or race.
On rode they to the Forum,
   While laurel boughs and flowers,
From house tops and from windows,
   Fell on their crests in showers.
When they drew nigh to Vesta,
   They vaulted down amain,
And washed their horses in the well
   That springs by Vesta's fane.
And straight again they mounted,
   And rode to Vesta's door ;
Then, like a blast, away they passed,
   And no man saw them more.

Mommsen says that this legend " bears a stamp thoroughly un-Roman, and was beyond doubt at a very early period modelled on the appearance of the Dioscuri—similar down to its very details—in the famous battle fought about a century before between the Crotoniates and Locrians at the river Sagras."

Similar stories are to be met with in mediaeval history. When in 1429, on the 6th of May, the Maid of Orleans took the fortress of the Tournelles from the English at the siege of Orleans, many of her adversaries stated that they saw in the air the forms of the Arch-angel Michael and of Aignan, the patron saint of the city. Both were mounted on white chargers and fighting on the side of the French.

The battle-cry of the Spaniards, " St. James," originated in the Middle Ages, when the Spanish army under King Ferdinand defeated the Moors in Estremadura. On this occasion the Christians, after besieging the stronghold of Coimbra unsuccessfully for seven months, had begun to regard it as impregnable, and were on the verge of abandoning their task in despair, when St. James appeared to a pilgrim and promised to give his aid the next day. The downcast soldiers were inspired anew by this message, and when the morrow came they placed themselves in battle array, and eagerly looked for the fulfilment of the saint's word.   And they were not disappointed.   An unknown warrior on a snow-white steed appeared among them and ever led the charge where the fight was hardest.   " Who is he ? " they breathlessly asked one another, but none could tell, till suddenly, as by one accord, the cry "St. James ! St. James ! " burst from their throats, and they rushed into the fury of the battle with new courage in their hearts. From this moment their fortune turned, and ere evening fell the citadel was taken.   From that day " St. James ! " was the favourite battle-cry of the Spaniards.   They have never forgotten the help given them by the stranger and his snowy steed.

Another occasion on which St. James and his battle-charger came to the rescue of hard-pressed Spaniards was when Hernando Cortés, the Spanish explorer who was known as " the Conqueror of Mexico," with his little band of soldiers was almost overwhelmed by hostile Indian warriors in the year 1519.   Cortés was expecting reinforce-ments, but they did not come, and he grew more and more anxious, since the foe's sheer weight of numbers was sufficient to crush his small force.

Suddenly he saw that the farthest columns of the enemy were agitated and thrown into confusion, which quickly spread through all their ranks.   Immediately following this arose the Christian battle-cry of " San Jago ! " and " San Pedro ! "

And now the Spaniards could see the longed-for reinforcements scattering the foe !   And to their wonder and astonishment the leader was none other than the patron saint of Spain, who, mounted on his beautiful grey battle-charger, was heading the rescuers and destroying the infidels.   It was the " glorious apostle James, the bulwark and safety of our nation," says Pizazzo y Orellana, though Cortés sup-posed it was his own " tutelar saint St. Peter," but " the common and indubitable opinion " was that St. James was the figure who so oppor-tunely arrived to save the day.   The Indians fled, many of them throw-ing away their arms, and Cortés drew off his men to a grove of palms that stood hard by, to offer thanks to God for the victory so miracu-lously given.   Most accounts agree that the Indian forces consisted of eight squadrons containing five thousand men in each, but the number of their slain is variously estimated at from one thousand to thirty thousand, whilst it is claimed that the Christians had only two of their small band killed.

During the awful nightmare of the late terrible war, it would not have seemed strange if the forces of evil it loosed had entirely blotted out things spiritual from mortal view. But it was not so. The privation and suffering entailed, the tremendous effort forced forth, the close and continuous presence of Death, all combined to bring about a curiously exalted condition of mind in the troops on the ghastly battlefield. Hence it was that large numbers of them had their spiritual eyesight quickened, and in times when all seemed hopeless, maintained that they had seen angels leading them and fighting on their side. Not unnaturally, the angel guardian of the English soldiers was seen as St. George, mounted upon his snowy steed. A typical instance of this was supplied by Miss Callow, secretary of the Higher Thought Centre at Kensington, in a letter to the *Weekly Dispatch*. She wrote :

" An officer has sent to one of the members of the Centre a detailed account of a vision that appeared to himself and others when fighting against fearful odds at Mons. He plainly saw an apparition representing St. George, the patron saint of England, the exact counterpart of a picture that hangs to-day in a London restaurant. So terrible was their plight at the time that the officer could not refrain from appealing to the vision to help them. Then, as if the enemy had also seen the apparition, the Germans abandoned their positions in precipitate terror. In other instances men had written about seeing *Clouds of Celestial Horsemen* hovering over the British lines."

To take one more instance of our national champion's appearance on horseback, which is all the more remarkable because it was the foe who saw the vision, and because the saint was accompanied by bowmen ; there appeared in the *Universe*, a Roman Catholic paper, a story told by a Roman Catholic officer at the front, of an apparition of men with bows and arrows. The officer states that when he was talking to a German prisoner afterwards, the man inquired who was the officer on a great white horse who led them, and said that though he had been such a conspicuous figure, none of them had been able to hit him.

Not alone the British Army had these glimpses of heavenly leaders. To the Russian soldiers their national hero, General Skobeleff, appeared on a snowy charger, sometimes to forewarn them of coming peril, at other times to fight on their behalf when they were in a tight place, and turn the fortunes of the day for them.

The French in similar circumstances saw sometimes St. Michael, and sometimes Joan of Arc, both mounted on magnificent white horses and leading them to victory.

We can afford to smile at such stories afterwards, but the fact remains that they are taken seriously enough at the time.

Rogers, in his *Italy*, describes " a most extraordinary deluge, accompanied by signs and prodigies," which took place early in the fourth century. " On that night, says Giovanni Villani, a hermit being at prayer in his hermitage above Vallombrosa, heard a furious trampling as of many horses ; and crossing himself, and hurrying to the wicket, saw a multitude of infernal horsemen, all black and terrible, riding by at full speed. When, in the name of God, he demanded their purpose, one replied, ' We are going, if it be His pleasure, to drown the city of Florence for its wickedness.' This account, he adds, was given me by the Abbot of Vallombrosa, who had questioned the holy man himself."

It is said that at the siege of Antioch a Turk named Pyrrhus saw an infinite army of soldiers on white horses, with white arms and vestments, who fought on the side of the Christians. These afterwards disappeared and were supposed to be angels and the souls of the blessed sent by God to succour the Christians.

In the great victory gained by Mohammed at Beder, he was stated to have been assisted by three thousand angels, led by Gabriel, who was mounted on his horse, Hiazum.

According to some authorities, Mahomet's mount when he ascended to heaven to learn the will of God was an ass named Al Borak, or The Lightning, but others say it was a horse brought to him by the Angel Gabriel, which he rode on this occasion. This steed " had the face of a man, but the cheeks of a horse; its eyes were like jacinths, but brilliant as the stars; it had the wings of an eagle, spoke with the voice of a man, and glittered all over with radiant light." It was one of the animals that were admitted into Paradise, its fortunate companions in this privilege being Al Adha, the prophet's camel, Balaam's ass, Tobit's dog, and Ketmir, the dog of the seven sleepers.

Another description of Al Borak says:

"Borak was a fine-limbed, high-standing horse, strong in frame and with a coat as glossy as marble. His colour was saffron with one hair of gold for every three of tawny; his ears were restless and pointed like a reed; his eyes large and full of fire; his nostrils wide and steaming; he had a white star on his forehead, a neck gracefully arched, a mane soft and silky, and a thick tail that swept the ground" (*Croquemitaine*, II. 9).

The Hindu deity Vistnou (or Vishnu, as the more modern spelling is), the second person of the Indian Trinity, whose function is the preservation of creation, has descended nine times upon the world in various forms. The first shape he took was that of a fish, the second a tortoise, the third a hog, the fourth a hybrid monster between a lion and a man, the fifth a mendicant Brahmin, the sixth a beautiful child, the seventh a hero named Ram, the eighth the god Kristna, the ninth the god Bodha (Buddha) or Fo. The tenth and last metamorphosis is not yet accomplished. Nor is it to be until the close of the fourth or Kali age, when the world has become wholly depraved.

Vishnu is then to be revealed in the sky seated on a white and winged horse which stands upright in the heavens on three of its legs, holding the fourth aloft. When the determined moment arrives, the horse will let fall this suspended hoof, and strike the earth with such tremendous power that the serpent, Sigpana, unable to support the world longer, will retire, leaving the tortoise to bear its entire weight. The tortoise will thereupon plunge into the sea, and the world will be drowned, and all incorrigible wrongdoers finally destroyed. All creation is then to be renovated, the good are to be redeemed, and the age of purity restored.

The poet Campbell (apparently confusing the second person of the Trinity and the first) writes:

Nine times have Brama's wheels of lightning hurl'd
His awful presence o'er the alarméd world;
Nine times hath Guilt, through all his giant frame,
Convulsive trembled, as the Mighty came;
Nine times hath suffering Mercy spared in vain—
But Heaven shall burst her starry gates again!
He comes! dread Brama shakes the sunless sky,
With murmuring wrath and thunders from on high,
Heaven's fiery horse, beneath his warrior form,
Paws the light clouds, and gallops on the storm!

The Persian Messiah, Sosiosh, is also to come seated on a horse, and the Pralaya, or period of cosmic rest, is to follow his arrival.

As we have just seen, St. John in the Apocalypse uses the same symbolism and represents the triumphant Christ as mounted on a white horse.

BIBLIOGRAPHY

Dictionary of the Bible, edited by James Hastings, M.A., D.D. (T. & T. Clark, Edinburgh.)

Encyclopædia Biblica, edited by T. K. Cheyne, M.A., D.D., & J. Sutherland. (A. & C. Black, London.)

Historical Essays, by Lord Mahon. (John Murray, London, 1849.)

History of the Conquest of Mexico, by Wm. H. Prescott. (London, 1863.)

The Myths of Greece and Rome, by H. A. Guerber. (Geo. G. Harrap, London, 1913.)

Myths and Legends of the Middle Ages, by H. A. Guerber. (Geo. G. Harrap, London, 1913.)

Universal History, Ancient and Modern, by Wm. Mavor, LL.D., Vol. XI, p. 252. (Richard Phillips, London, 1802.)

Dictionary of Phrase and Fable, by Rev. E. Cobham Brewer, LL.D. (Cassell.)

The Koran and its Commentators.

Brahmanism and Hinduism; or Religious Thought and Life in India, by Sir Monier Monier-Williams, K.C.I.E. (John Murray, London, 1891.)

The History of Rome, by Theodor Mommsen. Translated by Wm. Purdie Dickson D.D., LL.D. (Macmillan & Co., London, 1908.)

Lord Macaulay's Essays and Lays of Ancient Rome. New edition. (Longmans, Green & Co., London, 1897.)

CHAPTER III

Ghostly Horses

SOME seventy years ago there lived at Seend, in Wilts., an agricultural labourer named John Ovens, with his wife and family. They were poor and frugal, and their supper usually consisted of dry bread and cheese with some beer to help it down. John used to fetch their liquid refreshment from the " Bell " every evening, as they could not afford to buy it in bulk, but his rule always was to get a double portion on Saturdays that the Sabbath might not be broken. However, one Sunday a party of unexpected guests arrived, and the hospitable John went off to fetch more beer so that he might entertain his friends.

When he returned from his errand he was ghastly white and trembling with fear. At first he would not say what the trouble was, but finally was persuaded to tell.

He had met on his road a phantom funeral which was the replica of that of one of his friends who had been buried some thirty years or more. There was the hearse, with the same wreaths and crosses, drawn by a pair of coal-black horses. Following it was a long procession of carriages and carts pulled by horses of every description, decked with mourning ribbons, and in the carriages sat the very mourners who had followed their dead to the grave so long ago, many of them now themselves on the farther side. He had recognised the scene in detail; the same horses and carriages and people were re-enacting the funeral rite.

The memory of the ghostly procession haunted John to his death some twenty-five years later, and he could not speak of it without

31

trembling. He considered the vision had been sent to him to warn him of his sin in violating the Sabbath, and nothing ever again could persuade him to repeat the offence.

The story was told to the author by John's granddaughter Louisa Castle, who vouches for its truth.

Killarney is said to have been at one time haunted by the ghosts of the hero O'Donoghue and his favourite white horse.

For many years after his death his spirit is supposed to have been seen on May-day morning gliding over the lake on his steed, to the sound of unearthly music, and preceded by groups of youths and maidens, who flung wreaths of beautiful spring-flowers before him.

Among various stories connected with this legend of the lakes is one of a beautiful young girl whose mind became so possessed by the idea of this visionary chieftain and his snowy steed that she fell deeply in love with him, and one May morning threw herself into the lake so as to join him.

The following poem by Thomas Moore shows how large a part of the maiden's heart was given to the ghostly steed. It seems to dominate her fancy almost as much as the hero himself.

The Killarney boatmen still call the crested waves which sometimes arise on their lake " O'Donoghue's white horses."

The poem is called

O'DONOGHUE'S MISTRESS

Of all the fair months, that round the sun
In light-linked dance their circles run,
Sweet May, sweet May, shine thou for me !
For still when thy earliest beams arise,
That youth who beneath the blue lake lies,
Sweet May, sweet May, returns to me.

Of all the smooth lakes, where daylight leaves
His lingering smile on golden eaves,
Fair lake, fair lake, thou'rt dear to me ;
For when the last April sun grows dim,
Thy Naiads prepare his steed for him
Who dwells, who dwells, bright lake, in thee.

Of all the proud steeds that ever bare
Young plumèd chiefs on sea or shore,
White steed, white steed, most joy to thee,
Who still, with the first young glance of spring,
From under that glorious lake dost bring,
Proud steed, proud steed, my love to me.

While white as the sail some bark unfurls,
When newly launched, thy long mane curls,
Fair steed, fair steed, as white and free ;
And spirits from all the lake's deep bowers
Glide o'er the blue wave scattering flowers,
Fair steed, around my love and thee.

Of all the sweet deaths that maidens die,
Whose lovers beneath the cold waves lie,
Most sweet, most sweet that death will be,
Which under the next May evenings' light,
When thou and thy steed are lost to sight,
Dear love, dear love, I'll die for thee.

Another story of a spectral horse and rider is of a very different kind to the romantic one we have just related. An old house near Colne known as Wyecoller Hall is the home of these apparitions. The pair may be heard galloping up to the door on windy nights. The rider, who is garbed in a costume of the Stuart period, leaves his horse outside and goes upstairs. Screams and groans are then heard in a room on the first landing. Suddenly the ghostly horseman returns, and gallops off on his phantom steed, which breathes forth fire from its nostrils. The legend runs that one of the Cunliffes of Billington, who used to own the Hall, murdered his wife, and ever since, with his horse, has annually haunted the scene of the tragedy.

The Ilmington Hills, in Gloucestershire, used to be haunted by an apparition known as the " night coach." This was drawn by six dark horses, and would pass over places where no mortal could drive. It was generally abroad at midnight, but occasionally seen in the day.

One such appearance is recorded as occurring about the year 1780 to a farmer who was walking alone upon the hills one misty morning, absorbed in thought. As he wandered along he suddenly became aware that a vehicle was noiselessly and swiftly passing him by. So near to him did it approach that he might have touched it by stretching out his hand. The carriage was a heavy and old-fashioned coach drawn by six dark horses.

Before the seer had had time to realise how incongruous was its presence in such a place, the whole equipage disappeared over the brow of the hill into the mist below at a point where no material carriage could have kept its wheels. Then only did he become aware of the supernatural nature of what he had seen.

Somewhere about the close of the century a mysterious stranger who passed by the name of Staunton took up his residence in the neighbourhood. He was devoted to scientific pursuits, and these, together with his solitary life, gained for him the reputation of a necromancer, though, fortunately for him, the country people regarded him as a " white wizard." The night-coach yielded to his exorcisms and was laid to rest.

BIBLIOGRAPHY

" The Ilmington Hills," serial article by Scarlett Potter in *Time,* 1884.
Survey of the Lakes. (Clarke, 1789.)
Shropshire Folk-lore, by G. E. Jackson.
Abbeys, Castles, and Ancient Halls of England and Wales, by John Timbs. (F. Warne & Co., London.)
Satan's Invisible World Discovered.
Russian Chaps, by M. C. Lethbrige. (John Lane, London, 1916.)

DEMON · HORSES.

M. Oldfield Howey.

CHAPTER IV

The Demon Horse : Marë and Others

FROM ancient tale and monkish legend we learn not only that there are demon horses, but that the arch-fiend himself has occasionally assumed this form that he might more readily deceive poor, simple, unsuspicious mankind. He once made an attack on St. Peter of Verona in this guise, being impelled thereto by jealousy of the crowds who thronged the holy man's church. Having decided to disperse one of the large congregations that the saint's reputation had attracted, the devil took the form of a black horse, and rushing into the midst of the assembly stamped upon many and caused wild fear to all. But St. Peter recognised the foe in spite of his equine disguise, and proved himself equal to the occasion. He made the sign of the cross, and the demon horse fled, becoming invisible in a cloud of smoke.

To take another instance of the Devil's using the form of a horse for mankind's undoing, Mr. D. M. Rose, writing in the *Scotsman*, says :

" Let me give the story of the golden horse of Loch Lundie. Two men from Culmailie went one Sunday to fish on Loch Lundie, and they saw, pasturing in a meadow, one of the most lovely golden-coloured ponies they had ever seen. One of the men determined to seize the animal and bring it home. His companion, in a state of great alarm, tried to dissuade him, assuring him that the animal was none other than the Devil in disguise. The man, nothing daunted, began to stalk the pony, declaring that if he could get a chance he would mount on the beast, even if it were the Evil One.

" At length he managed to get within reach, and making a bound, he seized the bristling mane, and leaped on the animal's back. In an instant the pony gave one or two snorts that shook the hills, fire flashed from its eyes and nostrils, and tossing its tail into the air, it galloped away with the man to the hills, and he was never again seen by mortal being.

" According to another version, the yellow horse of Loch Lundie was last seen in a meadow near Brora by two boys who broke the Sabbath. They tried to mount the animal, and one of them succeeded in doing so. The other boy, getting alarmed, tried to withdraw, but found, to his horror, that his finger had stuck in the animal's side. With great presence of mind, he immediately pulled out his knife and cut off his finger. The pony immediately gave an appallingly shrill neigh and galloped madly away with his rider, who was never seen again. . . .

" There is a story told about a son of Rose of Tullisnaught, who was lost in the neighbouring Forest of Birse. When he and his servant were out hunting one day he suddenly came upon a beautiful yellow pony in a glade of the forest. The servant tried to persuade him that the pony was merely the Devil in disguise, but Rose determined to capture and mount the animal. He managed to do this, but in a twinkling horse and rider disappeared and were never seen again."

Mr. Rose comments on these tales unsympathetically : " Of course, in folk-lore the pony [of Loch Lundie] was undoubtedly regarded as Auld Nick, but the truth is that wild horses actually existed in the Sutherland Hills until after 1545."

We may here note that the word " hobgoblin " really signifies a demon horse, though not now used in this sense. Its derivation is *hob* from middle English *hoby*, "a small horse," whilst *goblin* means "demon" or "malicious fairy."

The suggestion is that the eccentric movements of these sprites is like the up-and-down motion of a cantering horse.

A coltpixie is also a mischievous spirit or fairy in the shape of a horse, which neighs and so misleads mortal horses into bogs. A colepixie is the will-o'-the-wisp, and according to some authorities coltpixie is merely a popular perversion of this word.

To come to demon horses proper, we must assign a leading place to the four coal-black steeds of Pluto. These drew his chariot on the occasions when he left his gloomy realm to visit the earth's surface and seek fresh victims to drag down with him to the Infernal Regions.

> Mark him as he moves along,
> Drawn by horses black and strong,
> Such as may belong to Night
> 'Ere she takes her morning flight.
> *(Barry Cornwall.)*

But our ancestors told of the existence of many demon steeds, besides those specially reserved for Pluto's use, and it would appear that these were at the call of certain powerful wizards, witches, and necromancers who greatly troubled the earth in those early periods.

One of the most celebrated of these wizards was Michael Scott, who flourished about the middle of the sixteenth century. According to one of the traditions related of him and still current in Scotland, he was chosen to go upon an embassy to France, to obtain from the French king compensation for certain piracies that his subjects had committed on the Scottish coast.

The new ambassador, disdaining the ordinary methods of transport available to mortals, by means of his occult knowledge and magical powers evoked a fiend in the shape of a huge black horse. He boldly mounted this uncanny steed and forced him to fly through the air to France. But the fiend was resourceful, and as they crossed the sea he put a question to his rider. "What is it," he asked, "that the old women of Scotland mutter at bedtime?" He hoped the wizard would answer that it was the Pater Noster, for then he could have thrown him from his back! But Michael was a match for him, and sternly replied, " What is that to thee ? Mount, Diabolus, and fly ! "

When he reached Paris he tied his horse to the palace gate, entered, and delivered his message. The French king was inclined to set him at naught, and was about to refuse his request with contempt, when Michael, seeing how things were trending, asked him to postpone his reply till he had seen his horse stamp three times.

At the first stamp every steeple in Paris was shaken and the bells set ringing ; at the second, three towers of the palace fell down ; and the infernal steed had lifted his hoof for the third time, when the king, struck with terror, offered the fullest concessions, and so averted further disaster. Sir Walter Scott introduces this legend in his *Lay of the Last Minstrel*.

In early mediæval literature may be found various *chansons de geste* celebrating the exploits of the demon horse Bayard, whom Malagigi the necromancer had brought from Hell and given to his cousin Aymon of Dordogne. The latter carried on a sort of guerrilla warfare against his sovereign, the Emperor Charlemagne, and thanks to his demon steed was always the victor. At last, after many years of desultory struggle, Charlemagne determined to strike a decisive blow at his foe, and came with a large army to besiege the castle where Aymon had entrenched himself. Just at this critical moment, Satan stole away the magic horse ! Poor Aymon was in terrible distress when he awoke one morning to find his beloved and invaluable Bayard had disappeared, but Malagigi comforted him, and promised he would recover the steed for his kinsman, even though he had to go to Mount Vulcanus, which was the Mouth of Hell, to fetch him.

Accordingly he journeyed thither, leaving Aymon to repel the foe. As soon as he arrived, disguising his true purpose, he offered himself as a servant to Satan. The unsuspicious Devil gladly accepted him in this capacity, and gave him the charge of a horse he had recently stolen which was none other than Bayard ! Malagigi took the precaution of lulling his employer to sleep with a drugged potion, and then hastened to the imprisoned steed, who was angrily pawing the ground. His master's name whispered in his ear was sufficient to

M. Oldfield Howey.

FROM "THE SPECTRAL HORSEMAN."

Then does the dragon, who, chained in the caverns
To eternity, curses the champion of Erin,
Moan and yell loud at the lone hour of midnight,
And twine his vast wreaths round the forms of the demons,
Then in agony roll his death-swimming eyeballs,
Though 'wildered by death, yet never to die !
Then he shakes from his skeleton folds the nightmares
Who, shrieking in agony, seek the couch
Of some fevered wretch who courts sleep in vain.—SHELLEY.

39

banish Bayard's ill-humour, and, springing on to the horse's back, Malagigi rapidly rode away.

The steed's joyful whinny as he escaped aroused Satan from his slumber, and realising that a trick had been played upon him, he quickly mounted a storm cloud and gave chase, hurling a red-hot thunderbolt at the wizard to stop his flight. But Malagigi had not come unarmed. He muttered a magic formula and held up a crucifix, so that the bolt fell short, and the Devil, losing his balance, was precipitated on to the earth and for ever lamed by the force with which he fell.

Meanwhile, things had gone so badly with Count Aymon that he had been obliged to flee from his fortress, mounted only on a sorry steed instead of his fleet Bayard. The enemy were in hot pursuit, and were aided by bloodhounds. These were about to seize him when Malagigi opportunely appeared with the demon horse. Bounding on to Bayard's back, Aymon drew his famous sword Flamberge, soon routed his now terrified foes, and quickly regained the castles and forts he had lost.

Charlemagne was forced to sue for peace at any price, and gave much gold and the hand of his sister Aya to secure it. Aymon did not rest on these hardly-won laurels, but, mounted always on Bayard, covered himself again and again with glory. At last, feeling himself about to depart this life, he sent for his sons to say farewell. To the three eldest he gave the spoil he had accumulated in his life of warfare, but to the youngest, Renaud, he promised his horse and sword provided he could mount and ride the former. Renaud succeeded at the second attempt and so became owner and master of Bayard.

Faithfully the demon steed served him, and saved his life and that of his brothers by its magic powers, but alas! the noble creature came to a tragic end. It was the old, old story of man's faithlessness to his fellow-creatures and betrayal of their trust. Aymon's sons, finding themselves again at the mercy of the Emperor, purchased his forgiveness by handing to him the demon horse to be put to death. Charlemagne had poor Bayard's hoofs heavily weighted, and caused him to be led to the centre of a bridge that spanned the Seine. There, before his master's eyes, the Emperor had him driven into the river to drown.

His demon origin did not save him. Twice the noble creature rose, each time turning a look of agonised appeal on his master, till Renaud, his heart breaking, fell to the ground. Once more the form of Bayard appeared above the water, but missing his master among the spectators, he sank again for the last time. Renaud, maddened, as well he might be, by the torture of his faithful friend, tore up the treaty of pardon so dearly bought, and flung it at the Emperor's feet. Then he broke his sword Flamberge and cast it into the river, declaring that never again would he use such a weapon.

Tradition asserts that after fighting (with a club) in the crusades, he died as a hermit known far and wide for his holy life.

The extraordinary thing about this demon steed is that his whole character appears to have been noble and beautiful, and his influence on his master such as a saint might have exerted. Even Satan himself, according to this legend, was more sinned against than sinning.

Ideas of abstract right and wrong scarcely existed in Christendom at this period, so that it is not unusual to find the Devil actually occupying a superior moral position to his heavenly antagonist. We need not be surprised therefore to find the demon steed rivalling the angelic horses in virtue.

The following legend of a demon horse comes from Cornwall, that treasure-store of ancient occult lore. Behind the town of Polperro is a deep fissure which modern geologists call a fault and ascribe to sub-terranean disturbance, but which the wise men of olden days named the Devil's Doorway, and believed to be the result of a very different cause.

The story is that his Satanic Majesty, wishing to take the air and see how his children in this world throve, burst through at this point from his kingdom below, the rocks making way for his exit. He came forth in a fiery car drawn by a coal-black horse of gigantic size. The steed was so delighted to find itself in the upper world that it reared wildly to express its joy, and with such force did it bring its feet down on the ground that not only was Great Britain shaken as by an earth-quake, but the deep impression of its burning hoof was left in the rock. There it remains to this day, now filled with water, a hoof-shaped pool, confounding the incredulous.

St. Augustine alludes to the tale of a battle between evil spirits which was seen upon a plain in Campania during the civil wars of Rome. This vision was accompanied by all the noise and din of warfare, and the saint declares that when it was over the ground was covered with the hoof-marks of horses and footprints of men. On the very spot where this was witnessed an actual fight took place not long after.

The following story is related by Cardinal Damiano in a letter addressed to Pope Nicholas II, written about the year 1060.

The horses mentioned therein induce us to include it here, although they form but a small portion of the interest of the story. The positions occupied by the witness and the narrator who has handed on to us the tale should be evidence at least of their good faith in so doing, if not of their critical faculty.

" A servant of God dwelt alone, near Naples, on a lofty rock hard by the highway. As this man was singing hymns by night, he opened the window of his cell to observe the hour; when lo ! he saw passing many men, black as Æthiopians, driving a large troop of pack-horses laden with hay; and he was anxious to ask who they were, and why they carried with them this fodder for cattle ? And they answered, ' We are evil spirits; and this food which we prepare is not for flocks or herds, but to foment those fires which are kindled against men's souls; for we wait, first for Pandulphus, Prince of Capua, who now lies sick; and then for John, the captain of the garrison of Naples, who as yet is alive and well.' Then went that man of God to John, and related faithfully that which he had seen and heard. At that time the Emperor Otho II, being about to wage war on the Saracens, was journeying towards Calabria. John therefore answered, ' I must first go reverently and meet the Emperor, and take counsel with him concerning the state of this land. But after he is gone I promise to forsake the world, and to assume the monastic habit.' Moreover, to prove whether the priest's story were true, he sent one to Capua, who found Pandulphus dead; and John himself lived scarce fifteen days, dying before the Emperor reached those parts; upon whose death the mountain Vesuvius, from which hell often belches forth, broke out into flames, as might clearly be proved, because the hay which those demons got ready was nothing else than the fire of that fell conflagration

prepared for these reprobate and wicked men ; for as often as a reprobate rich man dies in those parts, the fire is seen to burst from the
above-named mountain, and such a mass of sulphureous resin flows
from it as makes a torrent which by its downward impulse descends
even to the sea.   And in verity a former prince of Palermo once saw
from a distance sulphureous pitchy flames burst out from Vesuvius,
and said that surely some rich man was just about to die, and go down
to hell.   Alas for the blinded minds of evil men !   That very night,
as he lay regardless in bed, be breathed his last."

Other instances follow, but as they do not bear on our subject, we
refrain from a longer quotation.

We hope the demons are good horse-masters, and do not overload
and illtreat their steeds as men so often do.   Such negative evidence
as is available on this point is in their favour, and we never read of a
demon horse being abused by his owner, but, on the other hand, the
best of understanding seems to prevail between horse and master in
Satan's realms, if monks and saints may be credited.

Even in far-off China the belief in the existence of demon steeds is
found.   The Chinese attribute fits and convulsions " to the agency of
certain mischievous spirits who love to draw men's souls out of their
bodies.   At Amoy the spirits who serve babies and children in this
way rejoice in the high-sounding titles of ' celestial agencies bestriding
galloping horses ' " (Golden Bough).   It is so evident from the actions
of these spirits that they are demonic rather than celestial, that we
must take it the title is bestowed in the hope of appeasing by flattery
a dangerous foe !

It is interesting to find that what we call a nightmare was believed
by our ancestors to be the result of a visitation from the Saxon demon
Marë or Mara.   This was a sort of vampire which sat on the chest of
its sleeping victim, half strangling him and causing fearful visions.

The phrase " Away the mare " has reference to this incubus, and
means " Off with the blue devils. Farewell Care," or something
similar.   These demon nightmares were supposed to guard hidden
treasures when not occupied as we have seen above, and over these
they would brood as a hen over her eggs.   Hence comes the saying,
" A mare's nest," meaning the spot where the vampire mounts guard

over concealed stores of good things. This is the reason why, if someone announces that he has made a wonderful discovery, we ask if he has found a mare's nest.

In Devonshire those who would throw discredit on such an announcement, or say a story is nonsense, will call it a *blind* mare's nest, whilst in Gloucestershire they term a rambling, long-winded tale a horse-nest.

Here is a modern instance of a visitation of Marë culled from the *Daily Express* of February 5, 1920. It will be noted that though the writer does not refer to an outside occult agency, yet the symptoms he describes seem to demand such an explanation, and are entirely in accord with Marë's methods. The paragraph is headed " Nightmare of Death," and runs :

" Death during nightmare, the problem raised at the inquest on a convict who died in his sleep, was much discussed in medical circles yesterday. ' There is nothing improbable in the suggestion of death caused by nightmare,' said Dr. Welby Fisher of Harley Street, and formerly on the staff of St. George's Hospital, to a *Daily Express* representative. ' Victims of these unpleasant sensations always experience difficulty in breathing. With persons suffering from angina pectoris, the struggle for breath during nightmare would cause death. A normally healthy person would not be likely to die of these nocturnal terrors, but one who is physically weak would lack the power to withstand the terrible strain. Nightmare is more common with children than with adults, but I have never known a child die in these circumstances. Grown-up people who are subject to a recurrence of these distressing symptoms should exercise the greatest care . . . as neglect of the simple rules of health may bring the nightmare of death.' "

The *Express* further comments on this in a leading article :

" The dictionary interpretation of a nightmare is an incubus or evil spirit that oppresses people during sleep. . . . Whatever the cause, there is no question that the effects of a nightmare leave their mark on the human brain for a lifetime. The question is now raised whether such visions may not be the cause of many sudden deaths which occur during sleep. Leading medical authorities agree that this is a very frequent explanation in the case of persons suffering from extreme physical exhaustion."

The same paper a few weeks later—on March 4, 1920—gave us another " modern instance " of Marë's power to injure and affright. This is headed " Disaster in a Dream," and comes from the *Daily Express* correspondent at Washington :

" Mr. H. M. Jessen, a farmer of Onawa, in the State of Iowa, has become a white-haired mute following a dream in which he saw his wife and children crushed beneath an overturned motor-car. Mr. Jessen had planned a motor trip with his family to Sioux City, but, being detained by work, permitted the car, driven by one of his children, to leave without him, Mr. Jessen travelling later by train. He arrived at his destination, however, before his family, and while sitting waiting in the foyer of the West Hotel dreamed of the fatal accident. When he awoke he frantically waved his arms, but could not speak. His family, when they arrived, found him still dumb. They told him that their motor-car had stalled on a railway crossing, and that a train was only brought to a stop a few inches from it, so that the accident of which he had dreamed very nearly took place. The farmer appears to be permanently dumb, and his hair has since turned white."

The visitations of Marë being attended by such terrible consequences it is small wonder that our ancestors sought means to thwart her entry into their houses and stables, especially the latter, since to annoy and even torture horses is her chief delight. This protection they found was given by the hag, halig, or holy stone—that is, a stone with a hole through it, suspended over the door, or tied to the key. To this talisman they frequently added a piece of horn which they thought would ensure the protection of the God of Cattle, called by the Romans, Pan.

Many of the brass ornaments used now on the harness of cart-horses are really charms to protect them from Marë, witchcraft, and fascination. Such is the design of a Greek cross within a circle, the latter symbolising the sun, to which, as we shall see, horses are sacred.

The Turks, Arabs, and Abyssinians of to-day hang amulets consisting of passages from their sacred writings, copied on parchment on their horses and camels with the same object.   And here is the explanation of the popular custom of attaching a cotton-reel to a key.   It is the old holystone charm against Marë in its modern form.   I have often asked the followers of this practice—stablemen and others in my employ—what was the object of attaching to a key such an apparently useless encumbrance, but could never obtain an explanation, though some looked wise as if they could tell, an they would.   The majority, however, seem to be merely following the methods of their fathers without troubling themselves to ascertain the reason.

Sir Thomas Browne referred to the halig when in his work entitled *Vulgar Errors* he asked :   " What natural effects can reasonably be expected when, to prevent the Ephialtes, or Nightmare, we hang a hollow stone in our stables ? "

Ephialtes interpreted literally is " One who leaps upon," and is descriptive of Marë's methods.

Grose mentions that a stone with a hole in it hung at the bed's head " will prevent the nightmare, and is therefore called a hag-stone."

Indeed, the holy stone was considered to be a protection from evil spirits of every kind.

The ceauniæ, or bœtuli, and all perforated flint stones, were not only used for this purpose, but more especially for the protection of horses and other cattle by suspending them in stables or tying them round the necks of the animals.

The following fine descriptive poem from Harrison Ainsworth's novel *Rookwood* well illustrates Marë's doings :

EPHIALTES

I am the hag who rides by night
Through the moonless air on a courser white !
Over the dreaming earth I fly,
Here and there—at my phantasy !
My frame is withered, my visage old,
My looks are frore, and my bones ice-cold
The wolf will howl as I pass his lair,
The ban-dog moan, and the screech-owl stare.
For breath at my coming the sleeper strains,
And the freezing current forsakes his veins.

Vainly for pity the wretch may sue—
Merciless Mara no prayers subdue.
        To his couch I flit—
        On his breast I sit!
            Astride! astride! astride!
        And one charm alone
        (A hollow stone)
            Can scare me from his side.

A thousand antic shapes I take;
The stoutest heart at my touch will quake.
The miser dreams of a bag of gold,
Or a ponderous chest on his bosom rolled.
The drunkard groans 'neath a cask of wine;
The reveller swelts 'neath a weighty chine.
The recreant turns, by his foes assailed,
To flee! but his feet to the ground are nailed.
The goatherd dreams of his mountain tops
And, dizzily reeling, downward drops.
The murderer feels at his throat a knife,
And gasps, as his victim gasped, for life!
The thief recoils from the scorching brand,
The mariner drowns in sight of land!
Thus sinful man have I power to fray,
Torture and rack—but not to slay!
But ever the couch of purity
With shuddering glance I hurry by.
            Then mount! away!
            To horse! I say
                To horse! astride! astride!
            The fire-drake shoots—
            The screech-owl hoots—
                As through the air I glide!

Some peoples who have never heard of the holy stone and the protection afforded by it to horses yet recognise that such protection is needed, and have discovered other methods of thwarting Marë. Thus among the Moors, those who are wealthy keep a wild boar in their stables for the evil spirits to enter into, that their horses may be left in peace.

Among the Australian natives the nightmare is also recognised as a demon, but I have not ascertained what form it takes there, probably not the equine.

Shakespeare has the following enigmatic allusion to Marë which has given the commentators some trouble to explain. One of them indeed, not being able to make head or tail of it, has described it as a nonsense rhyme !   Let us see if we can throw any light on it.

> Swithold [i.e. Saint Withold] footed thrice the old [i.e. the wold] ;
> He met the nightmare, and her nine-fold :
>> Bid her alight,
>> And her troth plight,
> And aroint thee, witch, aroint thee.
>
> (*Lear* III. iv. 126.)

" Nine-fold " apparently is used elliptically for the nine-fold offspring, or nine-fold company of the nightmare, and may be taken to mean that she was fully escorted, since nine—the number of the Muses—is a symbol of perfection. Compare the phrase " to the nines." Nine does not seem to have any more direct connection with Marë, though it is curious to find it again associated with her, and almost in the same words, in the following extract from Irving (*Sketch Book*, p. 418) : " Stars shoot and meteors glare oftener across the valley than in any other part of the country, and the nightmare with her whole nine-fold seems to make it the favourite scene of her gambols."

The last line of the verse has the meaning " Get thee behind me, witch," and is used as a charm or exorcism by the saint, who hopes thus to scare off his ill-met foe.

Shelley has given us a most weird and wonderful imaginative picture of nightmares in his poem entitled *The Spectral Horseman*. It is itself a vision worthy of Marë's inspiration, and perhaps unsurpassed in horror by any other poetical description.

> Then does the dragon, who, chained in the caverns
> To eternity, curses the champion of Erin,
> Moan and yell loud at the lone hour of midnight,
> And twine his vast wreaths round the forms of the demons ;
> Then in agony roll his death-swimming eyeballs,

Though 'wildered by death, yet never to die!
Then he shakes from his skeleton folds the nightmares,
Who, shrieking in agony, seek the couch
Of some fevered wretch who courts sleep in vain.

In these nine lines is concentrated the agony of worlds, seen and unseen, throughout the ages. God grant that the light of Truth dispel the awful dreams of darkness that torture all the beings peopling the earth and realms below; that one day we may awake to find it was but a delusion of Marë's creation, and that all is well!

BIBLIOGRAPHY

Dictionary of Phrase and Fable, by the Rev. E. Cobham Brewer, LL.D., 2nd edition. (Cassell, Peter & Galpin, London.)

The Golden Bough, by J. G. Frazer, Part VII, Vol. II, p. 74, and Part II, p. 59.

The Lay of the Last Minstrel, by Sir Walter Scott, Canto II. xiii.

Vulgar Errors, by Sir Thomas Browne.

Rookwood, by Harrison Ainsworth.

The Spectator, No. 117.

Popular Romances of the West of England, new edition by Robt. Hunt, F.R.S. (Chatto & Windus, London, 1896.)

The Century Dictionary, Wm. Dwight Whitney, Ph.D., LL.D. (*The Times*, 1899.)

Damiani Epistolæ, lib. i. 9, quoted in *Pompeii : Its History, Buildings, and Antiquities*, edited by Thomas H. Dyer, LL.D. (Bell & Daldy, London, 1867.)

CHAPTER V

Demon Horses: The Wild Huntsman

THE legend of the Wild Huntsman with his demon steed and hounds is found in various forms in most European countries, and is of hoary antiquity. We think our readers will be interested to compare some of the various developments of this tradition. One of the most striking of these connects it with that of the Wandering Jew. According to this version, Christ, during His agony, asked leave to slake His thirst at a horse-trough, but the churlish Jew of whom He requested the boon rudely refused Him, and, pointing to where a horse's hoof-prints on the ground had become full of the overflowing water, said that there Christ might drink. Ever since the Wandering Jew has been condemned to drive a team of demon horses through the fury of the storm. Only when Judgment Day arrives will he be released from his dreary and terrible doom, and his hellish steeds cease from their task.

In the Middle Ages the Wild Hunt was also known as Cain's Hunt, and Herod's Hunt, these names being given to it because their bearers were, like the Wandering Jew, thought to be unable to find rest for their souls on account of their murderous crimes, and to occupy positions as leaders in the Wild Hunt.

In pre-Christian days Odin, in his double character as Wind-god and leader of disembodied spirits, rushing through the air on his famous steed Sleipnir, was often spoken of as "the Wild Huntsman." And when his worshippers heard the tearing winds rushing and roaring through the woodlands, they whispered, shuddering, that Odin was riding with his train of huntsmen, their steeds snorting and their hounds baying. As the winds blew more fiercely during autumn and winter, this was the time when Odin was supposed to prefer to hunt, especially on the days between Christmas and Twelfth Night, and the peasants always carefully left behind in the fields the last sheaf of corn that Sleipnir might not go hungry.

The passing of Odin's (or Woden's) Hunt (or Asgardreia) was often considered to be a forewarning of disaster, such as pestilence or war. Mrs. Hemans sings in her poem entitled *The Wild Huntsman* :

> The Rhine flows bright ; but its waves ere long
>   Must hear a voice of war,
> And a clash of spears our hills among,
>   And a trumpet from afar ;
> And the brave on a bloody turf must lie,
> For the Wild Huntsman hath gone by !

The quarry of the phantom hunt took many forms. Sometimes it was a wild spirit horse, sometimes a boar, or again it would be white-breasted fairy maidens, or wood-nymphs, known as moss-maidens. If any scoffer joined the wild hallo in mockery, he was likely to bring on himself the terrible retribution of being caught up and whirled away by the demon hunt ; but those who halloed with sympathy and good faith were rewarded. A horse's leg would be thrown at them, and if they carefully kept this till the following day, it would change into a lump of gold !

Many people in England to-day fear to hear a dog howling at night and consider it an omen of death. They have, however, forgotten the origin of their superstition—the passing of Odin's Wild Hunt and baying hounds foretelling disaster.

The horse of Odin was grey in colour (like the clouds), and had eight feet, making him as swift as the wind when he rushed through mid-air. From this originated the oldest Northern riddle that has reached our days : " Who are the two who ride to the Thing ? Three eyes have they together, ten feet, and one tail, and thus they travel through the lands." The reason why Odin and his horse could boast but three eyes between them was that Odin had voluntarily sacrificed one of his eyes that he might obtain in exchange the wisdom which is his chief characteristic.

In some districts of Germany Odin is identified with the Saxon god Irmin, whose image, known as the Irminsul near Paderborn, was destroyed by Charlemagne in 772. Irmin used to ride across the sky in his chariot along the track we name " the Milky Way," but which by the ancient Germans was called " Irmin's Way." The chariot he used can still be seen in the constellation of Charles's Wain, or, as it is called in the North, Odin's Wain. When it rumbles through the sky, we earth-dwellers say it thunders. Odin was the inventor of runes, the first alphabet used by Northern peoples, and these he engraved upon Sleipnir's teeth.

In Mecklenburg it is a goddess who is said to lead the Wild Hunt. She is known as Frau Gode or Wode, the female form of Wustan or Odin. She rides a white horse on these occasions, and her attendants take the shape of hounds and all manner of wild beasts. Her appearance is always looked upon as an omen of great happiness and prosperity.

The castle of Rodenstein in the Odenwald is also an abode of the Wild Huntsman, and the local peasantry most firmly and devoutly believe in his actuality. Here his origin is ascribed to an earthly being—a proud and lawless baron who lived formerly in the castle, and who, one Sunday morning set forth a-hunting. He owned a ferocious pack of hounds which terrorised the surrounding country. Calling these to his side, he blew a tremendous blast on his horn to summon his followers. As he did so, two strangers in hunting costume rode up and took their places, one on either side of him. The young man on his right was mounted on a most beautiful white horse and was fair-haired and sweet of countenance. But the other horse was coal-black and his rider was dark and savage in appearance.

The Earl and his attendants set forth and soon started a stag, which bounded into some fields of corn just ripening for harvest. The peasant owners, seeing their hopes about to be destroyed, prayed the Earl by all that was sacred not to follow. The fair rider joined his plea to theirs, but the dark hunter urged him on, and his was the counsel that prevailed. The corn was trampled into dust, and the peasants called to Heaven to avenge them.

The chase sped on, and next encountered a young man who tended a herd of cows and calves. The hounds sprang furiously upon these inoffensive creatures, and the herdsman entreated the Earl to call them off, explaining that they were the sole support of certain widows and orphans. Again the two strangers intervened with opposite advice, and it was that given by the dark rider which was followed. The Earl urged his hounds on, and cattle and herdsman were slaughtered.

On again sped the hunt, till it reached a wood where dwelt a pious hermit, who, shocked by the cruel violence of this terrible oncoming, arose to make remonstrance. Once more the two strange riders urged conflicting counsel, and the evil one was victorious. The Earl, in fury at the hermit's presumption, lifted his whip to strike him down. But in an instant all was changed. From that moment, mounted still on his fiery hunter, changed now to a demon steed, he was doomed to ride until the Judgment Day, with all his hounds in full career, chasing a spectral stag, and himself pursued by avenging spirits. Ever since he has been the harbinger of woe and war ; and in seasons of public trouble is heard issuing forth with whirlwind speed as the midnight hour sounds, accompanied by the noise of spectral horse and horns and hounds, though it is seldom that the phantoms are visible.

A little lower down the hill on which Rodenstein castle stands is the Bauer-hof, or farm-house belonging to it, and here in former ages the array of the Wild Huntsman has been heard going out when war was approaching and coming in when peace was about to return.

On one occasion when a benighted chasseur heard this infernal chase pass beside him, he could not refrain from answering the " hallo " with which the Wild Huntsman cheered on his hounds, and calling out " Good sport to you ! " " Do you wish me good sport ? Then share the spoils," replied a hoarse voice, and a huge piece of foul flesh was thrown at him.

Soon after this adventure the daring chasseur lost two of his best horses, and he himself never wholly recovered from the effects of the encounter.

Sir Walter Scott has a fine poem on the Wild Huntsman, too long to be quoted in full, but well worth looking up. We will content our-selves with two verses, though we would like to give it at length.

This is the horn, and hound, and horse
That oft the lated peasant hears ;
Appall'd he signs the frequent cross,
When the wild din invades his ears.

The wakeful priest oft drops a tear
For human pride, for human woe,
When, at his midnight mass, he hears
The infernal cry of " Holla, ho ! "

Another version of the legend is found in the ancient German *Book of Heroes*, and in the " Wilkina " Saga.   Dietrich von Bern, who has been identified by some authorities with the historical Theodoric of Verona, in his latter days became weary of and disgusted with life, and found in the chase his one remaining pleasure.   One day, whilst he was having a refreshing dip in a stream, his servant came to tell him he had sighted a splendid stag.   The king immediately shouted for his horse, but it was not forthcoming.   Seeing a coal-black steed standing near, and longing to be after his quarry, he sprang on to the strange animal's back.   Instantly it was away with him.   His servant followed as well as he could, but was unable to overtake his master, who was never seen again.   The peasants say that even now the king leads the Wild Hunt upon the demon steed and is doomed to do so until Judgment Day.

The valley of the Murg in the northern part of the Schwarzwald is haunted by a female counterpart of the Wild Huntsman.   Dressed in the costume of three hundred years ago, she rides through the glades of the Black Forest, or flies through the air on moonlight nights.   On her head she wears a large black hat, and she is followed by a pack of black hounds breathing fire from their nostrils, and rides a black horse.   The spectre is thought to be the ghost of a former Countess of Eberstein, who, because of a false oath sworn by her, has been condemned to follow for ever what on earth was her favourite pursuit.

According to the legend, when still a denizen of the physical world, she wrongfully laid claim to land which belonged to her neighbour, the Count of Würtemberg, as she wished to hunt in his portion of the forest. She met the Count, by arrangement, on the disputed territory, that they might discuss the boundary together.   The argument not going favourably to her case, she swore, and called upon Heaven to witness, that she was standing on her own land. This was in a perverted sense a fact, for the crafty Countess when setting forth to keep her appointment had placed a handful of earth from her own territory in each shoe ! To this oath she added that no power in Heaven or Hell should stop her from hunting for ever in the Forest if she so chose. Her punishment was to be taken at her word and doomed to hunt on a demon horse with the demon pack at her heels till the end of time.

French tradition provides still another variant of this legend. *Le Grand Veneur* was an aerial huntsman who haunted the Forest of Fontainebleau. He was occasionally visible riding a black horse and accompanied by hounds. At one period he hunted so close to the royal palace that the attendants came out into the court, thinking that it was the king they heard returning from the chase, and on another occasion the king himself (Henry II) was startled, whilst hunting in his favourite forest, by the sounds of horns, the shouts of huntsmen, and the barking of dogs and trampling of horses. At first they sounded faintly in the distance, but gradually came near. Some of the king's company who were riding ahead of him " saw a great black man among the bushes," who, in funereal voice called out, " M'entendez-vous ? " or " Amendez-vous ? " The king made inquiries among the peasants and foresters about the apparition, and was told it was often seen, riding, and accompanied by a pack of hounds, but that it never did any injury.

On the eve of the murder of Henry IV, and again just before the terrible French Revolution broke forth, it is said that the Wild Huntsman's shouts were distinctly heard as he rode across the skies.

Uller, the Winter-god of the Norsemen, was also the God of Hunting, and was supposed to ride in the Wild Hunt and at times even to lead it, during the absence of Odin in the winter months. In Christian times his place in popular worship was taken by St. Hubert, the Hunter, and the saint is consequently known as the Wild Huntsman in some parts of France, and also in the Black Forest in Germany. Here, especially at the harvest season and on the feast of St. Hubert, may be heard the unearthly sound of his phantom hounds and the galloping feet of his goblin horses. They hurtle through space over tree-tops and roofs, without bit or bridle to control them. They are four in number, and each carries a knight in armour of sable hue with his visor down. In Northern France the Wild Hunt was called " Mesnée d'Hellequin," from Hel, Goddess of Death.

Another version of the Wild Huntsman was born in our islands in prehistoric days. Gwyn ap Nudd, one of the most prominent of the gods who figure in early British mythology, is the Wild Huntsman of Wales and the West of England, and it is his hunt which is sometimes heard, hot on the scent, in desolate places when darkness has fallen.

He is mounted on a demon horse, round-hoofed, " the torment of battle," of blackest hue, before whose feet armies would fall more quickly than broken rushes to the ground, and thus horsed, and accompanied by a demon hound, this god hunts—not the deer, but the souls of men. He is, in fact, the God of Death and Hades.

Another supposed founder of the Wild Hunt in England of olden days was the mythical King Herla. After him the hunt was called the Herlathing.

Later, we find the Wild Huntsman and his demon horse reappearing in England under the title of Herne the Hunter. They are said to have flourished in the reign of Richard II and to have been seen on many occasions by Henry VIII.

The Forest of Windsor was the home of Herne and his spectral band of wood-demons. His appearance must have been most picturesque. Robed in deer-skins, he wore on his head a helmet formed of a stag's skull, with antlers branching from it, and on his left arm carried a rusty iron chain with phosphoric fire burning in its links. A large horned owl flew before him, as he rode, sometimes alone, sometimes at the head of his demon band.

The horses which carried the hunters were coal-black, with flowing manes and tails, and eyes that glowed like carbuncles. They appeared to breathe fire and smoke as they rushed with furious speed through the forest in chase of the terrified deer, accompanied by a pack of large black hounds of equally hellish aspect.

On some occasions Herne, horse, and hounds are said to have vanished in smoke and flame from before the eyes of startled spectators.

Returning to quite modern times, we find that the Wild Huntsman, accompanied by a pack of headless hounds, is often to be seen in Cornwall and is especially given to haunt the Abbot's Way on Dartmoor. The following instance is well known locally. A certain farmer who lived on Dartmoor was riding home one night after spending the day at Widdicombe fair, where he had done some satisfactory business, and partaken freely of the cider for which Devon is famous. Before leaving, he had a further fortifier in the form of some spirit to keep out the cold as he rode home. He met with no adventure until he had passed the great ridge of Hambledon, and was ascending to a plateau where a circle of upright stones told that the Druids had once celebrated their mysteries on its face, when suddenly the surrounding silence was broken by the sound of a horn and the baying of hounds in full cry. The farmer drew rein to await what was coming, and a pack of hounds rushed past him followed by a huntsman on a black horse and garbed in black. Being still a good deal " elevated " by his potations, he fearlessly shouted to the huntsman, " Hullo ! Old Nick ! What sort of sport ? Show us some of your game ! " The black huntsman grimly replied to his rash speech, " There you are ! " and threw him something which the farmer caught, ere Nick disappeared from view. To his horror and astonishment he discovered by the light of the moon that it was the body of a dead baby which he held in his arms, and to crown the terror, that baby was his own ! Putting his horse to the gallop, the now completely sobered farmer rushed over the moor in a manner which would not have disgraced the Wild Huntsman himself, until he reached his home. As he pulled up by the gate, his wife came running out to meet him, almost frantic with anxiety, to tell him their little one had disappeared. The window had been opened and the cot was vacant. The poor farmer was too heartbroken to speak. For reply he held up the small dead form he carried, and later, when he had somewhat recovered, told of his terrible adventure. The bereaved parents sold their home and left the haunted place as soon as they were able. This is a well-authenticated instance of the doings of the Wild Hunt, and a friend of the author had it from people who knew the place where it occurred.

The Hunt is known there as " the Wish Hounds," and dwellers

in that district say it is often heard on stormy nights, the baying of the hounds and the blasts of the huntsman's horn sounding above the beating rain and wailing wind. According to some accounts, the hounds, instead of being headless, have gleaming eyes, and are of monstrous size, and the horses flash fire from their nostrils.

The leader of this Cornish Wild Hunt is said to be the infamous Lord Tregeagle, and his evil deeds in life and weird and awesome doings since death would fill a volume. He was guilty of more than one murder, and there was hardly a crime he had not committed whilst in the flesh, so it need not surprise us to find him still the same character in the spirit-world.

To take another modern instance, also from Cornwall, Sir Alfred Robbins in a letter published in the *Daily Mail* of October 19, 1921, under the heading " Unseen Hands," writes of a Satanic Hunt as follows :

" *To the Editor of the ' Daily Mail.'*

" SIR,—The story which has been told in your columns of ' the Unseen Hands ' is not the first tale of eerie mysteries of the Devon roads. One such was narrated to me, when very young, by those who had the facts at first hand. Some seventy years ago there lived in my own native town of Launceston, in Cornwall, which is only two miles from the Devon boundary, a ne'er-do-weel who, after many reckless adventures, told his intimates of the most appalling of all. He said that on the previous night as he was crossing Yeolm Bridge, which spans the stream between the two counties, he discovered himself in the midst of Satan and his hounds engaged in hunting. The demon threatened him that if ever again he crossed that bridge at night and interfered with the hunt he would be struck dead. The story was laughed at as the creation of a possible drunken dream, but the man himself was so impressed by it that for several years he was known to make long detours rather than go over Yeolm Bridge by night. But one evening, being at a town some fifteen miles away, and seeing there a carriage which was returning empty to Launceston, he asked the driver whether he could have a ride back on the step.

Assent was given and the journey made, and the driver was not particularly astonished on arriving at his stable to find the man had gone.

"Meantime the daughter of a neighbouring farmer was crossing Yeolm Bridge late that night, when she stumbled over the body of a man stretched at full length. It was the body of the man who had been, according to his own story, threatened with this very fate.

"An inquest was held, and as there was no evidence of violence or external injury of any kind, a number of the jury, who were acquainted with the man's strange story, wished to bring in a verdict, more often returned at that period than now, of ' Death by the Visitation of God.' The foreman pointed out to them that, if it were truly a case of visitation, the stroke, according to the tale, must have come, not from the Almighty, but from the Evil One ; and ultimately, though with reluctance, the jury gave a verdict of ' Death from Natural Causes.'

"That foreman was my father (the late Richard Robbins, of Launceston), and in my boyhood I was acquainted with the two principal witnesses—the driver of the carriage and the girl who discovered the body.

"ALFRED ROBBINS."

A posthumous miracle of Father Lesly, a Scottish capuchin, was in connection with the Wild Huntsman. The remains of the sainted father were buried on a hill which was haunted by the unearthly noises of the chase. But after the holy relics had been placed there, the land had rest and the demon hunt was heard no more. This is recorded in the Life of Father Bonaventura.

The Wild Hunt used also to be heard in the wilds of Ross-shire.

> The broken cry of deer
> Mangled by throttling dogs ; the shouts of men
> And hoofs thick beating on the hollow hill.
>   . . . Aghast the herdsman eyes
> The mountain's height, and all the ridges round,
> Yet not one trace of living wight discerns ;

Nor knows, o'erawed, and trembling as he stands,
To what, or whom, he owes his idle fear,
To ghost, to witch, to fairy, or to fiend ;
But wonders, and no end of wondering finds.
(Scottish Descriptive Poems.)

BIBLIOGRAPHY

The Mythology of the British Isles, by Charles Squire. (Blackie & Son, Ltd., London, 1905.)

Sully's *Memoirs*.

Scottish Descriptive Poems.

The Wild Huntsman, a poem by Sir Walter Scott.

Myths and Legends of the Middle Ages, by H. A. Guerber. (Geo. G. Harrap & Co., London, 1913.)

Myths of the Norsemen, by H. A. Guerber. (Geo. G. Harrap & Co., London, 1909.)

Article in *Occult Review*, November 1917 : " The Weird in the West Country."

The Black Forest, its People and Legends, by L. G. Seguin. (Hodder & Stoughton, London, 1885.)

CHAPTER VI

The Headless Phantom Horse

I T is very curious to note in how many cases the phantom horses which haunt the scenes of their former activities are headless, and usually nothing to account for this phenomenon is to be discovered.

Sometimes these truncated ghosts are ridden or driven by human phantoms who have also lost their craniums, or who carry them snugly tucked beneath their arms, or hold them at arm's length to illumine their path.

We incline to the opinion that most of these unattractive beings belong to the goblin- or demon-world, though in some cases legend and tradition clearly link them with beings who once habited earthly tabernacles, and it seems impossible to lay down any general law. Each case must be judged on its merits.

According to a very old legend, Glasgow was at one time haunted by a ghostly coachman, coach, and horses. The most curious characteristic of these steeds was that they went to the river to drink, though both they and their coachman were headless. In life this equipage belonged to a certain Bob Dragon, whose income is said to have been one guinea a minute.

Edinburgh boasts a similar apparition known as Major Weir's coach. It used to haunt the city streets by night, and many were those who testified to seeing or hearing it. Its first appearance was somewhere about the year 1770.

As might be expected, Cornwall, with its rich stores of legend, can furnish many stories of headless horses.

On one occasion certain labourers at Lanreath were startled by a phantom of headless horses drawing a carriage and driven by a man in black. They told their Rector, Mr. Mills, about it, and he in his turn consulted the Rev. Richard Dodge, who lived near Looe, and was famed as an exorcist. Mr. Dodge met Mr. Mills by appointment, but the ghost failed to turn up, so the two clergy left each other to pursue their homeward ways. But soon after the parting Mr. Dodge's horse became restive and refused to go on, and he, thinking its psychic senses might be keener than his own, wisely humoured it, and allowed it to bear him back to where he had left Mr. Mills. What was his distress to find his colleague lying prostrate on the ground, with the headless horses, their coach and driver, close beside him ! Leaping quickly from his saddle, Mr. Dodge murmured a prayer, and the ghostly driver, screaming " Dodge is come, I must be gone," whipped up his steeds and vanished into the night, never to reappear.

Sir Thomas Boleyn, who is known to fame as the sire of the unfortunate Anne who married Henry VIII, is said to haunt his ancient seat of Bickling Hall, in Norfolk, where, in 1507, poor Anne was born.

According to the tradition current in the country around, Sir Thomas Boleyn is doomed for a period of a thousand years, annually, on a certain night, to drive a coach which is drawn by four headless horses a circuit which takes him over twelve bridges in the neighbourhood. These include Aylsham, Burgh, Oxnead, Buxton, Coltishall, the two Meyton bridges, and Wrexham. On these occasions Sir Thomas carries his head under his arm whilst flames come forth from his mouth. The apparition is much feared by the rustic population, and few are they who will venture to loiter near any of the bridges when it is Sir Thomas's night for driving abroad.

According to *Notes and Queries*, No. 29, an informant stated that on one occasion he was actually hailed by Sir Thomas and asked to open a gate, but that " he warn't such a fool as to turn his head ; and well a' didn't, for Sir Thomas passed him full gallop like," and a voice spoke and said that he (Sir Thomas) could not hurt those who refused his requests, but that had he stopped, he would have carried him off. The same informant added that he had only met one person who had actually seen the phantom equipage.

There is a Welsh belief that the Devil sometimes assumes the shape of a headless horse. Our English hero Sir Francis Drake appears to have been a special favourite of the Old Gentleman. Tradition relates that it was the aid of Satan that enabled him to destroy the Spanish Armada. To accomplish this feat he went to Devil's Point, in Cornwall, where he cut pieces of wood, which as they fell into the water were magically transformed into well-equipped gunboats. Many other equally wonderful feats were performed by Sir Francis with the aid of his powerful friend, but what we are now concerned with is that since his death he drives at night. His coach is a black hearse, and it is drawn by headless horses, who are urged on by running devils and yelping, galloping, headless hounds. His route is through Jump, on the road from Tavistock to Plymouth. At the risk of being considered a " devil's advocate," one cannot but note how useful was the service his Satanic Majesty rendered to our beloved country !

Another member of the Drake family—also a bold, bad man— haunts the road between Exeter and Exmouth, mounted on the charger that carried him in his last fleshly ride, now alas ! headless.

The following is the story of their exit from this life as told me by one of the rider's descendants.

Elliot Drake flourished in the eighteenth century. One day, whilst drinking with a friend, he challenged his comrade to race against him to a certain inn, and swore that he would be the first to reach it, even if he broke his neck for it. The challenge was accepted, and they mounted their steeds and galloped off pell-mell along the road, Drake leading. Close to the goal, a high gate barred their way, but nothing daunted, Drake put his horse to the jump. With a supreme effort the gallant animal topped the barrier, but fell upon the further side, breaking his own and his master's neck. Ever since this tragedy horse and man have celebrated the anniversary of their ride by rushing again at full speed down the highway.

Lord Angosteen is another ghostly driver of headless horses. These phantoms, which are known as " Angosteen's Headless Horses," are supposed to haunt Vamborough Hill, E. Greenwich, and pull up at the Ship and Billet Inn. Here, the ghost of Lord Angosteen is said to get on to the coach and drive to his house, which is in the neighbourhood.

The phantoms, it is averred, have been seen by passers-by at 6 a.m. on a November morning, and Lord Angosteen himself, dressed in black velvet breeches and silk stockings, is often met with, and is quite a familiar figure locally.

Near Liverpool " the Headless Riders," supposed to be some of the Pretender's soldiers accompanying him on his flight from Ormskirk, are still to be seen on the main Preston Road between Maghull and Lydiate. They gallop for about a mile where the road is bounded by a grey stone wall on which their fleeting shadows may be distinctly seen. There is no hedge opposite that could be held to account for the phenomenon. Some people who have actually ridden or driven through the spectral troop say that the experience was preceded by the sound of rushing hoofs and the clanking of accoutrements. Others only see the shadows on the wall.

An eyewitness wrote to a friend of the author in 1908 as follows :

" Anyone wishing to experience this phenomenon should go at dusk and wait just before the turn into the Maghull Road. Queerly enough, old M—— and I were in it, and I saw shadows and heard noises which were unaccountable, and my cob shied and stood trembling while the soughing noise lasted."

The author's friend had had a similar experience. The phantoms ride towards Liverpool and away from Maghull. The local inhabitants do not willingly pass that way when the riders and their uncanny steeds are due.

BIBLIOGRAPHY

Abbeys, Castles, and Ancient Halls of England and Wales, by John Timbs. (Fredk. Warne & Co., London.)

CHAPTER VII

The Saxon Horse

THE Great Western Railway between Didcot and Shrivenham affords to the traveller watching from the southern side of the line a view of the great white horse of the Saxons, which is carved on an almost precipitous part of Uffington Hill on its northern side, some two miles distant from the railway. The hill is composed of chalk, and the enormous white horse, 374 feet long and 120 feet high, may be seen from a distance of twelve miles. Uffington lies two and a half miles outside the boundary of Wiltshire and is within that of Berkshire. Nearly all the other white horses are in Wiltshire, but we take this one first as it is undoubtedly the original of them all.

The ensign is supposed to have been cut by the pious King Alfred to commemorate his victory over the Danes in the great battle of Ashdown (or Æscendum), which was fought in 871.

Asser writes of it: " Four days after the battle of Reading, King

THE BIRD-BEAKED HORSE OF UFFINGTON:

Æthelread and Alfred his brother fought against the whole army of the pagans at Ashdown. . . . And the flower of the pagan youths were there slain, so that neither before nor since was ever such destruction known since the Saxons first gained Britain by their arms."

This was the battle that finally broke the Danish power in England.

The white horse has been preserved by the zeal of the country people living in its neighbourhood, and has presided over the site of the battle for nearly twelve hundred years. It has given to the valley below the name of the White Horse Vale. At one time a ceremony called " Scouring the White Horse " was periodically held, and the whole countryside would assemble to celebrate the event with all kinds of festivities.*

In 1738 this custom was spoken of by Dr. Wise as an old one.

* We are sorry to see the following paragraph in the *Daily Mail* of August 26, 1922, but hope the remedy suggested by the writer will be adopted, since it would be a thousand pities to let these national symbols perish :

" NEGLECTED ' WHITE HORSE '

" FAMOUS LANDMARK WHICH REQUIRES CLEANING

" The famous White Horse on the Berkshire Downs near Uffington—to which reference is made in *Tom Brown's Schooldays*—is but a shadow of its former glory. It can scarce be seen for want of a scouring. It has become so dirty of late years that travellers on the Great Western Railway line who still remember it as it was many years ago, standing out clear and active on the long range of chalk hills, complain that something ought to be done to renovate it. The horse is in commemoration of Alfred's victory at Ashdown, and is scheduled by Act of Parliament as an ancient monument.

" Several other white horses which can be prominently seen from railway lines in different parts of the country are also stated to require scouring, and it is suggested that the Girl Guides and Boy Scouts in the districts should perform the task. The following is a list of some of those that are still in existence :—

Wiltshire.—Westbury Horse, Marlborough Horse, Winterbourne Bassett Horse, Devizes Horse, Pewsey Horse, Wootton Bassett Horse, Calne Cherhill Horse.
Berkshire.—Uffington Horse.
Hampshire.—Alton Barnes Horse.
Warwick.—Tysoe Red Horse.
Dorset.—Osmington Horse, Cerne Abbas Giant.
Sussex.—Wilmington Giant.
Yorkshire.—Northwaite Horse, Thirsk Horse.
Buckinghamshire.—Whiteleaf Cross, Princes Risborough ; Bledlow Cross, near Princes Risborough.
Scotland.—Mormond Horse, Aberdeen.

" The White Horse at Uffington is one of the most popular and the most ancient. It is nearly 350 feet long, and in shape and outline it is lean and scraggy. It is mentioned in the Abingdon Abbey records as early as 1571."

Two years later a pamphlet appeared in which the scourings were incidentally referred to as taking place every seven years, but later records show longer and irregular intervals.

It must be confessed that, considered as a work of art—whilst the figure is extremely decorative—the original designer certainly did not belong to the naturalistic school, but appears to have been a post-impressionist of the first water, as a reference to the illustration will show !

During the last 150 years the outline seems to have been scarcely modified at all, and we may therefore presume that the design before us is much as the original makers left it.

The Rev. W. C. Plenderleath, M.A., in his interesting work on *The White Horses of the West of England*, has pointed out that this horse has the head of a bird and is beaked.   And he does not deem this to be due to an accident, or want of skill on the artist's part, but considers it has a symbolical significance.

For the interpretation of this he refers us to some contemporary British coins of Boadicea in which the same feature may be found, and he points out that the bird-headed steeds fulfil the description of the horses of Ceridwen (see " Corn-horse "), who is sometimes described by the bards as a white mare, and at other times is spoken of as " the high-crested hen."   He adds that Mr. Davies, in his Druidical *Mythology*, refers to a coin of Boadicea, saying that he believes the horse depicted on it was intended to represent Ceridwen herself.

These bird-horses are referred to in several poems of Taliesin preserved in the Myvyrian Archæology as " hen-headed steeds."

Mr. Hughes is reported in *The Times* of June 10, 1871, as giving it as his opinion that it is uncertain whether the white horse was cut out on the hill after the battle.   He says : " Indeed, I incline to believe that it was there long before, and that Ethelred and Alfred could not have spent an hour on such work in the crisis of 871."

We cannot help thinking Mr. Hughes has probability on his side.

The horse on Bratton Hill, near Westbury (Wilts.), was also carved by an artist of the school that scorns the mere imitation of nature, to celebrate another great victory of King Alfred.   But unfortunately a vandal of the name of Gee, whilst employed on a survey of Lord Abingdon's estates in 1778, " new-modelled " it, and entirely altered

its whole character. There is luckily still extant a drawing of the
first horse—made six years previously to its destruction—by Gough,
the editor of Camden, and a most weird and uncanny creature it

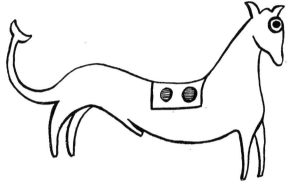

THE ORIGINAL HORSE OF BRATTON HILL.

would seem to have been, not one that an indifferent horseman would
care to mount, although it carried a saddle upon its back ! From the
appended sketch of the drawing (which the measurements show to be
much foreshortened) it will be seen that the horse was a male, and
that it bore the crescent moon upon its upturned tail.

The crescent was another symbol of Ceridwen, whom we have just
seen represented as a white mare ; and Taliesin, in the poem we referred
to then, speaks of the " strong horse of the crescent," and is supposed
by most commentators to mean thereby a son of Ceridwen by Nevion
(Neptune).

Apparently this is the steed here pictured. It should be remembered that the moon was regarded as masculine by the Saxons, so
that it was a fitter emblem of the son than of Ceridwen.

This horse is said to have been carved in A.D. 878 (that is, seven
years after the one at Uffington) to celebrate the battle in which King
Alfred, now not the mere lieutenant of his brother Ethelred, but King
of England and Commander-in-Chief, " fiercely warring against the
whole army of the Pagans with serried masses, and courageously
persevering for a long time, by Divine favour, at last gained the victory,
overthrew the Pagans with very great slaughter, and put them to
flight, and pursued them with deadly blows, even to their stronghold,
and all he found outside of it, men, horses, and sheep, he seized,

immediately killed the men, and boldly encamped before the entrance of the Pagan stronghold with all his army."

After a siege of fourteen days the enemy surrendered, and then came the carving of the white horse on the hillside to commemorate the triumph, or at least, so says local tradition. As usual, scholars are at variance, and in this case are doubtful if the battle took place in this neighbourhood at all !

We will next take the steed who reigns on Cherhill, Calne. Although the site is close to the spot where it is said that a great battle was fought in A.D. 821 between Egbert, King of the West Saxons, and Ceowulph, King of the Mercians, the horse has no claim to antiquity, and there is no local tradition of its superseding any previous horse. It was cut in the year 1780 by Dr. Christopher Allsop, who was Guild Steward of the borough, and living in Calne.

In this case the horse needs no label to tell us what species of animal we are viewing, for it is a truthful representation of a lively-looking cob that anyone might be proud to have in his stable.

It lies only about a quarter of a mile from the London high-road, and the traveller on this route can view it for several miles.

This horse is 129 feet in length and 142 feet in height, and the inner circle of its eye is 4 feet in diameter. At the time of writing (1922) this horse is sadly in need of scouring, as owing to the Great War all such things have had to be neglected, but we understand that a local lady has come to its rescue and asked permission to restore it. Formerly the Lord of the Manor was its groom !

This Pale Horse of the Saxons in olden days was credited with much mysterious power, and even its counterfeit was supposed to possess a life of its own and an ability of movement from which omens could be drawn, for it was a sacred link between Odin—the All-Father— and his people. The banner of the Pale Horse symbolised the presence of the god and was reverenced accordingly.

The standard of the ancient Saxons· was preserved in the royal shield of the House of Hanover. It was reintroduced into England by the Georges, and one of our more modern white horses bears the figure of George III mounted upon it.

This horse is carved on the hills between Preston and Osmington, in Dorsetshire, and was cut about the beginning of last century by a soldier whose regiment was quartered near, and was made to commemorate the King's visit to Weymouth.

The ensign now forms the badge of many British regiments. We find it on the hat of a Scots Grey in 1745, to whom, perhaps, this emblem was particularly appropriate. Certain modifications of the Saxon trotting white horse should here be noted, such as that it is now galloping, and is winged. The House of Savoy, which is also descended from the Saxons, has preserved the white horse as ensign, but its distinguishing feature is that it is rampant.

The galloping white horse, which is the ensign of Kent and may be seen to-day impressed on Kentish hop-pockets and bags, dates from the year 449, when Hengist (the stallion) and Horsa (the horse) landed on Kentish shores with the sacred emblem emblazoned on their banner. Bishop Nicholson, in his *English Atlas*, considers that the names Hengist and Horsa were not proper at all, but only emblematical ; " even as the Emperor of the Germans was called the Eagle, and the King of France the Lily."

There may still be seen at Aylesford, in Kent, the White Horse Stone. The legend attached to it is that one who rode a white horse was killed on the spot where it stands. In all probability this takes us back to the days of the great battle of Crayford, in which Horsa was slain. The two chiefs were brothers and boasted their divine descent from the god Woden (see " Hooden Horse "). They were joined by five thousand Saxons in their invasion of Britain and spared neither age nor sex in their bloody conquest.

Aubrey, in a transcript of his MSS. preserved in the museum of the Wilts Archæological Society at Devizes, says : " The white horse (Uffington) was made by Hengist, who bore one on his arms or standard," and this confirms the opinion of Mr. Hughes which we have already quoted as to its early date.

There are a number of other white horses carved on English hillsides, but all are of comparatively modern date. For instance, the White Horse of Kilburn, in Yorkshire, which is engraved on a hillside of the Hambledon Range, was cut in 1857 to the design of a local schoolmaster. It is 100 yards long and 76 yards high, and its making occupied 30 men and took six tons of limestone. It can be seen on a clear day from York Minster, 25 miles away. Those who wish to learn more about these modern white horses should consult Mr. Plenderleath's most interesting work, where old and new ones are pictured and described.

Mr. Craveth Read has well described the attitude of the English of to-day towards their ancient sacred symbol. " They have forgotten that they are horses," he says, " though the fact remains. Do they not still worship their totem at their chief festivals, abstain from eating it, and pay more attention to its breeding than to their own ? "

The abstention from eating horse-flesh, practised even to-day, by the Anglo-Saxons was of course originally a feature of their religion, and it was probably of the very strong views and feelings of the British converts to the Christian Church that Pope Gregory was thinking when in 732 he wrote to St. Boniface : " Thou hast permitted to some the flesh of the wild horse, and to most that of the tame. Henceforward, holy brother, thou shalt in no wise allow it."

This strict command, coming from the head of the Church which had thrown over all its Jewish parent's distinctions between clean and unclean meats, certainly must have had some strong reason behind it.

That most delightful of philologists, George Borrow, has given us further illumination on this point of the close connection of the English with their symbol. He informs us that the word " mare in old English stands for woman, . . . and likewise in vulgar English, signifies a woman."

No wonder we are a " horsey " people ! We cannot dissociate ourselves from our symbol.

BIBLIOGRAPHY

Gentleman's Magazine Library of Popular Superstitions.
Universal History, Ancient and Modern, by William Mavor, LL.D., vol. xix, p. 23. (Richard Phillips, London, 1803.)
The White Horses of the West of England, by the Rev. W. C. Plenderleath, M.A. Second edition. (Allen & Storr, London, 1892.)
Natural and Social Morals, by Craveth Read.
The Romany Rye, by George Borrow. (Thomas Nelson & Sons.)
The National Encyclopædia, by Writers of Eminence. Article : " Berkshire." (Wm. Mackenzie, London, about 1874.)

CHAPTER VIII

The Trojan Horse

AMONG all the figures of ancient history that most appealed to our youthful imagination, the horse of Troy surely wins in a canter, and a closer inspection of the famous steed only increases its fascination for young and old alike.

The horse seems to have been intimately interwoven with the destiny of Troy from the earliest inception of that fated city to its final destruction. According to Virgil, Troy was built by Neptune, and, as we shall see in a later chapter, that deity was the God of Horses as well as of the Sea.

From Plutarch we learn that the city was taken three times, and always the fateful animal was the cause. Hercules was the first who wasted the streets and broke down the walls, and his quarrel was that Laomedon, the first King of Troy, had enlisted his services to rescue his daughter Hesione from a sea-monster, and then refused to bestow on him the promised reward of six beautiful, and probably sacred, horses.

The next occasion on which Troy figures in history is in connection with the war waged by the Greeks for the recovery of the beautiful Helen, abducted by Paris, son of Priam, King of Troy. This led to Troy being taken for the second time, the captor now being Agamemnon, and his means, the famous horse of wood, whose story with its inner meaning we are about to consider.

The third and last occasion on which the city was taken it fell to Charidemus. A horse gave him the victory, for it stood in the way and hindered the Trojans from shutting the city gates in-time to keep out the foe.

73

The sacred character attached to this animal by the ancient Grecians is well illustrated in the story recorded by Pausanias of how Tyndareus, seventh King of Sparta, famed as the father of the beautiful Helen, being fearful of the revenge her rejected suitors might take, caused all her many lovers to swear to protect her. To ratify and give solemnity to this oath he sacrificed a horse, and having cut it in portions, he made them to swear whilst standing on parts of the sacred animal, for well he knew that none dare violate a vow so sanctified.

Eventually, the choice of the beautiful Helen fell on Menelaüs, the brother of Agamemnon ; but they had not long been wedded when Paris, universally acknowledged as the handsomest man of his age, appeared upon the scene, and so captivated the heart of Helen that she left her country and husband and was transported with all her treasure to the Trojan land.

Then it was that Menelaüs, acting on Agamemnon's advice, demanded the performance of the vow so solemnly made by Helen's princely admirers, and their assistance in an expedition against Troy, to avenge the wrong.

Thus commenced the famous ten years' war somewhere about 1700 B.C.

We may here note that one of the princes who had bound himself by the oath was unwilling, when the call came, to leave his vast possessions. This was Echepolus of Sicyon, but he offered to send in his stead his celebrated mare Œthe, of unsurpassed speed. This offer was accepted, it being considered that a good horse was a far more valuable help than an unwilling soldier.

An incident which occurred during the siege of the city further illustrates the religious veneration with which horses were regarded. According to Virgil's account, the Grecian soldiers were becoming depressed by their long-continued failure, and even King Agamemnon had begun to lose heart, when Diomede and Ulysses were specially inspired and aided by Minerva to capture the horses of Rhesus, King of the Thracians, at night, whilst the enemy slept.

These milk-white steeds were harnessed with gold and silver trappings and were reputed to be swifter than the wind. As they were sacred animals, a special significance was attached to their capture,

THE TROJAN HORSE.
(*By Holloway, after* **M**. *Oldfield Howey.*)

75

and as soon as the glad news that they were taken became known in the camp, the hearts of the soldiers revived at the happy omen. For had not the oracle said that Troy should be taken if the horses of Rhesus could be prevented from drinking the waters of the Xanthus or eating the grass of Trojan soil ?

Events certainly justified this prophecy, and not only so but its fulfilment was brought about by the ruse of the famous image of the sacred horse that we are now about to describe.

And here we must note that the title of " Trojan horse " by which it is generally known is a totally incorrect one. It should rather be spoken of as the " Grecian mare," for, firstly, it was conceived and created by the Greeks, not the Trojans, and secondly, Virgil's description makes it indisputably clear that it was a mare and not a horse. This is only what we should expect, since it was made by direction of, and as an offering to, the chaste and virgin goddess Minerva, to whom a male would scarcely be an acceptable gift.

According to Virgil's account, Ulysses, in the tenth year of the siege of Troy, despairing of taking the city by siege or combat, determined to do so by stratagem. Acting on the advice of Calchas, the priest and soothsayer, he had a monstrous wooden effigy of a mare, " the size of a mountain," built of planks of fir and maple, and so designed as to be capable of concealing a band of soldiers within its ample form. He proclaimed as his reason for the strange creation that he had decided to abandon the siege, and wished to make a peace-offering to Minerva that he might be assured of a prosperous voyage home to Greece.

Accordingly, after concealing some of the bravest of the chiefs in its womb, the rest of the besiegers withdrew as if they had departed to their homes, but really only to the island of Tenedos, within hail of their friends, to await a favourable moment to return and take Troy by surprise.

Now, Ulysses had a friend named Sinon, who was famous as a master of double-dealing and craftiness, and he undertook to so mislead and deceive the Trojans that they should take the monstrous mare within their gates, when he would find means to open the door concealed within its side and release the hidden Grecian warriors.

He further advised the Grecians to return from Tenedos to Troy by night to join up with those in the mare who would have the gates open and be awaiting them. His advice was followed, and all went as he had planned. The Trojans, believing that their enemy had really fled discomfited, issued joyously forth from their city gates and hastened to view the deserted Grecian camp. Their eyes at once turned in amazement to the enormous mare, the Grecian propitiation to Minerva, and one of the elders of the city advised that it should be brought within the walls and set in the citadel. But Capys and other prudent ones urged that it might be a trap, and should be drowned or burned, or that it should be pierced to see if it contained a hidden enemy.

Laocoon, the son of Priam and priest of Apollo, also came forward and warned the people of the mare's true nature, crying aloud :

> " Oh, wretched countrymen ! what fury reigns ?
> What more than madness has possessed your brains ?
> Think you the Grecians from your coasts are gone ?
> And are Ulysses' arts no better known ?
> This hollow framework either must inclose
> Within its blind recess our secret foes ;
> Or 'tis an engine raised above the town,
> T' o'erlook the walls and then to batter down,
> Somewhat is sure designed by fraud or force—
> Trust not their presents, nor admit the horse."

And, as he spoke, Laocoon hurled his great spear at the mare, so that its hollow sides rang. His action would have saved the city, had not the gods ordained otherwise. But at this juncture some shepherds appeared dragging a Grecian youth they had discovered hiding in the marshes.

Now, this man was none other than Sinon, who had suffered himself to be made prisoner that he might accomplish his perfidious scheme for the destruction of Troy. The Trojans crowded round the helpless captive, mocking and insulting him, but Sinon gained the sympathy of his generous foes by telling a piteous story of the persecution he had suffered from his own countrymen, from whom he said he had fled since they were about to offer him as a sacrifice to Apollo. He then professed to disclose the design of his compatriots in creating the mare, saying that their conduct to him had been so outrageously cruel as to leave him, free from all ties of honour or friendship, willing to reveal their dark plots.

He proceeded to relate how the Grecians were convinced that their only hope of success in the war lay in the favour and protection of Minerva, but that from the day when Diomed and Ulysses had dared with bloody hands to snatch her image from her holy place in Troy, her face had been turned from them, and the hope of the Greeks had ebbed.

Calchas, the priest and soothsayer, had told them they must cross the seas again and seek at home new omens for the war ere they could hope for victory. He had also directed them before embarking to make the likeness of a mare to be a peace-offering to Minerva. They were to make it of enormous bulk, continued Sinon craftily, so that the Trojans might not receive it into their gates, nor bring it within their walls, and get safety for themselves thereby. He deemed that, not knowing its sacred character, they would be certain to violate it in some way as the work of their enemy, and if they did so, a signal ruin awaited them. If, on the other hand, they drew the mare with honour into their city, they would so win the favour of Minerva as to be enabled to carry successful war into the very centre of Greece, and bring on her the doom she sought to inflict on Troy.

The unsuspecting Trojans believed Sinon's clever fabrication, and whilst they yet hung upon his words, a terrible portent was sent by the gods to deceive them to their own undoing. Laocoon, the priest of Neptune,[1] was sacrificing a bull at the altar of his god. Suddenly two awful serpents appeared upon the sea, their breasts erect above the waves, their tails lashing the waters, their eyes red as blood, making for the shore accompanied by loud rumbling noises and suffused with fire and blood. They made straight for the altar, their forked tongues hissing loudly with rage. The two little sons of Laocoon were standing beside him ; and twining round these boys, the serpents crushed them to death. Laocoon rushed to save his children, but only shared their fate. The unfortunate priest vainly raised cries of agony to heaven. The serpents accomplished their fatal work and

[1] Note: It should be remembered that Neptune was God of horses, and therefore naturally offended by Laocoon's affront to the mare.

then glided to the temple of the great Minerva and lay under the feet of the goddess.

No longer did hesitation and caution prevail. At any cost Minerva's favour must be regained. Laocoon was pronounced deservedly punished for his crime in assaulting the sacred mare with his weapon. Unanimously the populace urged that the Grecian offering should be brought within the city. They opened wide the Scæan Gate and pulled down the wall at its side. Rollers were placed under the mare's feet. Ropes were hung around its neck, and amid dancing and singing the emblematic monster was drawn into the very centre of the citadel. The temples were adorned with festive boughs in its honour, and the remainder of the day passed in feasting and rejoicing.

And yet there were not lacking omens of the trouble to come. Four times on the threshold of the gate the mare halted, four times the arms resounded within. Cassandra also opened her mouth and prophesied the doom of the city, but none heeded her.

At last night fell, and the men of Troy lay asleep. Then the Grecian soldiers emerged from their wooden prison, slew the Trojan guards, opened the city gates and set Troy ablaze.

When, long after these events, the poet Demodorus, at the request of Ulysses, sang their story at a feast, Homer tells us that :

> Full of the god, he raised his lofty strain,
>
> .   .   .   .   .
>
> How e'en in Ilion's walls, in deathful bands,
> Came the stern Greeks by Troy's assisting hands ;
> All Troy upheaved the steed ; of differing mind,
> Various the Trojans counselled ; part consigned
> The monster to the sword, part sentence gave
> To plunge it headlong in the whelming wave ;
> Th' unwise prevail, they lodge it in the towers,
> An offering sacred to th' immortal Powers :
> Th' unwise award to lodge it in the walls,
> And by the God's decree proud Ilion falls ;
> Destruction enters in the treacherous wood,
> And vengeful slaughter fierce for human blood.
> He sung the Greeks stern-issuing from the steed,
> How Ilion burns, how all her fathers bleed.
>
> (*Odyssey,* viii, 547–64, Pope's trans.)

Among the soldiers concealed in the womb of the mare was Diomede, the Tyrant of Thrace, who was the constant companion of Ulysses in his adventures. Dante speaks of them as inseparable even in hell, and thus refers to these heroes of the famous ruse :

> Ulysses there, and Diomede endure
> Their penal tortures, thus to vengeance now
> Together hasting, as erstwhile to wrath.
> These in the flame with ceaseless groans deplore
> The ambush of the horse.
>
> (*Hell*, canto xxvi.)

We must not think of Diomede as merely acting a part in the veneration he professed for the mare. That he regarded horses as sacred is proved by the legend that he fed his steeds with the strangers who visited his coasts. This was evidently a religious sacrifice, for strangers were regarded as the proper offering to certain deities. Thus Busiris, the King of Egypt, sacrificed to his gods all unknown persons who set foot on his territory :

> Oh fly, or here with stranger's blood imbrued
> Busiris' altars thou shalt find renewed.
> Amidst his slaughtered guests his altars stood
> Obscene with gore and baked with human blood.
>
> (Camoen's *Lusiad*, Bk. XI.)

The seventh labour of Hercules was the punishment of Diomede for this cruel religious custom. He threw Diomede to his own mares, and when they had devoured him, led them to Eurystheus, King of Argos—his taskmaster appointed by the gods—in token that this labour was completed.

The names of Diomede's mares were Dinos (Dreadful) and Lampon (Bright-eyed). They are known as the Thracian Mares.

After Diomede's death the Veneti, who dwelt by the Adriatic Sea, and were famed for their breed of swift horses, made a sacred grove where they sacrificed a white horse to this hero.

From the story of the horse of Troy arose the Latin proverb, " 'Tis a Trojan horse," meaning that under a religious cloak a venomous intent was veiled. Probably the device of the stalking horse (Anglo-Saxon *stælcan*, " to walk with strides ") was not derived from Ulysses' achievement ; but though it may have been independently evolved, we find the same root idea. The sacred figure of the horse —and it was as venerated by Anglo-Saxon as by Grecian religious thought—is used at once to deceive the intended victim and to propitiate the god.

Fowlers (not so very long ago) used to conceal themselves behind a canvas representing a horse grazing, and " stalked " step by step till they got within shot of their game.

Shakespeare alludes to this practice when he says :

" He uses his folly like a stalking horse, and under the presentation of that, he shoots his wit " (*As You Like It*, V, 4).

BIBLIOGRAPHY

Story of the Trojan War : an Epitome (from classic writers), with a Preface by the Lord Bishop of Gloucester and Bristol. (James Blackwood & Co., London, 1874.)

The Stories of the Iliad and the Æneid, by Alfred J. Church, M.A. (Seeley & Co., London, 1886.)

The Æneid, II, 257–64. Virgil.

M. *Oldfield Howey.*

CHAPTER IX

The Hobby-horse

" The hobby-horse is forgot."
(*Love's Labour's Lost*, Act III. sc. 1.)

SHAKESPEARE seems to have thought of this fact as a most remarkable omen or phenomenon, for he puts the same words into Hamlet's mouth :
" Else shall he not suffer thinking on, with the hobby-horse ; whose epitaph is, For O, for O, the hobby-horse is forgot."

This creature was not then the harmless toy of little children, or the pet foible of those who were older, but was regarded by the Puritans of those times as so dangerous to the soul that they exerted all their power and influence to banish it from the May games and other festal occasions on which it was wont to appear.

The common people, however, were just as unwilling to lose it, and clung to it with the most extraordinary pertinacity, which is probably the reason why when anyone cherishes some small folly and will not abandon it, we say it is his hobby-horse. At last the Puritans were successful in their campaign, and the hobby was banished from the May games, along with Friar Tuck and Maid Marian —probably on the ground that all were tainted with popery, though actually the hobby is of pagan origin.

We have already noted that Neptune is God of Horses as well

as of Waters. We will now review an old rite, that prevailed until recent times at Padstow in Cornwall, which seems to connect the hobby-horse with the sea-deity.

The hobby-horse took the place of honour in the May-day celebrations which were held in that town, and its form was composed in the following manner.

A horse's head with a horse-hair mane was attached to a body distended by a hoop, behind which hung a horse's tail. The rider wore a ferocious-looking mask with red eyes, and a dress of sailcloth painted black. These grotesque figures were accompanied by a flower-decked crowd, who danced and sang before all the principal houses in the town. When they had completed the circuit of the place, the hobby-horse was ridden to the sea and submerged in the waves, the belief being that the horses and cattle of the inhabitants would thereby be protected throughout the coming year. No doubt this custom was originally an appeal to Neptune, and the hobby-horse a substitute for an actual horse ; but some writers see in the rite the remnant of an ancient morality play, and say that the hobby-horse represented the Devil or Evil Principle.

It would seem that the first of May is known as " Dipping Day " in Cornwall, for then the boys of the village go out with buckets and syringes and half drown or " dip " anyone, without regard to person or circumstance, who is not wearing a sprig of may in his cap. In connection with this we may note that Hitchin's account of the hobby-horse rite as it was practised in his day differs a good deal from that given above, though it is the Padstow horse he is describing.

According to this writer, the " horse," with its attendant train of men, women, and children, would proceed to a place known as Traitor Pool, in which it was always supposed to drink. The hobby's head was here dipped into the water, then quickly withdrawn, and the muddy liquid shaken over the spectators, to their great delight and amusement. The day generally ended in riot and dissipation.

Some writers would see in the Padstow horse the commemoration of the escape of a white horse from the flood that submerged a large part of Cornwall, known as Lyonesse, many hundreds of years ago, but this hardly seems a sufficient *raison d'être*. Certainly the water-horse is a Celtic tradition, and at Minehead, in Somersetshire, where the ceremony of the hobby-horse has been kept up from remote antiquity on May-day Eve and the two following days by the seamen of the town, it is known as a Hobby, or " Sailor's Horse."

The ancient marine ritual of the Dead Horse has much in common with the Sailor's Horse just described, though it appears to have a totally different meaning. To throw light on this, we must consider certain slang expressions. For instance, " to horse a bill " is to try and obtain payment for work not yet done. " To pay for a dead horse " is to pay for something that has been consumed or lost, or from which one has received or will receive no return, as if it were a horse which had died before being paid for. " To pull the dead horse " is to work for wages that have been paid in advance, and this brings us to the old-time seaman's ritual.

In the days of sailing-ships the crew used to sign on at the shipping master's office the day before sailing, and each claimed an advance of a month's pay. This was not given to them in cash, but in the form of an advance-note payable some days after the ship left port. The store-keepers and crimpers of the dock used to cash these notes at a big discount, and the sailors would spend the proceeds in merry-making before they embarked.

And now, before the revellers of the previous night, lay thirty days of hard and unremunerative work, for the Dead Horse, until at length the month expired and they could bury his remains in triumph. The " Horse " would be constructed from oakum and timber dunnage, and to it was attached a long line that a score or so of sailors could lay hold on. Then, starting from the forecastle-head, a slow and mock-solemn procession would wend its way aft, along the weather-side of the ship, whilst the chantey-man sang this dirge :

> " They say, old man, that your horse is dead—
>   And we say so, and we hope so !
> Oh, they say, old man, that your horse is dead—
>   Oh, po-o-or o-old man !
> And when he's dead we'll tan his hide—
>   And we say so, and we hope so !
> Yes, when he's dead we'll tan his hide —
>   Oh, po-o-or o-old man ! "

The song would wind through many verses describing what was to be done to the dead horse ; until they brought it up before the skipper and mates, by the rail of the poop. The Boatswain would then announce to the Old Man that the Horse had got his sailing orders. This was the signal for the Old Man to hand out rum to the crew. Then the procession would advance again ; this time down the lee side, singing the dirge as they marched. The Boatswain would meanwhile have taken up his post upon the knight-heads to perform the last offices. He first anointed the corpse with (paraffin) oil, and then set a light to it. The effigy was quickly in flames, and the burning figure of the Dead Horse was flung into the surrounding ocean, illuminating the night with its flare, whilst the crew sang in chorus once more :

> " Your horse is dead, and a good job too—
> And we say so, and we hope so !
> Oh, your horse is dead, and a good job too—
> Oh, po-o-or o-old man ! "

Next day the crew would work with a new zest and spirit, for the Dead Horse was no more.

The water-horse may also be found in the *Arabian Nights* and in the legends of all southern European countries ; but we have gone into this aspect of our hobby's character more fully in the chapter on " Sea-horses," to which we refer the reader.

But yet another explanation has been given of the inner meaning of the hobby-horse. This is that since the Maypole is, in reality, a phallos, it is probable that the hobby-horse was originally a phallic stallion like the Indian horse Mamojī. In this connection it should be compared with the bridal horse of India, described and pictured in another chapter. Its position next to the Maypole seems to emphasise this possibility, though, on the other hand, it was often introduced on festivals of different origin—Christmas Day, New Year's Day, and Twelfth Day.

The hobby-horse occupies a place in a painted glass window at Betley, in Staffordshire, which Douce attributes to the reign of Edward IV, and which he says is the oldest representation extant of an English May game and morris dance. The window has twelve panes and in the twelfth is the Maypole. Knight's edition of Brand's *Popular Antiquities* (I, 145) has an illustration of this window.

It is somewhat difficult to know under what heading to place the ceremony we are about to describe, as in form it so much resembles the other Irish rite—described by Charlotte Elizabeth—which from the date of its celebration we have inserted in the chapter on Sun-horses. But from the circumstance that this custom is, or rather was, observed on May Day, I rather incline to connect it with the hobby-horse.

On the first of May the men and boys of Dublin would cut a may-bush—generally a white-thorn about 4 or 5 feet high—and having planted it, would affix candles to its boughs and set them alight in such manner as not to burn the tree. Then a large fire would be lighted, and in this would be cast a horse's skull and other bones obtained from the tanners' yards in a part of the suburbs called Kilmainham. This custom gave rise to a threat even now made use of locally, " I will drag you like a horse's head to the bone-fire." When the fire was burning, the boys, giving three huzzas, would dance and jump around it, and when the candles on the may-bush were burnt out, it was also thrown into the flames. The celebrants would remain until the fire was exhausted and then return to their homes at the end of the day.

Bromley Pagets (also called Abbots Bromley) was remarkable for an extraordinary sport which was known as the Hobby-horse Dance held on these occasions. In this a man representing Robin Hood would ride upon the image of the horse, which was made of boards, carrying in his hands a bow and arrow, with which he made a snapping noise, keeping time to music played upon the accordion by a musician who accompanied him. Six other performers, adorned with reindeers' heads fastened on to their shoulders, and breeches spotted to suggest the deers' dappled hides, danced the " hay " and other country dances. The hobby-horse held a pot, which the reeves of the town kept filled with cake and ale, towards the expenses of which the spectators were expected to contribute a penny. What remained of the collection repaired the church and supported the poor. This custom has survived to modern days.

Beaumont and Fletcher allude to the hobby-horse dance in their *Knight of the Burning Pestle*, IV. 5 :

" The morris rings, while hobby-horse doth foot it feateously."

Hobby-horsing used to be a great custom in Somersetshire, and on the first of May, in Dunster, a procession of persons carrying grotesque figures of men and horses, which hid the bearers from view, marched around the town, and then went to Dunster Castle, where they were hospitably rewarded with money, cakes, and ale.

The Hobby-horse also finds a place in the morris dance which is performed annually at Revesby, in Lincolnshire, on October 20, and seems to be represented in much the same manner as that of Dunster Castle.

We have already made reference to the hobby-horse of Minehead. Mr. Percy Maylam, in his interesting book, *The Hooden Horse*, says of this :

" The following description of this hobby-horse has been sent to me by Mr. H. W. Kille, of Avalon, Minehead, Somersetshire : ' The custom of the hobby-horse, as practised at Minehead, is exceedingly ancient, having been kept up from time immemorial. The structure which is termed the *horse* bears a very crude resemblance to that animal, the wooden frame-work of which it is formed being covered with gaudy-coloured drapery and a profusion of ribbons. There is a hole in the middle of the back of the horse through which a man thrusts his head, which is covered with a grotesque mask and head-dress, and the framework is thus borne on the man's shoulders, his body and legs being concealed by gay houselling which reaches to the ground. In this fashion he capers about the streets, occasionally swinging round the tail, which is a long rope to which is attached a cow's tail, with considerable force, thereby clearing his way. The horse is accompanied by a man with a tabor—an old-fashioned drum— and he keeps up a monotonous tum-tumming the whole time. Of course largesse is demanded of the spectators. A quaint ceremony called *pursing* or *booting* was once practised on such as refused to give, but this is rarely done now. The people of Minehead are inclined rather to look askance on the hobby-horse, but he still flourishes, the custom being kept up by the seamen, who believe that no one can interfere with their rights so long as three rules are observed.

The custom is kept up for three days at the beginning of May, and on the first day at six o'clock in the morning the party must visit a certain cross-road to the west of the town. The second rule is that on the evening of the third day at ten o'clock they shall finish at a cross-road in the opposite direction ; the third being that the custom must not be allowed to drop through, even for one year, and these rules have always been adhered to with the greatest strictness. The custom is also kept up at Padstow, but it is alleged by the Minehead sailors that the Padstow men stole the idea from them and copied their horse. . . . Mrs. Story Maskelyne, of Bassett Down House, Swindon, who was at Minehead this very last May Day (1909), informs me that the custom is still kept up—that on May-day Eve the town was alive with merry children dressed up as hobby-horses. One huge horse perambulated the streets later on, but the boys begin earlier, in small parties, each with a rattle and drum.' ''

Salisbury possesses a giant hobby-horse known as " Hobnob," which used to parade the streets, until its appearance led to so much ruffianism that the Corporation interned it in the museum, though it still figures in public processions on special occasions.

This hobby has a movable lower jaw with sharp teeth of iron. This is worked by a leather strap controlled by the man who supports the effigy on his shoulders. He imitates the motions of a spirited horse, and by means of the strap, grabs at, and often rends, the clothes of those near by.

Many other hobby-horses appear to have been suppressed in the towns that once supported them, for the reason that prevailed with the Salisbury authorities. We wish all had been preserved in a similar way, but no doubt numbers were destroyed because of the zeal of the Puritans. It is probable that it was the ruffianism of the crowd on these occasions that originated the term " horse-play."

The hobby-horse has many times been referred to and described by playwrights and novelists, and I think it will interest my readers if I quote one or two of these authors.

In an old play by William Sampson, dated 1696, we read : " He'll keep more stir with the Hobby Horse, than he did with the pipers at Tedbury Bull-running " (*The Faire Maide of Clifton*, Act V).

Sir Walter Scott gives a short description of the hobby-horse in one of his novels : " Here one fellow with a horse's head painted before him, and a tail behind, and the whole covered with a long foot-cloth which was supposed to hide the body of the animal, ambled, caracoled, pranced, and plunged, as he performed the celebrated part of the hobbie-horse, so often alluded to in our ancient drama " (*Abbot*, xiv).

We are indebted to Harrison Ainsworth for a fuller description of the hobby-horse's appearance in a May-day procession in the early part of the seventeenth century :

" Lastly came one of the main features of the pageant. This was the hobby-horse. The hue of this spirited charger was pinkish white, and his housings were of crimson cloth hanging to the ground, so as to conceal the rider's real legs, though a pair of sham ones dangled at the side. His bit was of gold, and his bridle red morocco leather, while his rider was very sumptuously arrayed in a purple mantle, bordered with gold, with a rich cap of the same regal hue on his head, encircled with gold, and having a red feather stuck in it. The hobby-horse had a plume of nodding feathers on his head, and careered from side to side . . . indulging in playful fancies and vagaries . . . to the huge delight of the beholders. Nor must it be omitted, as it was a matter of great wonderment to the lookers-on, that by some legerdemain contrivance the rider of the hobby-horse had a couple of daggers stuck in his cheeks, while from his steed's bridle hung a silver ladle, which he held now and then to the crowd, and in which, when he did so, a few coins were sure to rattle. After the hobby-horse came the May-pole."

We may derive the word hobby-horse from the early English *hobby*, " a nag," or small pet riding-horse, but some say it has reference to the movements of the effigy in imitation of the animal. In this latter case it is derived from the Dutch *hobben*, " to toss, or move up and down," as in the canter of a horse, and is a weakened form of *hoppen*, rendered in English by *hop*, " a leap, especially on one foot." It should be compared with the North Friesic *hoppe*, " a horse," the Danish *hoppe*, " a mare," the old Swedish *hoppa*, " a young mare." etc.

BIBLIOGRAPHY

Popular Romances of the West of England (a new edition), edited by Robert Hunt, F.R.S. (Chatto & Windus, London, 1896.)

Lancashire Witches, by Harrison Ainsworth.

The Golden Bough, by J. G. Frazer, Part 1, Vol. II, p. 68.

The Faire Maide of Clifton, by Wm. Sampson, Act. V. (1696.)

Abbeys, Castles, and Ancient Halls of England and Wales, by John Timbs. (Fredk. Warne & Co., London, 1869.)

The Mirror of Literature, Amusement, and Instruction, XIX, p. 228. (Printed and published by J. Limbird, London.)

Natural History of Staffordshire, by Dr. Plott, p. 434. (1686.)

Sir Benjamin Stone's Pictures. (Cassell & Co., London, 1905.)

The Hooden Horse: an East Kent Christmas Custom, by Percy Maylam. (Canterbury. Only 313 copies privately printed, 1909.)

Every-day Book, Vol. II, p. 595.

Notes and Queries, First Series, Vol. XII, p. 297.

History of Cornwall, by Hitchins, Vol. I, p. 720. (1824.)

History of Carthampton, by Savage, p. 583.

British Popular Customs, Present and Past, by the Rev. T. F Thiselton Dyer, M.A. (G. Bell & Sons, London, 1911.)

CHAPTER X

The Hooden Horse

MR. PERCY MAYLAM, in his most interesting and learned work on the subject of the Hooden Horse, gives the following account of the custom as practised in Kent. I quote with his permission

"Anyone who has spent a Christmas in a farmhouse in Thanet—it has been my good fortune to spend five—will not forget Christmas Eve, when, seated round the fire, one hears the banging of gates and trampling of feet on the gravel paths outside . . . and the sound of loud clapping. Everyone springs up, saying, 'The hoodeners have come; let us go and see the fun.' The front door is flung open, and there they all are outside, the 'waggoner' cracking his whip and leading the horse (the man who plays this part is called the 'hoodener'), which assumes a most restive manner, champing his teeth and rearing and plunging and doing his best to unseat the 'rider,' who tries to mount him, while the 'waggoner' shouts 'whoa!' and snatches at the bridle. 'Mollie' is there also! She is a lad dressed up in woman's clothes and vigorously sweeps the ground behind the horse with a birch broom. There are generally two or three other performers besides, who play the concertina, tambourine, or instruments of that kind. This performance goes on for some time, and such of the spectators as wish to do so try to mount and ride the horse, but with poor success. All sorts of antics take place. Mollie has been known to stand on her head, exhibiting nothing more alarming in the way of lingerie than a pair of hobnail boots with the appropriate setting of corduroy trousers. Beer and largesse are dispensed, and the performers go farther. Singing of songs or carols is not usually a part of the performance and no set words are spoken.

"... In Thanet occasionally, but not always, the performers, or some of them, blacken their faces. Years ago smock frocks were the regulation dress of the party.

" In a house which possesses a large hall, the performers are often invited inside ; at times the horse uses little ceremony, and, opening the door, walks in uninvited. ... On Christmas Eve it is difficult to obtain any very definite idea as to the make-up of the horse, but ... it consists of a horse's head crudely carved from a block of wood, and painted, the carver evidently being of the conventional school of art. The head is securely fixed to the end of a stout wooden staff about 4 feet in length. In connection with the head is a piece of stout sacking in the shape of a sack. Under this sack-cloth the hoodener conceals himself, so that only his legs are seen ; grasping with his hands the staff to which the head is fixed, he stoops down until the staff touches the ground, thus serving as a support. The lower jaw of the head works on a hinge, and attached to it is a leather lace or stout cord which the hoodener pulls repeatedly, bringing the lower jaw sharply into contact with the upper jaw, and as both upper and lower jaws are thickly studded with hobnails for teeth, the result is a loud snapping noise supposed to resemble the champing of a horse."

Further details of the " horse's " make-up supplied by Mr. Maylam are that its ears are formed of pointed pieces of leather, whilst its tail is made of horsehair adorned with " caytis," as the brilliantly coloured ribbons used to decorate cart-horses are called in Kent. Its mane is also of caytis, and it has all the ornamental trappings with which it is usual to deck farm-horses in that county on state occasions, such as the swinging brass disc between the ears, and the circular brass on the forehead, whilst its bridle is a long piece of leather covered with brass studs. The gratuity is placed within the ferocious creature's jaws.

Sometimes the " horse " has two holes bored in its forehead to form the eyes, and the interior of the head hollowed, so as to hold a lighted candle. In Deal, the " horse's " forehead " is covered with black plush in representation of a horse's coat, the ears are made of the same material, and the eyes are painted in. . . . The covering in this case is a dark green material."

Mr. M. Abbott, of Canterbury, describing the Thanet horse in a letter to the *Occult Review* of October 1921, says : " The one I saw was black, decorated with brass trappings and red ribbons, the men carrying it being covered by a black cloth."

This most interesting and ancient ceremony or ritual of the hooden horse, which we now know only in a grotesque and mutilated form, is, or not so very long ago was, widely diffused over Great Britain. Its birthplace appears to have been the Isle of Thanet.

At the first glance the passer-by might suppose the hooden horse to be merely a local variant of the hobby-horse, but though the origin of both emblems is very uncertain, being almost lost in the mists of antiquity, they seem to have arisen independently from different sources. Here, as in the case of the hobby-horse, more than one possible origin suggests itself.

There are various spellings of the word, but either " hooden " (pronounced to rhyme with " wooden ") or "hoden " are the most general, and the former is the one adopted by Mr. Maylam. Referring to the dictionary I find *hood* (v.t.) to be derived from Middle English *hooden* or *hoden*, " to cover with a hood," as " to hood a falcon."

As this is an exact description of the hooden horse it is probably the derivation of the term, but there is another suggestion. When not in use, the " horse " (and formerly in Thanet every team of horses was represented by one of these effigies) was kept in the stable until a feast-day called it forth again. Sometimes for a whole year it might be idle. Now, *hodden* is a dialect form of *holden*, and has the meaning " kept," " held," or " held over," as a " hodden yow," which being interpreted, is a ewe to be kept over the year. In the case of the " horse " it would have the further meaning of " guarded " as a sacred object, and if we are right in regarding the effigy as a substitute for a living animal, it was probably for the annual sacrifice that it was thus reserved or " hoden."

And here the *European Magazine* (Vol. LI, p. 358) for May 1807 furnishes us with the link we are seeking. After describing the ceremony (if we may call what is now but a ghostly remnant of it by this name) as performed at Ramsgate, in Kent, at that time, with the skull of a dead horse instead of a wooden figure, the writer goes on to say that the effigy is called a *hoden* or *woden* horse, and inquires if it is " a relic of a festival to commemorate our Saxon ancestors' landing in Thanet, as the term ' woden ' seems to imply ? "

Now although, as Mr. Maylam points out, the wooden head was in use as far back as 1824, according to " reliable oral tradition," and is of such " archaic " type that it cannot be regarded as " a modern substitution," yet doubtless originally it was used in place of a skull, just as the skull became the substitute for the living or newly sacrificed animal, in what was once a solemn religious procession to or from the altar.   So the question may be answered affirmatively.   Or again, *hoden* may be the same as *Odin* (the Norse form of *Woden*), since even now " h " is freely introduced or deleted from certain words in the conversation of the less educated classes, and in earlier days this tendency was much greater and the English language less fixed.   In fact the actual pronunciation is " 'ooden."   Even if we take the name of the " horse " to be " Wooden," as some writers suggest, it is still to the god that we must go for explanation, and not to the substance of which the effigy is sometimes formed.   The literal interpretation of *Woden* is the " furious," the " mighty warrior," and in Middle English we find that *wooden* meant " mad," " raging," or " furious."

The wooden horse is supposed to be filled with the spirit of Woden, and therefore, of course, possesses his characteristics.   Hence the snapping jaws, and the general disorderliness of conduct which has led to the suppression of the horse in so large a number of places.   In the original sacrifices the head and skin were probably used in the ritual to cover the celebrant, as where animals are sacrificed it appears to be a common custom for the priest thus to clothe himself, whilst the worshippers partook with him sacramentally of the flesh of the god-impregnated victim, thus mystically attaining union with the divinity.

If we remember that Woden was hooded (to conceal the loss of his eye), we shall be conscious of another link between the hooden horse and the god.

The date of the pagan festivities, when horses were sacrificed to Woden, being practically synchronous with Christmas, we need feel no surprise at finding the custom transferred to the Christian festival when the worship of Odin ceased.

It was condemned by Archbishop Theodore about the year 690, and in his *Penitential* he prescribes penances for " any who on the kalends of January clothe themselves with the skins of cattle and carry heads of animals." After this, artificial heads and skins were generally adopted.

In spite of this prohibition, the older form of the hooden horse still exists in places, notably in Wales and the border counties. It consists of the actual skull of the horse enveloped in a sheet and decorated with gaudy, variously coloured ribbons, and sometimes with the bottoms of two glass bottles inserted in the eye-holes. It is mounted on a short pole and is taken from door to door by the carrier and his leader, who sing carols and chant incantations. A photo of such a pair appeared in the *Daily Mail* of December 29, 1921.

In the parish of Lymm it is, or was, the custom for a week or ten days before November 5, for a horse's skull decked with ribbons, etc., with glass eyes inserted in the sockets, to be mounted on a short pole as a handle, and carried by a man who is covered by a horse-cloth. A chain is usually attached to its nose and held by a second man, and several other men accompany them. If admitted into a house, they go through a sort of performance, the " horse " rearing, opening its mouth, etc., as the man with the chain directs. The " horse " sometimes seizes people and holds them fast until they pay to be released ; but as a rule he is very peaceable, since if his captive shows fight, the poor " horse " is usually left by his companions to fight it out (*N. and Q.*).

In Wales the figure of the horse is known as the Mari Llwyd (or Lwyd), which may be interpreted as Pale Mary, Wan Mary, or White Mary. The reference appears to be to the Virgin, or perhaps to the Moon, as her symbol, and probably represents an attempt to Christianise the old pagan rite. But, on the other hand, Mr. Maylam says, Wirt Sykes mentions " a tradition linking this custom with enchantment in connection with a warlike princess reported to have flourished in Gwent and Morganwg in the early ages, and who is to be seen to this day mounted on her steed on a rock in Rhymney Dingle."

Very similar customs are found in Germany, all of which unmistakably point to the conclusion we have already reached : that the hooden horse is Odin's steed. It is, however, only fair to Mr. Maylam, to whose most interesting book on the subject we are indebted for most of the information contained in this chapter, to say that his researches have led him to quite a different conclusion, and he considers the hooden horse to be derived from Robin Hood, and adduces much evidence in support of his theory.

The two theories, however, are not necessarily contradictory, as some writers see in Robin Hood himself but a legendary figure who personifies Odin.

With regard to the presence of " Mollie," she probably points to the time when the office of priest belonged specially to the female sex. There is little doubt that when men first usurped the priesthood they were clothed as women, and we may see the relics of this in the robes of modern priests.

Some authorities consider that the stag's horns carried sometimes in Twelfth-day, May-day, and Midsummer-day celebrations point to their having originated in the worship of Diana, though now they often accompany the hobby-horse (as at Abbots Bromley, Staffs.), to which I have ascribed a different origin.

BIBLIOGRAPHY

The Hooden Horse : an East Kent Christmas Custom, by Percy Maylam. (Canterbury, 1909. Only 303 copies printed.)

The Century Dictionary, An Encyclopædic Lexicon of the English Language. (*The Times*, London, 1899.)

Article in *The Invicta* Magazine, December 1909 : " Some Curious Old Customs in Kent," by Sidney Beedgar.

Survivals in Belief among the Celts, by Geo. Henderson, M.A., etc. (James Maclehose & Sons, Glasgow, 1911.)

Notes and Queries, Vol. I, pp. 173 and 258.

British Popular Customs, Present and Past, by the Rev. T. F. Thiselton Dyer, M.A. (G. Bell & Sons, Ltd., London, 1911.)

CHAPTER XI
The Bridal Horse

IT is a great pity, both from the point of view of the student of psychic lore, and the lover of beauty, that the white horses which once were such conspicuous figures at English weddings have been almost entirely replaced by the motor-car, with its unromantic utilitarianism and entire lack of tradition.

The white horse was not present at our marriages by accident. It has ever been the sacred emblem of our race, and its presence at our bridals was of deep significance.

It is most interesting to find that in some parts of India the horse is introduced at betrothal ceremonies in an effigy which takes the form of a wickerwork figure. The author is indebted to Mr. William Lewis, whose photograph of the equine monster was published in the *Daily Mail* (November 1921), for the following account of its use. Mr. Lewis writes :

"At the time I obtained the photograph I was serving with H.M. Forces in India, and had occasion to cycle from Agra to Fatipur Sikri, both places being in the United Provinces. Near a village about midway between the two places I met a procession of Hindus, in the centre being two of these horses, on which were mounted a little boy and girl gorgeously dressed.

"Time did not allow of my making exhaustive inquiries. I was satisfied it was a betrothal or wedding, and could not wait to photograph the ceremony because of the denseness of the crowd. Reaching Fatipur Sikri, I discovered the 'horse' I photographed, drying outside the maker's hut. Military regulations and lack of time prevented my going into the city to make further inquiries, and I never again had the opportunity.

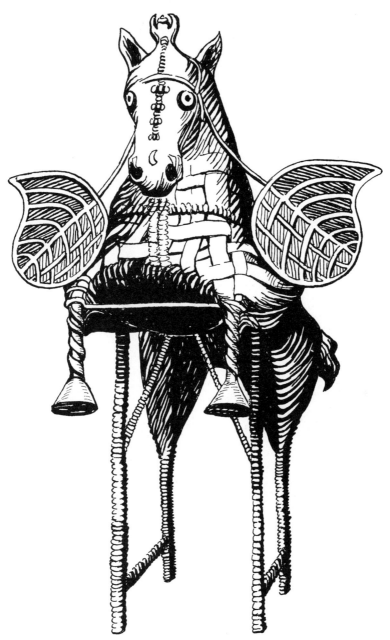

THE BRIDAL HORSE.

" The only connection of a horse with Indian religion or mythology I have been able to discover is in the Aswamedha, or horse sacrifice, referred to in the earliest Sanscrit literature."

Mr. Lewis has here laid his hand on the key to the problem. The high religious veneration in which the horse is held by the Hindus would add peculiar sanctity to a vow taken while sitting on horseback, and no true believer would lightly violate such an oath.

The student should turn to the chapter on the Trojan Horse, and note how the suitors of the fair Helen took the oath which resulted in the Trojan War, whilst standing upon portions of a dismembered horse, which had been sacrificed expressly for the purpose of making their vows inviolable.

The bridal horse is probably an image of Mamojī, the Indian phallic stallion.

The horse as the emblem of the Sun is the symbol of creative life, and the effigies, besides giving solemnity to the marriage vows, are, as it were, an unspoken prayer for the fruitfulness of their riders.

The student should turn to the chapters on the Sacrificial Horse and the Sun-horse for further information on this point.

M. *Oldfield Howey.*

CHAPTER XII

The Horse-shoe

AS the Sun is the God and Ruler of the Day, so the Moon is the Goddess and Queen of Night. The former symbolises the All-Father of creation, but the latter typifies the Mother-Principle, and has been recognised as doing so under various names in different countries and periods. Thus she who was once known as Isis is now the Madonna.

The horse-shoe represents the moon in her crescent form, and so is one of the principal symbols used to appeal to the Celestial Mother and attract her help and favour. It is nailed over doors that it may invoke her protection from bewitchment and the evil eye. But owing to ignorance of its meaning it is sometimes placed with the horns inverted. In this case it loses its significance, and is even said to " let the luck run out." It is in this sense that the horns of the altar are referred to in the Bible. " Bind the sacrifice with cords, even unto the horns of the altar " (Ps. cxviii. 27), i.e. to the avenues of approach. In Christian churches the corner on the left of the priest when he faces the altar is the gospel horn, and that at his right is the epistle horn, the two united being the means that enable him to stand with confidence before the All-Highest—the symbol of the Mother-love of God, the horn of salvation (Luke i. 69).

The horse-shoe as a charm is still greatly in favour almost everywhere in England, especially in country districts and the poorer parts of our towns, but about a century ago it was in still more general use.

Dr. Brewer, referring presumably to London, tells us that in 1813 there were seventeen in Monmouth Street, and seven could be counted in 1855. I do not know if any now remain.

Aubrey, in his *Miscellanies*, informs us that " it is a thing very common to nail horse-shoes on the thresholds of doors ; which is to hinder the power of witches that enter the house. Most of the houses of the West-end of London have the horse-shoe on the threshold. It should be a horse-shoe that one finds." He continues—" Under the porch of Staninfield Church, in Suffolk, I saw a tile with a horse-shoe upon it, placed there for this purpose, though one would imagine that holy water alone would have been sufficient. I am told that there are many other instances."

Nelson was a great believer in the protecting power of the horse-shoe and had one nailed to the mast of his ship *Victory*.

Douce thinks that the custom of nailing horse-shoes to thresholds is similar to that of driving nails into the walls of houses which was practised by the Romans as an antidote to the plague, but the idea there embodied is probably the objection fairies and witches have to iron, whereas a special virtue seems to be ascribed to nails that have been used to attach a horse's shoe to his foot. Occasionally they are used as a healing charm, as in Ireland, where if a child pines away and no cause can be assigned for it, the cure is to hang up a charm made of old horse-shoe nails, hen-manure, and salt. This scares away the fairies, who are enticing the child from the physical world to their own unsubstantial but attractive realm.

The horse-shoe is a remedy if the milk of a cow has been bewitched away. It must be boiled in a little of the milk, along with nine hairs from the cow. As the ingredients boil, the originator of the trouble begins to pine and sicken, and unless the milk is given back, before a week is out the evil-doer will be dead !

Saint Dunstan was noted for his skill in shoeing horses, and, according to an old legend, the devil one day appeared to him with a request that he would shoe his " single hoof." But the wily saint was one too many for the unwary devil ! Guessing immediately who his customer was, he first tied him securely to a wall, and then proceeded to inflict on him all the pain he could. At last the devil could bear no more, and roared for mercy. St. Dunstan thereupon exacted from his victim a promise that if he released him, he would never again enter any place where a horse-shoe was displayed.

The poet Gay referred to the horse-shoe's power to guard from witches in his fables. A witch is the supposed speaker of the following lines :

> Straws laid across my path retard,
> The horse-shoes nailed each threshold's guard.
>
> (Fable XXIII, Part I.)

And Scott refers to the same superstition. One of his characters says : " Your wife's a witch man ; you should nail a horse-shoe on your chamber door " (*Redgauntlet*, chap. xi).

Whittier, in his poem, " The Witch's Daughter," says :

> And still o'er many a neighbouring door
> She saw the horse-shoe's curvèd charm
> To guard against her mother's harm.

Peasantry, in almost all countries where the horse has been known, ascribe this power over witches to the horse-shoe. It is nailed on the threshold as well to keep witches in as to keep them out, and one that has been picked up by chance in the road is supposed to be specially efficacious.

According to Mr. J. G. Frazer, it is the custom in the Konkan, a province of the Bombay Presidency, " to drive iron nails and horse-shoes into the threshold at full moon or on the evening of the last day of the month, for the purpose of preventing the entrance of evil spirits."

This practice emphasises the connection between the horse-shoe and the moon.

Whittier was evidently much impressed by the horse-shoe charm, for again in another poem, *The Demon of the Study*, he describes how, in his efforts to exorcise his haunted room from " the demon that cometh day by day," he " nailed a horse-shoe over the grate," but even this failed, and the demon remained, sitting " like a visible nightmare " beside him.

The same poet in " Extract from ' A New England Legend ' says :

> How has New England's romance fled,
> Even as a vision of the morning !
> Its rites foredone,—its guardians dead,—
> Its priestesses, bereft of dread,
> Waking the veriest urchin's scorning !
>
> .   .   .   .   .
>
> The cautious goodman nails no more
> A horse-shoe on his outer door,
> Lest some unseemly hag should fit
> To his own mouth her bridle-bit.

The purple honesty—or, as it is often called from its shining seed-vessels, moonwort (*Lunaria annua*), in olden days was held to possess a strange attraction for horse-shoes and a power of drawing them off the feet of horses.   Thus Du Bartas writes :

> And horse that, feeding on the grassy hills,
> Tread upon moonwort with their hollow heels,
> Though lately shod at night goe barefoot home,
> Their maister musing where their shooes become.
> O moonwort ! tell us where thou hidst the smith,
> Hammer, and pincers, thou unshod'st them with ?
> Alas ! what lock or iron engine is't
> That can thy subtile secret strength resist,
> Sith the best farrier cannot set a shoe
> So sure, but thou (so shortly) canst undo ?

Another herb also known as " moonwort," the *Botrychium lunaria*, was credited with a similar power, and is referred to by Sir. T. Browne : " That ferrum equinum (lunary) . . . hath a vertue attractive of

Iron, a power to break lockes, and draw off the shooes of a horse that passeth over it. . . . Which strange and magicall conceit seemes unto me to have no deeper root in reason then the figure of its seed, for therein indeed it somewhat resembles an horseshooe, which notwithstanding Baptista Porta hath too low a signation, and raised the same unto a Lunatic representation."

We have given fairly fully the view of those who consider the horse-shoe the symbol of the Divine Mother, but there is an entirely opposite explanation of this mystic charm connecting it with devil propitiation.

Mr. Hargrave Jennings is an exponent of this opposing theory, and we give his case in his own words :

"The horns of the merry-andrew . . . and the horns of Satan, indeed the figure of horns generally, even have a strange affinity in the consecrate and religious. The horse-shoe, so universally employed as a defensive charm, and used as a sign to warn off and to consecrate, when—as it so frequently is—displayed at the entrance of stables, outhouses and farm buildings in country places, speaks the acknowledgment of the Devil, or Sinister Principle. The rearing aloft, and throwing out, as it were, of protesting and—in a certain fashion—badge-like magic signs, . . . fixed upon barn-doors, we hold to be the perpetuation of the old heathen sacrifice to the harmful gods, or a sort of devil propitiation. Again, in this horse-shoe we meet the *horse*, as indicative of, and connected with, spirit-power. . . . The horse-shoe is the mystic symbol of the wizard's foot, or the *sigma*, or sign, of the abstract 'Fourfooted,' the strangely secret, constantly presented, but as constantly evading, magic meaning conveyed in which (a tremendous cabalistic sign) we encounter everywhere. May the original, in the east, of the horse-shoe arch of the Saracens, which is a foundation form of our Gothic architecture, may the horse-shoe form of all arches and cupolas (which figure is to be met everywhere in Asia), may these strange, rhomboidal curves carry reference to the ancient mysterious blending of the horse and the supernatural and religious ? It is an awing thought ; but spirits and supernatural embodiments—unperceived by our limited vulgar senses—may make their daily walk amidst us, invisible. . . . It may indeed be that they are sometimes suddenly *happened upon* and, as it were, surprised. The world—although so silent—may be noisy with ghostly feet. The Unseen Ministers may every day pass in and out among our ways, and we all the time think that we have the world to ourselves. It is, as it were, to this *inside* unsuspected world that these recognitive, deprecatory signs of horse-shoes and of charms are addressed ; that the harming presences, unprovoked, may pass harmless ; that the jealous watch of the Unseen over us may be assuaged in the acknowledgment ; that the unrecognised presences amidst us, if met with an unconsciousness for which man cannot be accountable, may not be offended with carelessness in regard of them for which he may be punishable."

Mr. Jennings's solemn warning should not be lightly disregarded, *but* the required propitiation should be offered to the *Highest*—should be offered in love, and not in fear. If we can attain to the consciousness of the Celestial Mother-love surrounding all, perhaps we may help to raise our unseen antagonists until they too become vehicles of God's love. This shall be our meaning when we nail the horse-shoe to our door : the all-embracing arms of the Motherhood of God.

Sacred as the Cross ! We no longer wonder why nothing evil can approach those portals which it guards.

All this, and much more, is visioned by the initiate when he gazes in contemplation on the metal plate that has guarded a horse's foot.

BIBLIOGRAPHY

Redgauntlet, by Sir Walter Scott.
Fables, by the late Mr. Gay. Fable 23. Fourth edition. (Printed for J. Tonson and J. Watts, London, 1733.)
Folklore in the Old Testament, by J. G. Frazer, III, 12.
The Rosicrucians, by Hargrave Jennings.
Miscellanies upon Various Subjects, by John Aubrey, F.R.S. Fourth edition. (London, 1857.)
Pseud. Epid., II. 6, p. 100. Sir T. Browne. (1646.)
The Poetical Works of John Greenleaf Whittier. (Published by W. P. Nimmo, Hay, & Mitchell, Edinburgh.)

CHAPTER XIII

The Corn-horse

THERE is an ancient and widespread belief that a spirit presides over and resides in cornfields, whose mission it is to guard from harm and bring to fruition the growing corn.

In a large number of cases, though not invariably, this spirit is in the form of a horse or mare, which is invoked with mystic ritual at harvest time.

The origin of this custom in Europe may be traced in the pictured cave of Phigalia, in Arcadia, where Demeter, the Grecian Goddess of Agriculture, whose name means " the Corn-Mother," was imaged as a woman with a horse's head and mane. An altar was dedicated to her on Mount Æleus.

She is said to have assumed this shape that she might elude the attentions of her unwelcome lover, Poseidon, and then to have hidden from him in the cave of Phigalia. There she remained so long that the harvests, no longer the objects of her fostering, motherly care, began to perish, and famine threatened to exterminate the human race. However, to avoid this calamity, the God Pan came to the rescue, and pacified the angry goddess, and persuaded her once more to resume her wonted tasks. To celebrate Demeter's return to the harvest fields, the Phigalians placed her image in their cave.

The Romans adopted the Grecian worship of Demeter with some slight modifications.

The name by which they knew the Corn-mother was Ceres, probably from the root *creare* = " create," because she caused the earth to bring forth fruit and was the inventor of husbandry.

They imaged her as tall and majestic, with yellow hair crowned by a wreath of corn-ears, her right hand holding poppies and corn.

In the Roman version of the legend Neptune fell in love with her (see chapter on " Sea-horses "), and to avoid his embraces she hid in the midst of a drove of mares, taking the form of one herself. But Neptune had perceived her ruse, and the God of Horses quickly became a horse. From this union the horse Arion sprang.

The Romans celebrated the festival known as Ambarvalia (*ambi*, " around " ; *arvum*, " a cultivated field ") in Ceres' honour during the month of May. It consisted in the sacrifice of a pig, a sheep, and a bull, which were first led round the growing crops, and also in ceremonial dancing and singing, and the offering of an oblation of wine mixed with honey and milk.

But besides these sacrifices, according to Fraser's *Golden Bough*, if we examine the pages of Roman history we find that the annual sacrifice of a horse representing the Corn-spirit was one of the most important religious rites of the period, and considered necessary to secure the fertility of the earth and the increase of flocks and herds. An annual chariot-race took place on the fifteenth of October, in the Field of Mars, near the river Tiber, and the horse on the right-hand side of the winning team was the one that was honoured as the chosen sacrifice to Mars, and was called the " October horse."

Stabbed by a spear, its head was cut off and decorated with a string of loaves to symbolise the Spirit of the Corn. And a ghastly representation of the beautiful corn-horse it must have been ! Then ensued a hot contest, between the inhabitants of the ward known as the Sacred Way and those who lived in the ward of the Subura, for the possession of the sacred symbol.

If the former were successful in obtaining the coveted object, in the earliest days of Rome, they fastened the head on a wall of the King's palace ; but if the latter were the victors, it was the Mamilian Tower that was adorned with the trophy.

The tail was also severed, and carried with such haste to the King's dwelling that blood from it dripped on his hearth. The remainder of the blood from the victim was caught, and most carefully preserved till the shepherds' festival, known as the Parilia, which was held on April 21. This day was called the birthday of Rome, and was one of the most important feasts in the calendar. The Roman vestal virgins then took the ashes of unborn calves which had been sacrificed six days previously, and mingled them with the blood of the horse. This decoction they gave to the assembled shepherds for the fumigation of their flocks and herds, that thus they might increase their fecundity and ensure an abundance of milk.

This last-described sacrifice was offered to the pastoral deity Pales. Ovid gives us a description of the ceremony (*Fasti*, IV, 637--734), which was supposed to ensure the blessing of the Corn-spirit upon the whole nation.

Examining some early British coins of Boduo—or, as she is more generally called, Boadicea—we find pictured on them a mare. This is the symbol of Ceridwen, the Druidical Ceres, referred to by the bards as the White Mare, which form she is said to have assumed. It is supposed therefore to represent the goddess herself, and shows that the Corn-horse (or rather Mare) was known to the Britons in pre-Roman days.

In many parts of pre-war Germany the belief in the horse-shaped Corn-spirit was accepted unquestioningly by the peasants, and when they saw the shadow made by the wind passing over the bending corn, they would exclaim " There runs ' the Horse,' "—as if to their eyes the equine shape was a visible and palpable thing. Perhaps to these simple-minded folk it did so appear ! Faith can remove mountains which shut out vision from too learned people !

Be this as it may, the idea specially prevailed between Kalw and Stuttgart ; and at Bohlingen, in Baden, a further development was found. There the last sheaf of oats to be tied was named " the Oats-stallion," and supposed to be the tabernacle of the spirit that so long had lived in the crop.

We do not know if the hard experiences of wartime have eliminated all these poetic visions, but we hope not. The world still needs its spirit and fairy-workers. It is curious that here, as in some other instances we shall note, the original feminine character of the Corn-spirit has been overlooked, and the goddess has become a stallion ! Whether this can have been due to the indirect but rapidly growing influence of Eastern religious thought (so exclusively male in character) upon the European Continent, or was merely local and accidental, we leave our readers to decide.

Around Lille, also, this idea that the Corn-spirit lives in the harvest-fields in equine form is, or was until recently, the common belief, and clearly reflected in the customs of the peasantry. Thus, for example, if one of the band of harvesters appeared tired and overdone by his work, the others would exclaim " He has the fatigue of the horse."

And in this district a most curious ceremony is preserved, which the reader is advised to compare with the account given in the chapter on Sacred Horses, of the symbolism of the cross in Mexico. There the cross typifies the God of Rain, and it is probably with some such connection of fertilisation that it appears in this ritual. Certainly it is not as the Christian emblem that the cross is introduced.

The first sheaf made is named " the Cross of the Horse," and is laid upon a cross formed of boxwood which is inside the barn. The youngest horse on the farm is then brought in and made to trample upon it. When the corn is nearly harvested the reapers dance around the last blades, shouting " See the remains of the horse ! " From these last ears a special sheaf is made which is presented to the youngest horse of the parish to be eaten. No doubt the idea is, as Mannhardt remarks, that this youngest horse of the parish is the representative of the Corn-spirit who shall guard the fields next year—the corn-foal, who, by eating the sheaf in which the old corn-horse had taken his final refuge, provides a dwelling-place for his spirit, until the fields are ready to receive him once again.

If we look in our own islands for evidence of the Corn-spirit, we find that in Scotland a custom prevails very similar to that we have just been examining. The last sheaf of harvest is there given to a horse or mare to eat, but if this is omitted by a greedy farmer and it is threshed, then the thresher is said to " beat the horse."

Near Berry, the harvesters are in the habit of taking a midday sleep in the field, and they name this " seeing the horse." They do not commence their rest until their leader gives the signal ; but if he is tardy in doing so, one of their number will start to neigh in imitation of a horse, his comrades will do likewise, and then all will go to " see the horse."

Mr. J. G. Frazer, in his famous work *The Golden Bough* (" Spirits of the Corn and the Wild "), gives the following most interesting account of an English version of the ritual :

" In Hertfordshire, at the end of the reaping, there is, or used to be, observed a ceremony called ' Crying the Mare.' The last blades of corn left standing in the field are tied together and called ' the Mare.' The reapers stand at a distance and throw their sickles at it ; he who cuts it through ' has the prize with acclamations and good cheer.' After it is cut the reapers cry thrice with a loud voice, ' I have her ! ' Others answer thrice ' What have you ? ' ' A mare ! a mare ! a mare ! ' ' Whose is she ? ' is next asked thrice. ' A. B.'s,' naming the owner thrice. ' Whither will you send her ? ' ' To C. D.'s,' naming some neighbour who has not reaped all his corn.

" In this custom the Corn-spirit in the form of a mare is passed on from a farm where the corn is all cut to another farm where it is still standing, and where therefore the Corn-spirit may be supposed to take refuge.

" In Shropshire the custom is similar. . . . ' Crying, calling, or shouting the mare ' is a ceremony performed by the men of that farm which is the first in any parish or district to finish the harvest. The object of it is to make known their own prowess, and to taunt the laggards by a pretended offer of the ' owd mar ' (old mare) to help out their ' chem ' (team). All the men assemble (the wooden harvest-bottle being of course one of the company) in the stackyard, or better, on the highest ground of the farm, and there shout the following dialogue, preceding it by a grand ' Hip, hip, hip, hurrah ! '

" ' I 'ave 'er, I 'ave 'er, I 'ave 'er ! '

" ' Whad ast thee, whad ast thee, whad ast thee ? '

" ' A mar' ! a mar' ! a mar' ! '

" ' Whose is 'er, whose is 'er, whose is 'er ? '

" ' Maister A.'s, Maister A.'s, Maister A.'s ! ' (naming the farmer whose harvest is finished).

" ' W'eer sha't the' send 'er ? ' etc.

" ' To Maister B.'s ! ' etc. (naming one whose harvest is not finished). ' 'Uth a hip, hip, hurrah ! ' (in chorus).

" The farmer who finishes his harvest last, and who therefore cannot send the mare to anyone else, is said " to keep her all winter.' . . .

" At one place, Longnor (near Leebotwood), down to about 1850, the mare used really to be sent. The headman of the farmer who had finished harvest first was mounted on the best horse of the team . . . both horse and man being adorned with ribbons, streamers, etc. Thus arrayed, a boy on foot led the pair to the neighbouring farm-houses."

We have to travel far to get our next glimpse of the corn-horse. It is to the modern inhabitants of Assam that we must go, so widely flung is the symbol. There the agricultural tribe of the Garos celebrate the harvesting of their rice—to them the chief event of the year, with a festival in which the horse is the principal ceremonial figure.

An effigy of a steed is made from plantain and bamboo, and placed in the house of the headman of the tribe. All night long the assembled Garos dance and sing around it. When morning dawns, they take it to the nearest river and there launch it on the waters that it may float away with the current.

Sometimes this effigy of the horse is built around a man. The head, fashioned of straw and cloth, is carried on a stick, and used by the performer as a mask, whilst a priest, dancing in front of him, beckons him along the route. This is a lengthy ceremony occupying two days and three nights, so that the actors have to be continually relieved by others as they become worn out by the strain of their exertions. Finally, the body of the symbolic horse is thrown into the river, but the head is preserved for the next annual rice festival. Those who come to do honour to the occasion, and watch the effigy borne away by the stream, bring rice with them and eat a farewell meal by the water's side.

BIBLIOGRAPHY

The Pantheon, representing the Fabulous Histories of the Heathen Gods, by Andrew Tooke, A.M. Thirty-fifth edition. (Longman, Hurst & Co., London, 1824.)

The Century Dictionary, an Encyclopedic Lexicon of the English Language. (*The Times*, 1899 edition.)

Ovid, *Fasti* IV, 637–734.

The Golden Bough : " Spirits of the Corn and the Wild," by J. G. Frazer.

The White Horses of the West of England, by the Rev. W. C. Plenderleath, M.A. Second edition. (Allen & Storr, London, 1892.)

CHAPTER XIV

Sun-horses

NEARLY all ancient nations, especially Eastern nations, have represented the Ruler of the Day as being drawn in his chariot by celestial horses on his diurnal journey across the skies. Hence horses figure largely in solar rites, and used to be led in procession before the Sun-god's shrine, and in many countries were annually sacrificed to him.

Even the Israelites at times followed these customs, as can be seen by referring to 2 Kings xxiii. 11, where we read that Josiah " took away the horses that the kings of Judah [his predecessors] had given to the sun, . . . and burned the chariots of the sun with fire."

There is a good deal of difference of opinion about the rites in which these horses and chariots participated. Some think that the horses were sacrificed to the sun ; others that they were harnessed every morning to the chariots dedicated to the sun, which are mentioned in the same passage, and that the king, or some high officials, rode to meet the sun as it rose, as far as from the eastern gate of the temple to the suburbs of Jerusalem.

In 2 Kings xi. 16 reference is made to " the way by which the horses came into the king's house," showing how regularly the custom must have been followed, whatever it may have been, and disposing of the idea advanced by some critics that the horses were effigies of stone, wood, or metal, erected in the temple.

The *Tradition of the Sanhedria*, fol. 21, mentions Solomon's love for horses and his determination to have a large stud, although the prohibition of Moses had been clearly expressed, saying that the king shall not multiply horses to himself, nor cause the people to return to Egypt, to the end that he should multiply horses " (Deut. xvii. 16). We read in Kings that " Solomon had forty thousand stalls of horses for his chariots, and twelve thousand horsemen . . . whom he bestowed in the cities for chariots, and with the king at Jerusalem " (1 Kings iv. 26, x. 26).

In the same chapter we also learn how, with his proverbial wisdom, he evaded the second part of the commandment, for " Solomon had horses brought out of Egypt " to him, instead of sending his people to fetch them. Though perhaps most of these animals were intended for military purposes or for display, some of them were probably sacred.

Muhammad refers to Solomon's infatuation for them, which caused him first to forget the hour of evening prayer, and then in his bitter repentance cruelly to slaughter them, as being the cause of his failing. The passage describing this runs :

" Remember when at eventide the prancing chargers were displayed before him [Solomon], and he said, ' Truly I have loved the love of earthly goods above the remembrance of my Lord, till the sun hath been hidden by the veil of darkness. Bring them back to me.' And he began to sever the legs and the necks."

The reader should note the reference to the sun. Probably it was some equine solar rite that had so entranced Solomon. The chargers appear to have been mares, for the commentators say that the word here translated " prancing " implies that the *mares* stood on three feet, and touched the ground with the edge of the fourth foot. It would seem as if they were trained to perform a kind of dance, which corroborates our idea that they were sun-horses.

Their being sacred to a rival of Jehovah would also account for Solomon's sudden and savage revulsion of feeling under the influence of the priests of his own deity, when he returned too late for the evening worship.

Xenophon testifies that both the rites mentioned in the beginning of this chapter were followed by the Persians and the Armenians. He describes a solemn sacrifice of horses, which, with much ceremony, was made to the sun. The steeds were all chosen for their beauty, and were harnessed to a white chariot, crowned, and consecrated.

The ancient Greeks shared these customs of the idolatrous kings of Judah, and the Rhodians, who worshipped the Sun as their chief deity, every year dedicated a chariot and four horses to him, and cast them into the sea for his use.

Pausanias (III. 20) tells us that horses were sacrificed to the Sun at Mount Taletum, a peak of Taygetus.

Virgil describes how King Latinus, wishing to honour King Æneas, sent a chariot for him with two horses breathing fire from their nostrils, which were of the breed of the horses of the sun. With them he also sent one hundred horses, one for each man of Troy, decked with trappings of purple, and champing on bits of gold, and all very fleet of foot, from his stable of three hundred fleet horses. Æneas already

WINGED PEGASUS ON COIN OF CORINTH IN THE BRITISH MUSEUM.

had sacred horses of his own, of the breed which Zeus himself gave to King Tros, and would know how to appreciate the honour, which was perhaps the highest that could be bestowed on him.

In the mythology and ancient religions of India the horse holds a most important place, even representing Surya, the bright sun-god and the second person of the Indian Trinity (Trimurti).

Thus Surya is described as " the horse who neighed as soon as he was born, emerging out of the waters (or mist)," or " the Steed with the falcon's wings, and the gazelle's feet," and the Dawn is said to lead forth " the white and lovely horse " (Rig-Veda, X, 177).

In other hymns Surya is represented as being drawn in a chariot over the skies by seven red mares called " Harits " (" brilliant, ruddy "), his charioteer being Aruna, God of the Dawn. Thus : " Seven mares bear Thee on, O far-seeing Surya, in Thy chariot, god of the flaming locks. Surya has harnessed the seven Harits, daughters of the car, self-yoked " (Hymn I, 50).

Soma, the moon, is also represented as a heavenly steed, as is

Agni, the lightning. Surya is really identical with Agni (" he of the three abodes," i.e. Sun, Lightning, and Fire), and Soma, too, is only Agni's other self, hence the horse is their common symbol.

According to another authority the second person of the Indian Trinity is known as Har. He has already passed his ninth incarnation : and in the tenth will take the forms first of a peacock, and then of a horse, when all the followers of Muhammad will be destroyed.

In Rajputana the Indians celebrate the sun's birthday, on the seventh of the month Mágh Sudi, by a grand procession, in which the chariot of the sun, taken from the temple dedicated to the Sun-god, is drawn by eight horses.

The following verses are taken from a translation of one of the hymns of the Rig-Veda by R. T. Griffith.

HYMN TO THE SUN

Look ! his horses mounted high,
  Good of limb, and stout and strong,
In the forehead of the sky
  Run their course the heavens along.
Praises to his steeds be given
Racing o'er the road of heaven.

Such the majesty and power,
  Such the glory of the sun ;
When he sets at evening hour,
  The worker leaves his task undone.
His steeds are loosed, and over all
Spreadeth Night her gloomy pall.

The distinctively royal sacrifice of India is the Aswamedha, or Horse Sacrifice. This is certainly of solar origin, and was probably a custom belonging to the early dwelling-place of the Hindus in northern Asia, where the Scythians and the Massagetæ used to offer horses to the sun.

Later it was considered as an emblematic ceremony—the horse typified the sun, and the sun represented the universal soul.

The sacred writings describe the horse as being " bathed and decorated with rich trappings, the variously coloured goat going before him." The goat is killed first that it may make known to the gods that the horse is coming to them. Three times the horse is led around the sacrificial fire. He is then bound to a post and immolated by an axe. His flesh is roasted on a spit, boiled, made into balls, and eaten by all who have assisted at the sacrifice. " The priest, the assistant, the carver, he who lights the fire, he who works the pressing stones, and the inspired singer of hymns "—all eat their fill.

There is a most graphic and detailed account of the ceremony in two hymns of the Rig-Samhità (I. 162 and 163). These describe the slaughtering and burning of the horse with a naked realism that is almost horrible. Yet they also address the soul of the victim in mystic strains, recognising it as identified with the gods through the sacrifice, as even on earth he had been their symbol. Now that he is thus specially devoted to their service by his death, he " goes to them," and is of their race—*devajata*. He is therefore spoken of as " sprung from the gods," " fabricated from the sun," and is said to have " three forms," his highest birth-place being with Vàruna. His winged head " speeds snorting along the easy, dustless paths of heaven." His body, too, is winged, his spirit pervading as the wind, " intently fixed on the gods." Finally, " the horse proceeds to that assembly which is most excellent, to the presence of his father and his mother [Heaven and Earth]. Go [Horse] to-day rejoicing to the gods, that the sacrifice may yield blessings to the donor " (Rig-Veda, II, p. 112).

The hymn (I. 162) shows a tender solicitude for the feelings of the sacrificed that is perhaps unique in religious ceremonies that involve the shedding of a victim's blood. It thus addresses the consecrated steed :

" May not thy breath of life oppress thee when thou goest to the gods ; may not the axe injure thy bodies [the three forms referred to above] ; may not a hasty, unskilled carver, blundering in his work, cleave thy limbs wrongly. Forsooth, thou diest not here, nor dost thou suffer any injury ; no, thou goest to the gods along fair, easy paths ; the two harits [Indra's] and the dappled deer [the Maruts] will be thy comrades."

We cannot refrain from contrasting the spirit of this sacrifice with that which inspires the Jewish offerings of slaughtered beasts. No happy, glorious hereafter is promised to the creatures slain on Israel's altars. They are, on the contrary, accursed by the sins of the offerer, in whose place they suffer to appease Jehovah's wrath ; and if we may trust the Christian Churches, the bloodshed is all in vain.

> Not all the blood of beasts,
>   On Jewish altars slain,
> Could give the guilty conscience peace,
>   Or wash away the stain.

Jehovah was *not* appeased. He required a greater sacrifice yet !

To return to the Indian ceremony. Though the victim was thus honoured and blessed alike by gods and men, so that its fate was one to be envied, yet in later years, as further enlightenment came, the sacrifice, which had always been disliked by the Brahmans, was performed symbolically, and the actual slaughtering of the animals omitted.

In a Brahmana (or treatise) appended to the Yajur-Veda, an Aswamedha is described in which the creatures were tied to posts, and after prayers had been offered up, were set free uninjured.

In the post-Vedic ages of the Brahmanas men were sometimes the offerings. Then the horse was substituted for man as sacrificial victim. Later, the ox took the place of the horse, then the sheep and the goat, and lastly the vegetable products of the earth.

It was prescribed by the ritual of the Aswamedha that the horse should be slain by a golden knife, because " gold is light," and by means of the golden light the sacrificer also goes to the heavenly world (see the Satapatha-Brahmana). This clearly points us to the solar origin of the rite.

The Aswamedha is altogether travestied in the writings of a much later date known as Puranas. In these a mortal rajah performs the sacrifice that he may dethrone the god Indra, and it is upon this version that Southey's " Curse of Kehama " is based. As Professor Wilson observed, it is correct enough according to the authority which he followed, " but the main object of the ceremony, the deposal of Indra from the throne of Swarga, and the elevation of the sacrificer after a hundred celebrations, to that rank, are fictions of a later date uncountenanced by the Veda."

The importance attached to the Aswamedha may be gauged by the following paragraphs from the " Laws of Menu " :

" The man who performs annually for a hundred years an Aswamedha, or sacrifice of a horse, and the man who abstains from flesh meat, enjoy for their virtue an equal reward " (V. p. 53).   " A Bráhmen with abundant wealth, who presents not the priest that hallows his fire with a horse consecrated to Praja Pati, becomes equal to one who has no fire hallowed " (XI. p. 38).   " The sacrifice of a horse, the king of sacrifices, removes all sin " (XI. p. 261).

The reverence given to the consecrated victim before the consummation of the sacrifice has been beautifully described by Southey in his " Curse of Kehama."

Along the mead the hallowed steed
Still wanders whereso'er he will
O'er hill or dale, or plain ;

No human hand hath tricked that mane,
From which he shakes the morning dew ;
His mouth has never felt the rein,

His lips have never frothed the chain ;
For pure of blemish and of stain,

His neck unbroke to mortal yoke
Like Nature free the steed must be,
Fit offering to the Immortals he.

A year and a day the steed must stray
Wherever chance may guide his way,
Before he fall at Seeva's shrine

The year and day have passed away,
Nor touch of man has marred the rite divine.

The story of Phaëthon is so well known, I hesitate to insert it ; but as the account of the Sun's horses would be incomplete without it, I will briefly recount it. Helios, the Sun, having sworn to his son

Phaëthon, upon the Stygian lake—an oath which none of the gods
dare violate—that he would grant him any boon he wished, Phaëthon
said his desire was to drive his father's chariot and horses for one
day.   Helios begged him not to persist in his idea, for no mortal was
capable of managing these fiery steeds, and he would inevitably perish
in the attempt.

> In vain to move his son the father aim'd ;
> He, with ambition's hotter fire inflamed,
> His sire's irrevocable promise claimed.

The father, greatly grieving, was forced to comply with his son's
rash wish.   He carefully instructed him how to guide the horses and
especially advised him to observe the middle path.   Phaëthon was
frantic with joy as, climbing into the chariot, he took up the reins and
began to drive.   But the steeds, recognising a strange hand, and finding
quickly that Phaëthon was no match for them, ran away, and set both
heaven and earth ablaze.   Jupiter, horrified at the havoc, to put an
end to the conflagration, struck Phaëthon out of the chariot with a
thunderbolt, and cast him into the river Padus (Po).

> At once from Life and from the Chariot driv'n,
> Th' ambitious Boy fell thunder-struck from Heav'n.
> The Horses started with a sudden Bound,
> And flung the Reins and Chariot to the Ground :
> The studded Harness from their Necks they broke,
> Here fell a Wheel, and here a Silver Spoke,
> Here were the Beam and Axle torn away ;
> And scatter'd o'er the Earth the shining Fragments lay,
> The breathless Phaeton with flaming Hair,
> Shot from the Chariot like a falling Star,
> That in a Summer's Ev'ning from the Top
> Of Heav'n drops down, or seems at least to drop ;
> 'Till on the Po his blasted Corps was hurld,
> Far from his Country, in the Western World.
> Ovid's *Met.* Bk. II.   (Addison's translation.)

Greek and Latin mythology agrees with that of India in assigning
seven horses to the chariot of the Sun.   They were named as follows :
Bronté (Thunder), Eos (Day-break), Ethiops (Flashing), Ethon

(Fiery), Erythreios (Red-producer), Philogeia (Earth-loving), Pyrois (Fiery), and they are all described as breathing fire from their nostrils.

Scandinavian mythology, on the other hand, gives only two horses as drawing the Sun's chariot, their names being Arra'kur (the Early Waker) and Alsvin (the Rapid Goer). These steeds were protected from the fierce rays of the sun by great skins filled with air placed under their withers, and the gods also fashioned the shield Svalin (the Cooler), and fixed it in front of the car to shelter their horses from the scorching heat. Sol, the Sun-maid, daughter of the giant Mundilfari, and spouse of Glaur (Glow) was appointed to be the charioteer, and guide the steeds across the heavens.

Dag, the Norse God of Day, was drawn in his chariot by a most beautiful white steed called Skin-faxi (Shining Mane), from whose mane the light darted forth in golden gleams lighting the whole world, and giving health, joy, and gladness to its inhabitants.

> Forth from the east, up the ascent of heaven,
> Day drove his courser with the shining mane.
> Matthew Arnold, " Balder Dead."

In the beautiful ode " To the Sun," by Shelley, the same imagery is pursued :

> The immortal Sun,
> Who borne by heavenly steeds his race doth run
> Unconquerably, illuming the abodes
> Of mortal men and the eternal Gods.
>
> .   .   .   .   .
>
> His rapid steeds soon bear him to the West,
> Where their steep flight his hands divine arrest,
> And the fleet car with yoke of gold, which he
> Sends from bright heaven beneath the shadowy sea.

Marlowe writes :

> The horse that guide the golden eye of heaven,
> And blow the morning from their nostrils.

The following should be read with reference to the chapter on the Hooden Horse, though I have included it here as the custom described appears to be a survival of pagan sun-worship. This ritual is still in use in many parts of Ireland, though now it is nominally undertaken in honour of some Christian saint.

In *The Personal Recollections of Charlotte Elizabeth* may be found this most interesting description given by an eye-witness of a ceremony observed on Midsummer Eve :

After a great bonfire had been lighted and had " burned for some

AURORA.
(From an old engraving, 1616.)

hours and got low, an indispensable part of the ceremony commenced. Everyone present of the peasantry passed through it, and several children were thrown across the sparkling embers, while a wooden frame of some 8 feet long, with a horse's head fixed to one end, and a large white sheet thrown over it concealing the wood and the man on whose head it was carried, made its appearance. This was greeted with loud shouts of ' the White Horse ! ' and having been safely carried by the skill of its bearer several times through the fire with a bold leap, it pursued the people, who ran screaming and laughing in every direction. I asked what the horse was meant for, and was told that it represented all cattle."

Midsummer-day celebrations have been Christianised by naming the 24th of June after St. John the Baptist, but it is quite beyond doubt that the fire-festivals, which are, or were until recent date, held all over Europe on that day, or its eve, are survivals from a much earlier religion, and that the original idea was to honour and possibly even to aid the Sun, who then attains his highest altitude in the heavens, and whose position from that time gradually declines.

Probably the white horse, now drawn in effigy through the sacred flame, was formerly an actual steed offered in sacrifice to the ruler of the skies, that its spirit might join in effort with those heavenly horses who drew the Sun's chariot, and who now might be supposed to be failing and weary, as their achievement was every succeeding day less and less.

A similar custom to that we have just been examining used to be observed in Meissen or Thuringia, but in this case it was a horse's head that was thrown into the midsummer bonfires.

The following account by John Pinkerton describes a fire ceremony in Russia, more or less disguised as a Christian festival.

The Russians hold the feast of two martyrs, Florus and Laurus, on August 18, Old Style.

" On this day the Russians lead their horses round the church of their village, beside which on the foregoing evening they dig a hole with two mouths. Each horse has a bridle made of the bark of the linden-tree. The horses go through this hole, one after the other, while opposite to one of its mouths a priest stands with a sprinkler in his hand, with which he sprinkles them. As soon as the horses have passed by, their bridles are taken off, and they are made to go between two fires that they kindle, called by the Russians *givoyagon*, that is to say, ' living fires,' of which I shall give an account. I would first observe, that the Russian peasantry throw the bridles of their horses into one of these fires to be consumed. This is the manner of their lighting these *givoyagon*, or living fires. Some men hold the ends of a stick made of the plane-tree, very dry, and about a fathom long. This stick they hold firmly over one of birch, perfectly dry, and rub with violence and quickly against the former ; the birch, which is somewhat softer than the plane, in a short time inflames, and serves them to light both the fires I have described."

The Dawn (Eos or Aurora) has been called the " White-horsed." Her steeds were named Lampos (Shining) and Phaëthon (Gleaming), but sometimes she is spoken of as the " One-horsed " Eos (Orest, 1001).

Pegasus is said to have become her steed after he had thrown Bellerophon to the earth. By some of the early artists she is represented as driving a four-horsed car.

BIBLIOGRAPHY

The Golden Bough, by J. G. Frazer.

Story of the Nations : " Vedic India," by Z. A. Ragozin.

Life in Ancient India, by Mrs. Speir.

Voyages and Travels, by John Pinkerton.

Dictionary of Phrase and Fable, by Dr. Brewer, LL.D. (Cassell, Peter & Galpin, London.)

Personal Recollections by Charlotte Elizabeth.

Theosophy, Religion, and Occult Science, by H. S. Olcott. (Geo. Redway, London, 1885.)

Rajasthan, Tod.

The Pantheon, representing the Fabulous Histories of the Heathen Gods and most Illustrious Heroes, by Andrew Tooke, A.M. Thirty-fifth edition. (Printed for Longman & Co., London, 1824.)

Ovid's *Metamorphoses* in Fifteen Books. Translated by the most Eminent Hands. (Printed for T. Daviss, etc., London, 1773.)

The Stories of the Iliad and the Æneid, by Alfred J. Church, M.A. (Seeley & Co., London, 1886.)

The Koran. Translated from the Arabic by the Rev. J. A. Rodwell, M.A. (J. M. Dent & Co., London, 1909.)

Institutes of Hindu Law : or the Ordinances of Menu, according to the Gloss of Cullúca. Verbally translated from the original Sanscrit. With a preface by Sir William Jones. (Calcutta : Printed by Order of the Government. London : Reprinted for J. Sewell, Cornhill ; and J. Debrett, Piccadilly, 1796.)

M. Oldfield Howey.

CHAPTER XV

The Moon-horse

FAMILIAR as we are with the idea that the sun is drawn in his chariot on his daily round by horses, perhaps few of us have thought that the moon used the same means of progression. At least in the good days of old, when she was properly honoured on earth and so able to reveal her mode of travel to mortals, this seems to have been the case, if legends may be believed.

According to the myths prevailing among the Norsemen, the car of the moon was drawn by a single horse named Alsvider (the All-swift) and driven by the goddess (Mani, the Moon) herself—the beautiful daughter of the giant Mundilfari.

Every night Mani fulfilled her mission to mankind by guiding her steed along the heavenly way, although the terrible wolves Sköll (Repulsion) and Hati (Hatred) incessantly pursued and sought to devour both horse and goddess, so that the world might again be abandoned to the horrible darkness which formerly enveloped it. Occasionally the wolves were almost successful in their chase. They overtook the chariot and all but devoured their prey. This was the reason of an eclipse.

But Mani would be aided by the terrified shouting of the people of earth, which so frightened the wolves as to cause them to loose their hold again, so allowing her to escape once more. Then she would flee with increased rapidity whilst the horrid monsters hastened after her, longing for that day when at last they would prevail and the world would cease to be. By day they chased the sun, by night the moon, never weary in their deathly purpose.

One of Mr. J. C. Dollman's beautiful pictures represents these weird wolves pursuing the radiant chariots of the sun and moon across the pathless sky.

According to Roman mythology, Diana or Jana (the feminine corresponding to Janus) was the Goddess of the Moon, and like the Sun-god she had her horses and chariot. Only her steeds were milk-white in hue. (To this day a white horse is called among the Arabians a moon-coloured horse.) Every evening when the sun had finished his course, Diana mounted her moon-car and drove across the heavens amid the watching stars.

As Shelley, in his verses " To the Moon," sings :

> And having yoked to her immortal car
> The beam-invested steeds, whose necks on high
> Curve back, she drives to a remoter sky
> A western Crescent, borne impetuously.

According to other writers, the chariot of the moon is drawn by a white and a black horse, because it is only at night that she sends forth her rays, and sometimes, says Festus, a mule is added to her team, because she is barren, and shines by the borrowed light of the sun.

Diana is not merely a charioteer of horses. In one aspect she is herself a horse. She is known as Triformis and Tergemina because, according to the poets, she has three heads—the head of a horse on the right side, of a dog on the left, and a human head in the midst.

> Behold far off the goddess Hecate
> In threefold shape advance.

Hecate or Proserpine is the title by which Diana is known in Hell for her kingdom, like her form, is threefold and comprises Heaven Earth, and Hell.

Milton sings:

> The Moon
> With borrow'd light her countenance triform
> Hence fills and empties.

And Lowell says:

> Goddess triform, I own thy triple sway.

BIBLIOGRAPHY

Myths of Greece and Rome, by H. A. Guerber.   (Geo. G. Harrap & Co., London, 1913.)
Myths of the Norsemen, by H. A. Guerber.   (Geo. G. Harrap & Co., London, 1909.)
The Pantheon, representing the Fabulous Histories of the Heathen Gods, by Andrew
     Tooke, A.M.   Thirty-fifth edition.   (London, 1824.)
Paradise Lost, III. 730, Milton.
Endymion, VII, Lowell.

M. Oldfield Howey.

CHAPTER XVI

The Wind-horse

THE swiftness of horses naturally suggested to our forefathers its only rival, the swiftness of the wind. Consequently it was a very common belief among the nations of classical times that in the region of the West, whence the fleetest horses were derived, the mares were with foal by the wind of that quarter, which was, of course, conceived of as a personality. Thus these people accounted for the wonderful swiftness of their steeds, which rivalled in speed the strong West Wind from the Atlantic.

The earliest reference to this belief is the myth of Xanthos and Balios, the marvellous horses of Achilles, whose story we have given elsewhere. These were celebrated for their fleetness, and were said to have been born of the harpy Podarge to Aquilo, the West Wind. He saw her as she grazed on the meadow by the stream of Oceanus. Her name means " the Swift-footed," so these favoured steeds inherited the coveted quality from both parents.

> The winged coursers harness'd to the car ;
> Xanthus and Balios of immortal breed,
> Sprung from the wind, and like the wind in speed.
> Whom the wing'd harpy, swift Podarge, bore,
> By Zephyr pregnant on the breezy shore.
>   (*Iliad*, XVI, 181 *sq.*, Pope's translation.)

A similar idea is expressed in the following lines from Tasso's *Jerusalem Delivered*, which describes the horse of Raymond as being begotten by the Gale :

> Aquiline of matchless speed ;
> The banks of Tagus bred this generous steed :
> There the fair mother of the warrior brood
> (Soon as the kindly spring had fired her blood)
> With open mouth, against the breezes held,
> Receiv'd the gales with warmth prolific filled :
> And (strange to tell) inspir'd with genial seed,
> Her swelling womb produc'd this wondrous steed.
> Along the sand with rapid feet he flies,
> No eye his traces in the dust descries ;
> To right, to left, obedient to the rein,
> He winds the mazes of th' embattled plain.
>
> Bk. VII. 555.

Probably the North Wind was the sire of Aquiline, as Aquilon is a name of Boreas, though not in very general use. Anyhow, it is the North Wind who is the hero of Trojan legend. This relates that King Erichthonius not only possessed fabulous wealth, but also three thousand mares which pastured in the marshland meadows around the city walls, with their tender foals. Boreas, having seen them as they grazed, became enamoured of them, and taking the form of a black-maned horse he sired twelve fillies. " These, when they bounded over the Earth—the Grain-giver—would run upon the topmost ripened ears of corn and break them not, and when they bounded over the broad back of the sea, they would run upon the crests of the breakers of the hoary brine."

On another occasion Boreas took the form of a horse, and joined the mares belonging to Dardanus, the King of Troy. This time also he became the sire of twelve steeds, so swift of foot that they outdistanced all competitors.

The Ulemas of Algeria have the same idea that the wind is the parent of the fleet steed. According to their account, when God wished to create the mare, He spoke to the Wind, saying, " I will cause thee to bring forth a creature that shall bear all My worshippers, that shall be loved by My slaves, and that will cause the despair of all who will not follow My laws." After God had fulfilled His word, He addressed the newly created mare as follows : " I have made thee without an equal : the goods of this world shall be placed between thy eyes ; everywhere I will make thee happy and preferred above all the beasts of the field, for tenderness shall everywhere be in the heart of thy master ; good alike for the chase and retreat, thou shalt fly, though wingless, and I will only place on thy back the men who know Me, who will offer Me prayers and thanksgivings ; men who shall be My worshippers from one generation to another."

Would that this prophetic promise had not been so cruelly travestied by facts, and the glorious new creature of His conception dragged into the dust of corruption by man !

In India, also, we find the qualities of the wind cause it to be closely linked in legendary lore with the horse. Indra's companions in battle are the warlike Maruts (the Storm-winds), and their chariots are drawn across the skies by self-yoked, dappled mares, fleet as birds. These appear always in troops and act in a body as if of one mind. Sometimes they drive along with " golden mantles waving," sometimes they are " cloaked in rain," or it may be that their chariots are " laden with lightning," or with buckets of water which they pour out as they travel along. They are boisterous and noisy, and sing loudly, and crack their whips as they go. No one in heaven or earth can withstand them. The mountains tremble before them, and the very earth quakes with fear at their coming. The hymns to them are numerous and often very beautiful.

Another famous Wind-horse is Hofvarpnir (the Hoof-thrower), the fleet-footed steed of Gna, messenger of Odin's wife, Frigga. Upon this heavenly mount she could fly with extraordinary speed through fire and air, over sea and land, and from her rapid flights became the personification of the refreshing breeze.

BIBLIOGRAPHY

The Origin and Influence of the Thoroughbred Horse, by Wm. Ridgeway, M.A.
Jerusalem Delivered, by Tasso, Bk. VII. 555.
The Myths of Greece and Rome, by H. A. Guerber. (Geo. G. Harrap & Co., London, 1913.)

Myths of the Norsemen, by H. A. Guerber. (Geo. G. Harrap & Co., London, 1909.)

The Volsunga Saga (Danish).

The Place of Animals in Human Thought, by the Countess Evelyn Martinengo Cesaresco. (T. Fisher Unwin, London, 1909.)

The Mythology of Ancient Greece and Italy, by Thomas Keightley. (Whittaker & Co., London, 1838.)

HIPPOCAMPUS. *From a Pompeian painting.*

CHAPTER XVII

Sea-horses

NEPTUNE is said to have produced the horse when contesting with Minerva for the honour of naming the newly founded city of Athens.

To decide which deity should be accorded this privilege without showing favour to either, Jupiter decreed that the protection of the city should be entrusted to the god who should create the most useful object for the service of the human race. Thereupon Neptune struck the earth with his trident, and from the ground a glorious horse sprang forth. This evoked tremendous admiration and applause from the assembled gods, and the creator proudly proceeded to explain the many qualities and uses of the new creature. Everyone thought Minerva could now have no chance of victory, and when she produced an olive-tree, they laughed aloud at her creation. But soon they changed their minds. For when she told them of the extraordinary number of uses to which almost every part of her tree could be applied, and further pointed out that the olive was the symbol of peace and prosperity, whilst the horse was the emblem of war and all its evils, the palm of victory was unhesitatingly awarded to her, and she thus became the tutelary goddess of the city, and gave it her own name of Athene.

Those who would explain away everything tell us that the meaning of this fable is that the horse was originally introduced into Greece by way of the sea, but this hardly seems a sufficient reason to account for the close connection of Neptune with the horse, though we shall refer to it again.

The naming of the breakers as sea-horses at once occurs to the inquiring mind, and possibly it is this fancied resemblance of the waves to horses' forms that is responsible, for the simile is as widespread as it is ancient.

However this may be, it is quite clear from passages in ancient Greek writings that Neptune was looked upon as an equestrian deity, as well as God of the Sea. For instance, Homer writes :

> Neptune, the mighty marine god, I sing ;
>
> .   .   .   .   .
>
> O thou earth shaker ; thy command, twofold
> The gods have sorted ; making thee of horses
> The awful tamer, and of naval forces
> The sure preserver.
>
> (Chapman's translation.)

Again, Neptune's titles, Hippius and Hippodromus, and his presidency of the horse-races clearly indicate that he was accepted as the God of Horses (*hippos*, Greek = " horse "). And horses and mules were decked with garlands in the month of August when the solemn games named Consualia were held in the Sea-god's honour. The Cloud-bearer was named Hippa, and her connection with the steeds of Neptune is an obvious one, drawing her waters from their watery forms. The mariner who rides the white horses (or waves) is thence called Hippion. For this reason, too, the ship Argo was known as Hippodameia, that is " the Horse-tamer," because she rode over the billows. Hippodamé was also an epithet of Castor as a tamer of horses.

The Sea-horse, or Hippocampus, had a horse's head, body, and forefeet, but its body terminated in the tail of a dolphin or other fish. Pompeian paintings abound with representations of sea-horses drawing

SEA-HORSES WARRING WITH SEA-SERPENT.
(An ocean tragedy witnessed by the artist in a dream.)
By Holloway, after M. Oldfield Howey.

135

the car of Neptune and other deities. Spenser was probably thinking of the hippocampus when he wrote :

> The raging billowes . . . made a long broad dyke,
> That his [Neptune's] swift charet might have passage wyde
> Which four great Hippodames did draw in teme-wise tyde.

Virgil has given us many descriptions. The following will serve as instances :

> Through the vast seas he glides,
> Drawn by a team half-fish, half-horse he rides.
>
> *Geo.* 4.

> Where'er he guides
> His finny coursers, and in triumph rides,
> The waves unruffle and the sea subsides.
>
> *Æneid,* 1.

The subjoined verses from Statius may be quoted in further illustration.

> Shaking his trident, urges on his steeds,
> Who with two feet beat from their brawny breasts
> The foaming billows ; but their hinder parts
> Swim, and go smooth against the curling surge.
>
> *Achilleis,* 1.

Ships were always safe under Neptune's protection, for whenever he rides on the waves the weather immediately becomes fair and the sea calm.

Our English poets have shown no backwardness in adopting the Grecian symbol, and many are their references to Neptune's steeds. Byron, for instance, in *Childe Harold's Pilgrimage,* writes :

> The waves bound beneath me as a steed that knows his rider.

And in the *Two Noble Kinsmen* of Beaumont and Fletcher we find a similar thought :

> Oh, never
> Shall we two exercise, like twins of Honour,
> Our arms again, and feel our fiery horses
> Like proud seas under us.

The sea-god Poseidon, to whom horses were sacred, was the grand-sire of Hippolytus, whose name has the meaning of " horse-looser or horse-loosed," and whose story is remarkable because horses figure so largely in it. He met his death whilst driving in his chariot along the shores of the Saronic Gulf. Poseidon, to avenge an imagined wrong, sent a bull out of the waters, and the fierce creature so terrified the horses Hippolytus was driving that they bolted, threw him from his seat, and dragged him to death at their heels. But Æsculapius, at the request of Diana, restored him to life, and in gratitude his patient dedicated twenty horses to him. Because of their part in the death of Hippolytus, horses were excluded from the Arician grove and sanctuary. It is a remarkable coincidence, if nothing more, that the Christian saint of the same name was also dragged to death by horses, and that twenty members of his household were martyred at the same time, the number corresponding exactly with the twenty horses dedicated by the " Horse-loosed " Grecian hero to Æsculapius. The 13th of August, which is the day on which the saint suffered martyrdom, is also the special day of Diana, who, as the Goddess of Hunting, may be presumed to feel a keen interest in horses, and, as we have just seen, by her intercession, saved Hippolytus from death at their heels.

Poseidon is often identified with Neptune, and is usually repre-sented in symbolic art as having the body of a fish and the head of a horse. He is said to have loved the goddess Ceres, and to have followed her whilst she sought for her lost daughter, Proserpina. At last, to escape his unwelcome attentions, the goddess took the form of a mare, but the Sea-god, nothing daunted, immediately assumed the shape of a horse and renewed his wooing. He thus became the sire of Arion, a marvellous winged steed who was able to speak, and who was educated by the Nereides. They taught him to draw his father's chariot over the waves with matchless speed. Afterwards he was given to Copreus, the son of Pelops, and then belonged successively to Hercules and Adrastus. The last-named won all the chariot races when he had him.

According to the account of Antimachus, Adrastus was the first of the Danaans to drive " two high-praised steeds " in his chariot as a pair, and both were of divine birth, one being " Fleet Cracus " and the other " Thelpusian Arion," " whom, near the Oncean Grove of Apollo, Earth herself brought forth, a wonder for mortals to see." Arion is described in the Iliad as the " dark-maned, swift steed of Adrastus," and it was on his back that his master fled from Thebes. Arion had human feet on his right side.

Poseidon was also the sire of Pegasus, whose mother was the Gorgon Medusa. When the blood-drops from her severed head fell into the sea-foam, he created from them this famous winged steed, who was the first of the equine race to bear a human rider on his back. Pegasus was snowy white and was gifted with extraordinary speed and with immortality. Apollo and the Muses constantly used his broad back to fly through the air. The bold mortal who first mounted him was Bellerophon. A well-nigh hopeless task had been assigned to this hero. He had to slay the terrible Chimera, " a mingled monster of no mortal kind " (Homer, Pope's translation). It had the upper part of a lion, the lower of a serpent, and the middle of a goat, and it breathed forth flaming fire.

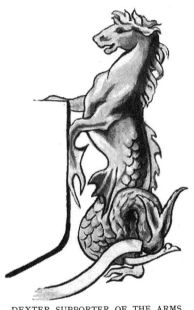

DEXTER SUPPORTER OF THE ARMS OF THE CITY OF CARDIFF.

Many other heroes had previously attempted this feat, but so far from being successful, none had survived to tell the tale. Bellerophon, being about to undertake the adventure, wished to possess Pegasus, and Pindar has told us how he obtained him. Bellerophon knew that occasionally this heavenly steed came down to earth to refresh himself by drinking of the Hippocrene fountain which had burst from the ground when his hoofs touched the earth for the first time. Or again, sometimes he might be found near Corinth at the spring of Pirene. This last was the city where Bellerophon reigned, and after many fruitless attempts to catch Pegasus, he applied to the soothsayer Polyeidos, and was by him told to sleep beside the altar of Athene.. He followed the prophet's directions, and in the dead of night the goddess appeared to him in a dream, and giving him a golden bridle, bade him sacrifice a bull to his sire Poseidon-Damæos (Tamer), and show the bridle to the steed. On waking Bellerophon found the bridle lying beside him, and hastened to raise an altar to Minerva (Athene) as " Hippeia " (Of the Horse).

Then, bridle in hand he went to watch for Pegasus at the spring of Pirene, and presently was rewarded by seeing the bird-like horse sailing down to where he lay in wait hidden by a thicket. Pegasus at once recognised the magic bridle and became kind and tractable, and our hero mounted him and sallied forth in search of the Chimera. In the Theogony it is said of the Chimera that she was slain by Pegasus and the " good Bellerophon."

After this adventure Bellerophon took many flights on Pegasus, until at last he decided to ascend to Olympus and join the gods. His faithful steed ascended heavenward with him, but Jupiter, in wrath at such presumption on the part of a mere mortal, sent a gadfly which stung Pegasus so severely that he involuntarily shied frantically, and Bellerophon was flung to the earth far below. He was blinded by this fall, and was never again able to ride the immortal Pegasus.

The Hippocrene, or Horse's Fountain, the origin of which we have just noted, was situated on Mount Helicon in *Bœotia*, and was sacred to the Muses, its waters being said to possess the power of poetic inspiration. Keats thus refers to it :

> Oh for a beaker full of the warm south,
> Full of the true, the blushful Hippocrene.
>> (*Ode to a Nightingale.*)

And Longfellow writes of the

> Maddening draughts of Hippocrene.
>> (*Goblet of Life.*)

In this myth we find that mysterious connection between Poseidon and Pallas-Athene (or Minerva) and the Horse more fully revealed than elsewhere. They are the parents of Pegasus (for Athene and

Medusa are the same), that is, probably of the ship ; and he is worshipped as the Breaker and she as the Bridler. There was a temple of Athene under this name at Corinth (*Paus. II.* 4, *I.* 5), and Poseidon was there named Damæos. Bellerophon was originally named Hipponoös.

Some writers consider this hero only represents one of the forms of Poseidon. The god is his father, and also, as we have seen, the sire of Pegasus. In the two combined we have Poseidon-Hippios, the Rider of the Waves—a symbol of navigation. Pegasus therefore may be taken to symbolise a ship. But others would find the interpretation of this marvellous horse, sired by the Sea-god, to be the same as that of the fable of its creation (already given in the first part of this chapter) —that is, that when horses were first introduced into Peloponnesus in the days of Adrastus (about 1350 B.C.), they came by way of the sea and were as much objects of wonder to the people of Argolis as they were to the Aztecs when Cortes arrived with his horses in Mexico (see " Sacred Horses "). The same result followed in each case. They were regarded as divine, and in Greece were additionally considered the actual offspring of Poseidon.

Neptune was widely worshipped throughout Northern Africa, Spain, Greece, and Italy, and indeed his cult extended almost universally in the earliest ages of Europe.

Horses were the chief objects favoured for sacrifice to this god by the ancient peoples of the historical period. Usually, they were killed and cast into the sea from high precipices. The sacred horse festivals of the Scandinavians were a survival of this Neptune worship, which was once practised along all the coasts of Europe.

The ancient inhabitants of Pontus were also counted among the Sea-god's worshippers, and occasionally they would make offering to him of a chariot to which were harnessed four milk-white steeds. They drove these into the sea until they were drowned, presumably that their shades might serve him in his watery kingdom ; for these people of other days had no doubts as to the immortality of the souls of animals, such as sometimes trouble those of a later day and newer creed.

It was only after the conversion of the peoples to Christianity that these rites were discontinued, and then it was with great difficulty the Church suppressed them.

The principal votaries of Neptune were sailors and horse-trainers, and these constantly sought his aid by invocation and sacrifice. Many imposing temples were exclusively dedicated to him.

We may note that Neptune's wedding-gift on the marriage of King Peleus of Thessaly with Thetis, the Nereides—a sea-goddess— was the pair of divine horses, Xanthus and Balius (see " Wind-horses ").

According to the account of the fabled continent of Atlantis given us by Plato, there was in the centre of the Atlanteans' citadel a holy temple dedicated to Cleito and Poseidon which was surrounded by an enclosure of gold. Poseidon's own temple also stood there, and in it were statues of gold.

" There was the god himself standing in a chariot—the charioteer of six winged horses—and of such a size that he touched the roof of the building with his head. Around him were a hundred Nereids riding on dolphins, for such was thought to be the number of them in that day."

The Atlanteans honoured horses by providing special baths for their use " with as much adornment as was suitable for them." They also set apart special gardens and places of exercise for their steeds, and a race-course, a stadium in width, extended all around the island citadel " for horses to race in."

It is interesting to find the sea-horse figuring in early Irish mythology.

Among the Gaelic gods described in the ancient manuscripts of Erin is Ler, who we may consider to be the Poseidon of the Gaelic Pantheon, though it is his son Manannán mac Ler who was the special patron of sailors, and journeyed to and fro between Ireland and the Celtic Elysium in the West with a chariot and horses that ran along the surface of the sea. This god had also a wonderful horse named Splendid Mane which was swifter than the wind of spring, and travelled with equal ease and speed on earth or sea. This horse he loaned to the Sun-god Lugh.

The name Ler means " the sea," and " mac " is " son of." Splendid Mane had a wonderful magic bridle, which in living Highland folk-lore is attributed to the Willox family. It has the property of causing the image of a worker of evil magic to appear in a pail of water produced for the purpose. The bridle or its bit was said to have been obtained from the water-horse.

When a tempest breaks over the sea in Ireland, the breakers are said to be the white horses of Manannán mac Ler.

The ancient Irish deity Brian also seems to have been partly a sea-god, and his place in later times was usurped by St. Michael of the White Steeds, who became the Gaelic Neptune, whilst Brian was thrust into outer darkness and now is looked upon as a demon by his

HORSES OF NEPTUNE.

former votaries. The following lines, which are quoted in Carmichael's *Carmina Gadelica*, refer to the steed of the god-saint, and belong to the transition stage of thought :

> Thou wert the warrior of courage
> Going on the journey of prophecy ;
> Thou wouldst not travel on a cripple,
> Thou didst take the steed of Brian Michael,
> He was without bit in his mouth,
> Thou didst ride him on the wing,
> Thou didst leap over the knowledge of Nature.

It should be noted how the freedom and power of this steed of god and saint are insisted on by the poet. His wonderful service is all willingly given. No taint of slavery is here.

We find our saint figuring again in Highland myth as God of Mountains and Seas. His title still is Michael of the White Steeds, or sometimes "Michael the Victorious."

According to another Irish legend, St. Bairre of Cork has annexed some of Neptune's attributes. His full name is the poetically suggestive one of Find-bharr ("Whitecrest"), and he rides across the Irish Sea on St. David's horse, which he begged the loan of to enable him to make the journey more speedily.

To turn to a rather different aspect of our subject. The water-horse is spoken of in the *Life of St. Féchin of Fore*: "It came to them and was harnessed to the chariot, and it was tamer and gentler than any other horse." Comparing this description of its character with the tales of its deeds given below, we feel that the saint's influence must have been a powerful one !

There are many legends of water-horses haunting the Scottish lochs and rivers and as it were personifying their raging floods. Loch Ness and the Beauly River are examples, but it would really be difficult to name any lochs in the Highlands that were not in olden times associated with the water-horse.

Boswell, in his *Journal of Johnson's Tour to the Hebrides*, relates the following myth, which was told by an old man of the lochs of Raasay : "There was once a wild beast in it, a sea-horse, which came and devoured a man's daughter, upon which the man lighted a great fire and had a sow roasted in it, the smell of which attracted the monster. In the fire was put a spit. The man lay concealed behind a low wall of loose stones. The monster came, and the man with the red-hot spit destroyed it."

Some uncanny tales are related by Hugh Miller about the strange behaviour of a sea-horse which had its abode in the waters of the River Conon, Ross-shire. It was known as the Black Glen kelpie, and very early one morning was seen near the source of the river, making very unusual noises. Shortly after it left the water altogether, and with fearful bellowings ran towards Loch Uisge and Kingairloch, since when it has neither been seen nor heard of.

Another supposed kelpie used to haunt the road near Loch Ness, until a bold brave Highlander, meeting it one night, drew his sword in the name of the Trinity, and laid it for ever. Other districts afford legends of the kelpie or water-horse temporarily taking the form of a handsome youth that it might win the love of an earthly maid, and finally, when her suspicions became aroused, revealing its true nature and ultimately destroying her in a lake, river, or well.

In fact it must be confessed that the kelpies are both mischievous and malicious in their actions. They give to the seer warning of his approaching death by drowning, and are often accused of hastening this fate and dragging the unfortunate one below the surface :

> These ponderous keys shall the Kelpies keep,
> And lodge in their caverns so dark and deep.
> (*Queen Mary's Escape from Lochleven.*)

The kelpies are especially Scotch fairies, and Scotland is also the native land of the Boobrie, an equally treacherous and malicious creature, to whom we will now introduce our readers.

The Campbell of Islay MSS. give the following account of the Boobrie (a fictitious monster of living Highland tradition, with the power of assuming at will three different animal forms, viz. water-horse, water-bull, and water-bird) as water-horse or " each-uisg " :

" On the banks of Loch Freisa, a fresh-water loch on the property of Lochadashenaig, in the island of Mull, the tenant was ploughing some land that was so hard that he was compelled to use four horses. Early one day one of the horses cast a shoe; they were nine miles from a smithy, and the nature of the ground prevented any possibility of the horse ploughing without one. ' Here's the best part of our day's work gone,' said the tenant to his son, who was leading the foremost horses. ' I am not sure,' replied the son ; ' I see a horse feeding beside the loch, we'll take a lend of him, as we don't know who he belongs to.' The father approved of the proposal. The son went down and fetched up the horse, which appeared to have been quite used to ploughing, drawing first uphill, then down, perfectly steadily, until they reached the end of the furrow, close to the loch. On an attempt to turn the horses, this borrowed one became rather restive, which brought the whip into use, though lightly. No sooner had the thong touched him than he instantly assumed the form of a most enormous Boobrie " (i.e. the monstrous bird form which is his favourite shape), " and uttering a shout which appeared to shake the earth, plunged into the loch, carrying with him the three horses and plough. The tenant and his son had both the sense to let go their respective holds. The Boobrie swam out with his victims to the middle of the loch, where he dived, carrying them along with him to the bottom, where he apparently took his pleasure of them. The tenant and his son got a most awful fright, as may well be imagined, but remained hid behind a large stone for seven hours in the earnest hope of even one of their horses coming ashore. But no such luck awaited them."

Besides the sea-horses, so famous in myth, there are the less-known river-horses, such as those who bore from view the Lorelei on the last occasion when she was seen by mortal eyes.

This famous siren maiden used to sit upon the rock that bore her name, near St. Goar on the Rhine, and her entrancing songs lured many mariners to their death. Forgetting time and place, those who heard her song wafted upon the breeze became enchanted with the sound, and allowed their boats to drift upon the cruel rocks, where they were quickly battered to pieces.

At last so many were lost in this manner, that it was determined some remedy must be found, and an armed force was organised, which, at nightfall, was to surround and seize the water-nymph. But when they drew near to her the siren-maiden soon had them all at her mercy by her enchantments, and the captain and his men stood spellbound, unable to move hand or foot. Meanwhile, the Lorelei, encircled by the motionless men, took off her ornaments and threw them into the water below. Then chanting a spell, she called the waves to the summit of her rocky throne, and we may imagine the amazement of the soldiers when the rising waters revealed in their midst a sea-green chariot drawn by white-maned horses into which the siren lightly leapt. As she did so, her magic equipage disappeared from the view of the astonished spectators. A few minutes later the river fell to its normal level, and the spell-bound men regained the use of their limbs, and made off to tell of their astounding experience.

The Lorelei has never since been seen, and the peasants say that she was so deeply offended by the insult offered her, that she will not again leave her coral caves.

In Spain, too, the water-horse is to be found, if ancient local tradition can be believed. Strange tales are told of the vast mountain range of Caballero. "It is said that in certain places there are deep pools and lakes in which dwell monsters, huge serpents as long as a pine tree, and horses of the flood, which sometimes come out and commit mighty damage." So wrote George Borrow in 1842, and

FROM A ROMAN BAS-RELIEF.
Illustrating how the ancients connected the horse with the sea; and probably intended to propitiate Neptune by introducing its form.

the mischievous character ascribed to it well accords with what we have learnt of water-horses in other places.

We have seen how in Grecian myth Pegasus represents a ship. The ferry-boats used on the Tsangpo River in Tibet remind us how universal is the connection of the horse with water, for they bear on their prow a beam carved into the semblance of a horse's head, and, moreover, the boat itself is known to the natives as "the Wooden Horse," just as in our idiom the railway-engine is sometimes called "the Iron Horse."

These boats have not the graceful outline of the Assyrian boat illustrated on the next page, but are huge barges of walnut planks, with square corners and flat bottoms, and are capable of carrying in one journey as much as twenty ponies, a dozen men, and a ton of goods.

Before closing this chapter we will just note the case of the substitution of Pegasus—the winged horse—for the Pascal Lamb in the arms of the Inner Temple.

For nearly five centuries the leading lights of the law have possessed the circular church and its appurtenances that formerly belonged to the lawless Knights Templars. When the Knights Hospitallers —to whom the forfeited estate of the Knights Templars had been granted by the Pope—were dissolved by King Henry VIII, their property was leased to the lawyers by the Crown at an annual rental of ten pounds. The law-students increased so much in number and importance that it became necessary to divide the Inn into two separate bodies, the Honourable Societies of the Inner and Middle

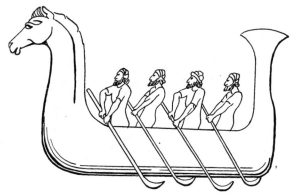

ASSYRIAN BOAT AS USED ABOUT 700 B.C. AND PICTURED IN THE PALACE OF SARGON.
Note that the form combines horse and fish.

Temple, with separate halls, but using the same church. The Middle Temple still bears the arms of the Knights Templars : argent [1] on a cross gules, a pascal lamb, or, carrying a banner of the first, charged with a cross of the second (such as may still be found in certain towns in the degenerate form of the Lamb and Flag public-house sign). The winged horse was substituted for the Holy Lamb by the Inner Temple early in the reign of Elizabeth, but no one has been able to suggest a satisfactory reason for the change.

BIBLIOGRAPHY

The Mythology of the British Isles, by Charles Squire. (Blackie & Son, Ltd.)
Dictionary of Phrase and Fable, by E. Cobham Brewer, LL.D. Second edition. (Cassell Peter & Galpin.)

[1] Note: argent = silver, gules = red, and or = gold in heraldry.

The Golden Bough, by J. G. Frazer.

The Origin and Influence of the Thoroughbred Horse, by Wm. Ridgeway.

The Myths of Greece and Rome, by H. A. Guerber. (Geo. G. Harrap & Co., London, 1913.)

Prehistoric Nations. Atlantis : The Antediluvian World, by Ignatius Donnelly. (Harper & Bros., New York, 1882.)

Faerie Queene, III, XI, 40, by Spenser.

Mavor's Universal History, Vol. IX, p. 1, by Richard Phillips. (1802.)

The Myths of the Norsemen, by H. A. Guerber. (Geo. G. Harrap & Co., London, 1909.)

Lhasa and Its Mysteries, by L. Austine Waddell, LL.D. (John Murray, 1905.)

Survivals in Belief among the Celts, by George Henderson, M.A. (James Maclehose & Sons, Glasgow, 1911.)

Campbell of Islay MSS. Advocates' Library.

The Mythology of Ancient Greece and Italy, by Thomas Keightley. Second edition. (Whittaker & Co., London, 1838.)

The Bible in Spain, by George Borrow, 1842.

CHAPTER XVIII

The Night-horse

ALTHOUGH the Grecian poets usually represented those deities who had long journeys to perform as possessed of a chariot and horses, we do not find either Homer or Hesiod attributing one to the Goddess of Night. But later poets did so, and we find Æschylus speaking of her " dark chariot " (*Coeph*. 656), Euripides describing her as driving through Olympus (*Fr. Androm.* 28), and Theocritus saying that the stars are " the attendants of the car of quiet Night " (*Idyll*, II. 166), whilst Apollonius represents Night as yoking her horses at sunset (*Argonaut*. III. 1193), and Statius makes Sleep her charioteer.

Our English poet Milton says :

> The yellow-skirted Fayes
> Fly after the night-steeds, leaving their moon-loved maze.
> *(Nativity*, I. 236.)

In the Vedic myth we find the horse used as an emblem of the moonless night-sky in the beautiful passage where the Pitris are said to have adorned the Black Horse with pearls.

Although not strictly night-horses, we will include in this chapter the shadowy steeds of the Ashvins, or Horse-men (*ashva*, " horse "), the famous twin brothers of the Sun and the Dawn, who are so often invoked in the Vedic hymns. They never ride, but drive in a chariot which is sometimes drawn by horses, but also by grey asses, figuring the grey twilight hour that precedes the dawn. They are described as " dispellers of darkness," and their chariot appears " at the end of the night."

They are represented as twins to typify the dual nature of the twilight, beginning in light and ending in darkness, or vice versa, and they are said to be inseparable companions, with the same symbolical setting forth of the close relation between the disappearing darkness and the returning light.

In character they are kind and gracious ; they heal the sick and give sight to the blind. They refresh and rejuvenate the weary Sun, when at the end of his long day's travail he sinks exhausted and overcome by his foe, the Night. They are the protectors and physicians of gods and men, and are ever young, though ancient as the skies.

Perhaps the more correct translation of their name would be " Descendants of the Horse " rather than Horse-men. They fill many offices, presiding over weddings, rescuing travellers from storms, working miracles for the good of mankind, and other such beneficent actions.

Scandinavian mythology has an equally poetical simile. The Night, personified as the Goddess Nott, a daughter of the giant Norvi, is said to be drawn in a dark chariot by a black horse called Hrim-faxi (Frost-mane). From his bit and his long flowing mane the rime drops fall upon the earth.

> Hrim-faxi is the sable steed,
> From the east who brings the night,
> Fraught with the showering joys of love :
> As he champs the foamy bit,
> Drops of dew are scattered round
> To adorn the vales of earth.
>> (*Vafthrudni's-mal*, W. Taylor's translation.)

CHAPTER XIX

The Horse in Charm and Incantation

IF we have realised the immensely important position held by the horse in ancient religion, we shall not be surprised to find that its aid is constantly invoked in charm and incantation.

The following incantation is one of the oldest known, and can be found in nearly all volumes of Scandinavian folk-lore. It appears to refer to some forgotten legend about a ride of Odin and Balder the Beautiful. It would seem that the horse on which the latter rode, slipped and broke a leg. This was miraculously healed by tying round the fracture a black thread in which seven knots had previously been made, and reciting this formula :

> Baldur rade. The foal slade (i.e. slipped).
> He lighted, and he righted,
> Set joint to joint, bone to bone,
> Sinew to sinew,
> Heal in Odin's name.

The spell was evidently found to be a potent healer, for it has survived to modern times. On the introduction of Christianity its form was slightly altered and was now referred to a supposed accident in Christ's triumphal ride into Jerusalem, and thus adapted it ran :

> The Lord rade. The foal slade.
> Set bone to bone, etc.
> Heal in the Holy Ghost's name.

Even to-day this spell is practised in remote corners of the British Isles, not only on animals but on human beings also, and apparently success still follows its use.

An interesting case of this was given in the *Occult Review* of May 1917 by Mr. Brodie Innes. He writes :

"Three years ago, being in Penzance, and driving out to see some Druidic remains, I fell into conversation with the driver. At first, with true Celtic caution, he denied that any witchcraft remained in Cornwall. But after I had told him some experiences of my own in the West Highlands, he told me that once he had a poisoned thumb that defied all the doctors to cure. He was told that his thumb must be amputated, but before agreeing to this he consulted a ' wise woman.' She anointed the thumb with a special salve of which she had the secret, and solemnly tied seven knots in a black thread, which she bound round the thumb, chanting something under her breath. I asked him if he could remember the words, but these he had barely heard, only he knew it was something about our Lord riding. Anyhow the thumb got perfectly well in a short time."

The " wise woman " was quite correct in chanting the charm under her breath, as the words must not be heard by bystanders.

The Scotch version is slightly fuller than that given above. It runs :

> Our Lord rade, His foal's foot slade :
> Down he lighted, His foal's foot righted.
> Bone to bone, sinew to sinew.
> Blood to blood, flesh to flesh ;
> Heal, in the name of the Father, Son, and Holy Ghost.

The divine Rider's quick and ready practical sympathy with his suffering mount is worthy of note. Whether we name Him Baldur or Christ, His love makes us say " Lord ! "

In Ireland there is a strange superstition current in some districts that a pure white horse confers upon its owner the gift of great wisdom in the cure of physical ills, provided he is riding or driving the horse when consulted. Suppose, for instance, that one of a family has fallen a victim to whooping-cough. The head of the household keeps a watch upon the road until the longed-for white horse appears. Then he will step forward, and after the usual Irish salutation of " God save you " will ask the rider or driver of the animal what is the remedy for whooping-cough. Sometimes the reply may be chicken, grapes, cream, and other enjoyable dainties, but occasionally the white horse's owner may be churlishly minded, or resent the interruption when perhaps he is hurrying to reach his journey's end. Then he may recommend bread and water or gruel as the cure for the trouble. But no matter what his advice may be it is rigorously enforced on the patient by his friends.

Many examples of the power ascribed to white horses can be found in Irish folk-lore.

A Spanish charm against the evil eye, the belief in which is very prevalent amongst the lower classes in Spain, and especially in Andalusia, consists of a stag's horn attached to a cord made from the hair of a black mare's tail.

Should the evil glance fall on the wearer, it is instantly intercepted by the stag's horn, which snaps asunder. Children are often to be seen wearing this charm, and small horns tipped with silver used to be on sale in some of the silversmiths' shops in Seville.

Although it does not really belong to this chapter, we should like to include here a charm which protects the horse and his rider from ill.

The turquoise was supposed to have this virtue by Europeans of the middle ages. No horseman wearing this gem could be thrown by his horse, neither could his horse be overtired whilst his rider used the charm.

If it is suspected that a vampire is lurking in a grave, the following is a sure method of discovering its whereabouts : A virgin youth must mount upon a virgin black stallion. He must ride the steed about the suspected burying-ground. If it halts at any spot and refuses to go any further, the suspicion is justified, and that place is without doubt the abode of a vampire ! This rite appears to have been practised in England in olden days.

But the belief in the existence of vampires is very widespread, especially in Eastern Europe, and a similar method of discovering their lurking-places is followed in Montenegro at the present day, as, though the authorities are opposed to such superstitious practices, the peasants are so certain that the safety of their own lives and the lives of their cattle depends on the continuance of such rites that they have actually threatened to desert their homes and villages *en bloc*, unless allowed to ensure their well-being in this way.   A black horse without blemish is led to the cemetery to discover the grave where the vampire has made its home.   The suspected corpse is then dug up, pierced with stakes, and burnt.

BIBLIOGRAPHY

Zincali, Vol. I, chap. ix, by George Borrow.
The Occult Review, May 1917, Sept. 1917, March 1918, Nov. 1906.
Hero Tales and Legends of the Serbians, by Woislav Petrovitch.   (George G. Harrap
    & Co., London, 1914.)
Popular Rhymes of Scotland.   (Chambers.)

CHAPTER XX

The Prophetic Horse

IN ancient days, when the gods made known their will and spoke to man by means of signs and auguries, the horse was esteemed as the medium of expression most favoured by the deities, and so was an object of the greatest veneration and consulted in every crisis.

It is probable that it was no jest or freak of mind on the part of the corrupt Roman Emperor Caligula, when he spoke of raising his horse Incitatus to the consulship, but was with the idea of paying a delicate compliment to his Gallic and British subjects, who held the horse in such high honour. He would no doubt have carried out this intention had his death not intervened. As it was, he built for it a stable of marble, with an ivory manger, and provided it with a well-furnished house that had a kitchen attached, so that its visitors might be properly honoured, and sometimes invited it to his own table.

One cannot but feel that had Caligula's human friends and counsellors possessed equal virtue with his steed, Rome might have escaped many of the horrors that befell her.

Perhaps Dean Swift had been meditating on this when he evolved his bitter satire, *A Voyage to the Houyhnhnms.*

Tacitus, in his treatise *De Moribus Germanorum*, says :

" These people have certain horses, which are kept in their sacred groves, untouched and free from any sort of mortal labour ; and when they are harnessed to the sacred chariot, the priest and the king, or the chief man of the city, go with them and observe their neighings and whinnyings. Nor is there any sort of augury to which more importance is attached—both in the minds of the people and also in that of the nobles and priests—for they imagine themselves to be the servants, but the others the favourites of the gods."

And Camden in his *Britannia* (Holland's translation, p. 135) speaks of the same thing, saying :

" Moreover this nation of the Saxons was very much addicted to superstition, and for that cause when they were to consult of weighty and important matters, besides soothsaying by inspection of beast's entrails, they observed especially the neighing of horses as presaging things to come. And thence perhaps it is that the Dukes of Saxonie in ancient times gave the horse in their Armes."

The ancient Saxons were not the only people who placed faith in the inspiration of their steeds.

In 521 B.C. the Persians wished to select a king to reign over them. To accomplish their choice it was agreed that the competitors for the sovereignty should meet on horseback at an appointed place near the city, and that he whose horse first neighed should be the chosen ruler. Darius was one of the candidates, and his groom, having heard of the agreement, determined to secure the throne for his master. To effect this he resorted to a stratagem and led a mare to meet Darius's horse at the appointed place the night before. Next morning when the Persians assembled, the horse of Darius at once neighed, and the other competitors immediately dismounted and proclaimed him king. Thus was given to Persia one of the wisest and most virtuous monarchs that the world has known.

During the wanderings of Æneas in search of a dwelling-place for himself and those who had escaped with him from fallen Troy, they beheld one morning from their ship a land with dimly seen hills and low-lying shores. And Anchises cried, " Lo ! there is Italy," and filling a cup with wine, invoked the gods to give them favouring winds to shore. And even whilst he prayed his request was granted, and a stronger wind arose behind. And as the harbour mouth grew nearer, upon the hills was seen a temple of Minerva. And, prophetic omen ! upon the shore were standing four horses white as snow. But here a difficulty confronted the seers. How was the augury to be interpreted ? Anchises did not know, and said : " Thou speakest of war, land of the stranger, for the horse signifieth war ; yet doth he also use himself to run in the chariot, and to bear the bit in company ; therefore also will we hope for peace."

Thus, two directly opposite interpretations being possible, and no soothsayer to decide which was the true one being of the party, it was decided to act cautiously. Sacrifices were made to Minerva and Juno. Then sails were trimmed and a speedy departure taken for fear some enemy should set upon them, as the Greeks were known to be on those shores. Nothing further came of the omen, so doubtless its purpose was served.

Later, in the same voyage, still upon the same quest, Æneas came to the city of Carthage, and in the midst of it was a wood thickly grown with trees. This was evidently a sacred grove, and here it was that the men of Carthage, when first they came to land from their voyage seeking a site whereon to build a city, had dug out of the ground the sign that Juno had promised them, even a horse's head. Finding this, they were to know that their city would be victorious and great in war and full of riches. The omen had been abundantly fulfilled. Æneas tarried many months among them and was most hospitably entertained by their Queen Dido.

In the cases we have just been considering the prophecies of equine augurs were delivered by somewhat indirect means requiring skilled interpretation. We will now take an instance in which the horse-prophet was enabled to give its message directly in the human speech, though we must note that this steed was of no mortal breed.

Xanthus was one of the two immortal horses, " Xanthus and Balius, noble progeny of swift Podarge," who drew the chariot of Achilles. These steeds had been given to his father Pelius by Neptune, and were of wondrous beauty with long drooping manes. Their names are descriptive of their colouring, for Xanthus means dun, or reddish yellow, and Balius is an adjective regularly applied to the deer and the lynx, and when used of horses means dappled.

The occasion when Xanthus became numbered with the prophets was as follows : The immortal steeds had been lent by Achilles to Patroclus to draw his chariot on the Trojan battlefield, and this hero had been slain there by the god Apollo—though the god had chosen to remain invisible, and give the honour of the achievement to Hector.

Xanthus and Balius were deeply grieved over the loss of their driver. They kept apart from the battle after his death, "weeping since first they were aware that their charioteer was fallen in the dust beneath the hands of the man-slaying Hector. They stood abasing their heads unto the earth. Hot tears flowed from their eyes unto the ground as they mourned in sorrow for their charioteer, and their rich manes were soiled as they drooped from the yoke-cushion on both sides beneath the yoke."

When Achilles next had occasion to ride behind the immortal steeds himself, he rebuked them for having left Patroclus dead, and then it was that the noble Xanthus, bowing his head till his streaming mane touched the ground, was enabled by the goddess Juno to speak what was in his heart, and unburden himself of his sad foreknowledge that Fate had also unalterably decreed his loved master's death.

> Yes, great Achilles, we this day again
> Will bear thee safely; but thy hour of doom
> Is nigh at hand; nor shall we cause thy death,
> But Heav'n's high will, and Fate's imperious pow'r.
> By no default of ours, nor lack of speed,
> The Trojans stripp'd Patroclus of his arms:
> The mighty god, fair-hair'd Latona's son,
> Achiev'd his death, and Hector's vict'ry gained.
> Our speed of foot may vie with Zephyr's breeze,
> Deem'd swiftest of the winds; but thou art doom'd
> To die, by force combin'd of god and man.
> (Translation: Anon.)

Before the noble animal could utter more, the Furies interposed and hushed his voice for ever.

"Oh! Xanthus!" cried Achilles, "why dost thou predict my death? Well do I know that it is my fate to perish here, far from my well-loved parents and my native shores. I am resigned to sink when Heaven ordains. Now perish Troy!" Saying which he rushed into battle.

The reader should note that Xanthus was not a mere mouthpiece used by Juno. The goddess enabled him to speak, that he might give vent to the crowding, bitter thoughts of his *own* heart. This story should be compared with the biblical narrative of Balaam's ass, where the same thought is expressed. The long-pent-up emotions and ideas confined in the animal's mind by its inability of giving them voice, suddenly released by the angel's power, and pouring forth in indignation at the injustice of its master and his blindness to the spiritual world around them, is the point emphasised.

BIBLIOGRAPHY

Universal History, Ancient and Modern, Vol. VIII, p. 51, by Wm. Mavor, LL.D. (Richard Phillips, London, 1802.)

De Moribus Germanorum, by Tacitus.

Britannia, by Camden (Holland's translation.)

Story of the Trojan War : an Epitome (from Classic Writers), with a Preface by the Lord Bishop of Gloucester and Bristol. (James Blackwood & Co., London, 1874.)

CHAPTER XXI

The Symbolic Horse

TO avoid repetition of information given in other chapters it has been necessary to omit a great deal properly belonging under this heading, because it has already been included under titles that seemed to claim it, or had such large developments as to demand a chapter of their own.

Perhaps courage was the quality of the horse that most appealed to early peoples, and we frequently find the steed used as an emblem of this virtue. The matchless description of the horse in the Book of Job (xxxix. 19–25, A.V.) gives us the key as to why it was thus considered :

"Hast thou given the horse strength ? Hast thou clothed his neck with thunder ? Canst thou make him afraid as a grasshopper ? the glory of his nostrils is terrible. He paweth in the valley, and rejoiceth in strength : he goeth on to meet the armed men. He mocketh at fear, and is not affrighted ; neither turneth he back from the sword. The quiver rattleth against him, the glittering spear and the shield. He swalloweth the ground with fierceness and rage : neither believeth he that it is the sound of the trumpet. He saith among the trumpets, Ha, ha ; and he smelleth the battle afar off, the thunder of the captains, and the shouting."

In Christian art the horse is the emblem of both courage and generosity, and where the artist wished to indicate that the saints he portrayed possessed these virtues he represented them as mounted on horseback.

St. Martin, St. George, St. Victor, and St. Maurice are therefore usually drawn as equestrians.

The Hebrew name of the horse, *abbir*, means " strong and valiant," and is applied metaphorically to horses, as, for instance in Jeremiah viii. 16 : " The whole land trembled at the sound of the neighing of his strong ones." And again in xlvii. 3 : " The noise of the stamping of the hoofs of his strong horses " (R.V. " strong ones ").

In the catacombs we find the horse representing the swiftness of the passing of human life. The steed's wondrous speed when motors were undreamt-of naturally suggested the flight of time which overtook all things. Occasionally a palm wreath is pictured above the horse's head as a warning that the race is not to the swift.

The following fine poem by Eliza Cook shows how aptly the horse illustrates the passage of time.

THE GALLOPING STEED

There's a Courser we ne'er have been able to rein—
He careers o'er the mountain, he travels the main—
He's Eternity's Arab—he trieth his pace
With the worlds in their orbits, and winneth the race.
Oh ! a charger of mettle, I warrant is he,
That will weary his riders whoe'er they may be ;
And we all of us mount, and he bears us along,
Without hearing our check-word or feeling our thong ;
No will does he heed, and no rest does he need ;
Oh ! a brave Iron-Grey is this Galloping Steed.

On, on, and for ever, for ever he goes—
Where his halting-place is, not the wisest one knows ;
He waits not to drink at the Joy-rippled rill ;
He lags not to breathe up the Pain-furrowed hill.
Right pleasant, forsooth, is our place on his back,
When he bounds in the sun on Life's flowery track ;
When his musical hoofs press the green moss of Hope,
And he tramples the pansy on Love's fairy slope ;
Oh ! the journeying then is right pleasant indeed,
As we laugh in our strength on this Galloping Steed.

But alack and alas ! he is soon off the grass,
With dark, stony defiles and dry deserts to pass ;
And his step is so hard, and he raises such dust,
That full many are groaning, yet ride him they must

On, on, through the gloomy morass of Despair—
Through the thorns of Remorse, and the yew-trees of Care ;
Our limbs and our forehead are sore to the quick,
But still we must ride him, bruised, weary, and sick :
Gentle hearts may be shaken and stirred till they bleed,
But on they must go with this Galloping Steed.

In the stone-hurdled churchyard he maketh no stop,
But the boldest, perchance, of his riders will drop ;
They may cling to him closely, but cannot hold fast,
When he leaps o'er the grave-trench that Death opened last.
Betrapped and bedecked with his velvet and plumes,
A grand circle he runs in the show-place of tombs ;
He carries a King—but he turneth the crypt,
And the Monarch that strode him so gaily, hath slipped ;
Yet on goes the Barb at the top of his speed,—
What's the fall of such things to this Galloping Steed ?

Right over the pyramid walls does he bound ;
In the Babylon deserts his hoof-prints are found ;
He snorts in his pride—and the temples of light
Wear a shadowy mist like the coming of night.
On, on, and for ever—he turns not aside ;
He recks not the road, be it narrow or wide ;
In the paths of the city he maketh no stay ;
Over Marathon's Plain he is stretching away.
Oh ! show me a pedigree, find me a speed,
That shall rival the fame of this Galloping Steed.

He hath traversed the Past ; through the Present he flies ;
With the future before him, right onwards he hies ;
He skims the broad waters, he treads the dark woods,
On, on, and for ever—through forests and floods.
Full many among us are riding him now,
All tired and gasping, with sweat on our brow ;
We may suffer and writhe, but 'tis ever in vain,
So lets sit on him bravely and scorn to complain ;
For we know there's a goal and a glorious meed
For the riders of Time—that old, Galloping Steed.

The same poet again refers to Time's iron-grey steed in her *Song
of the Old Year* :

Oh ! I have been running a gallant career
On a courser that needeth nor bridle nor goad ;

But he'll soon change his rider, and leave the Old Year
Lying low in the dust on Eternity's road.

.   .   .   .   .

My race is nigh o'er on Time's iron-grey steed,
Yet he'll still gallop on as he gallops with me ;
And you'll see that his mane will be flying again
Ere you've buried me under the Green Holly-tree.

The horse has always been a favourite emblem of speed wherever
its powers were known. Jeremiah speaks of horses "swifter than
eagles" (iv. 13).

The horse is also used as the emblem of pride, and in this connection the phrase "to ride (or mount) the high horse" should be noted.

Pierius in the fourth book of his hieroglyphics informs us that the
horse was the hieroglyphic emblem of pride.

The mystical Book of Revelation is full of occult allusions to the
horse.

St. John uses a somewhat mixed symbolism in Rev. ix., but the
horse predominates. Apparently he was endeavouring to describe
something he had seen in his vision which was totally unfamiliar
and hitherto unconceived of, either by himself or by those to whom
he spoke, and in his effort to convey a meaning he passes rapidly from
one image to another.

An ingenious interpreter might suggest that what he saw were the
aeroplanes of to-day during an air-raid. He describes how on the opening of "the bottomless pit" by the fifth angel, "the sun and the air
were darkened by reason of the smoke of the pit. And there came out of
the smoke locusts upon the earth. . . . And the shapes of the locusts
were like unto horses prepared for battle ; . . . and the sound of
their wings was as the sound of chariots of many horses running to
battle. And they had tails like unto scorpions, and there were stings
in their tails."

And later, when the four angels were loosed, he says : "And thus
I saw the horses in the vision, and them that sat on them, having
breastplates of fire, and of jacinth and brimstone : and the heads
of the horses were as the heads of lions [1] ; and out of their mouths

---

[1] i.e. Fierce or savage. See 1 Chron. xii. 8.

issued fire and smoke and brimstone. By these three was the third part of men killed, by the fire, and by the smoke, and by the brimstone, which issued out of their mouths."

Certainly these terrible fiery, winged horses, with the sound of their wings so wonderfully pictured, form a vivid image of the modern battle-plane and its death-dealing bombs, and perhaps conveyed a truer impression to the people of that age than a more literal description could have done.

The pale horse of St. John's vision was ridden by Death : " I looked, and behold a pale horse : and his name that sat on him was Death, and Hell followed with him. And power was given unto them over the fourth part of the earth, to kill with sword, and with hunger, and with death, and with the beasts of the earth " (Rev. vi. 8).

Long before St. John wrote the mystical Book of Revelation the horse was a symbol of Death and linked with Hell, for in ancient writings, Ninki-gal, the Queen of Hell, is represented as kneeling on a horse. The imagery that has thus been persistent through the ages must have appealed to mankind as well founded.

The prophet Isaiah foresaw in a vision the fall of Babylon by the Medes and Persians under the figure of " a chariot with a couple of horsemen, a chariot of asses, and a chariot of camels. . . . Behold, here cometh a chariot of men, with a couple of horsemen. And he answered and said, Babylon is fallen, is fallen ; and all the graven images of her gods he hath broken unto the ground " (Isa. xxi. 7–9).

Here the interpretation of the vision appears to be purely arbitrary, but this may be because the prophet has not more fully described what he saw. Perhaps the chariots were in flight, or broken, or perhaps in pursuit of a fallen foe. He does not even tell us to what nationality they belonged, but he saw in them the death of a city.

Shelley writes of

> The Horse of Death, tameless as wind.
> (*The Masque of Anarchy*, 33.)

But this imagery does not seem to have appealed to poets in the same measure as to prophets, for examples of it are rare.

The second horse of St. John's vision is thus described by the seer :

" And there went out another horse that was red : and power was given to him that sat thereon to take peace from the earth and that they should kill one another, and there was given unto him a great sword."

The dread god Mars is obviously indicated as the rider of the red horse. He is often represented on horseback. When he would drive abroad, his chariot is drawn by two horses named Fear and Terror. These are harnessed for him by his wife or sister Bellona, the Goddess of War.

> Mars rests contented in his Thrace no more,
> But goads his steeds to fields of German gore.
> (Cowper's trans. : Milton's Latin Poems.)

The horse, from its connection with war, was not only its natural emblem, but was also offered in sacrifice to Mars, and considered to be sacred to that god.

The Hebrews evidently were affected by this doctrine, for they used the horse only for military riding, and but two instances occur in the Bible of persons without military rank being mounted on horseback. Mordecai, who rode the King's horse as a special honour, is one of these (Esth. vi. 9) ; and the other case is where the king sent out letters by posts on horseback (Esth. viii. 10). Though the Preacher says, " I have seen servants upon horses, and princes walking as servants upon the earth " (Eccl. x. 7), he evidently considered it a paradox.

Hosea says, " We will not ride upon horses " (xiv. 3), meaning " We will not be militaristic." Zechariah, foretelling the coming of Christ, says He will be " lowly, and riding on an ass." That is, He will not come as a military conqueror, who would of course be on horseback. And wishing further to emphasise the peaceful character of Christ's reign, he says : " I will cut off the chariot from Ephraim, and the horse from Jerusalem." War without the horse was unthinkable.

A little later in the next chapter he says triumphantly : " The Lord of Hosts hath visited his flock the house of Judah, and hath made them as his goodly horse in the battle." A priest of Mars would have rejoiced in such imagery. And truly in those olden days the Lord of Hosts was a very war-god,—a fit Rider of the red horse, re-morseless, cruel, and vengeful. Why have our theologians endeavoured to place this being on the throne of the Supreme ? Thank Heaven !

at last we are emerging from such idolatry, but oh ! what suffering and sin it has entailed.

The Hebrews noted how " the horse rusheth into the battle " (Jer. viii. 6), the noise " of the pransing horses, and of the jumping chariots " (Nah. iii. 2) as the armies contended, and how " the horse-hoofs were broken by means of the pransings " (Judg. v. 22), how hands became feeble " at the noise of the stamping of the hoofs of his strong horses " (Jer. xlvii. 3), how the whole land " trembled at the sound of the neighing " (Jer. viii. 16), and how " the horse is prepared against the day of battle " (Prov. xxi. 31).

Searching ancient Assyrian and Babylonian records that were written about five thousand years ago, we find no mention or repre-sentation of horses being used as beasts of burden. The ox and the ass were the labourers, but the horse was regarded only as a warrior, and is frequently described as " glorious in war." It appears often on the Assyrian monuments, and it is easy to see with what veneration it was regarded, by the care of the sculptors in portraying the details of its mane, tail, and trappings.

To return to the red horse of the Apocalypse. Its secondary mean-ing may be the red races of mankind and their warlike character.

The black horse which immediately occurs to the mind seeking instances of its symbolism is that which was ridden by one of the four dread horsemen of the Apocalypse. And, not Death, as perhaps we might have expected, but Famine, was the rider.

" I beheld, and lo a black horse ; and he that sat on him had a pair of balances in his hand. And I heard a voice in the midst of the four beasts say, A measure of wheat for a penny, and three measures of barley for a penny ; and see thou hurt not the oil and the wine " (Rev. vi. 5, 6).

The balances indicate that food is so scarce as to be weighed out. The penny, or rather the Roman denarius, was the daily wage of a soldier or labourer. The prices were high, but not those of actual famine, the measure being just sufficient for one man's daily con-sumption.

Some would see in this black horse the symbol of the black races of mankind. In this case the balance might suggest the termination of the long period of slavery and injustice from which they suffered, and the tardy recognition of their rights.

The white horse has also many meanings. In the Apocalypse one of the four dread horsemen is mounted on a white horse, and here it would seem to be the emblem of Conquest.

" I saw, and behold a white horse : and he that sat on him had

THE FOUR HORSES OF THE APOCALYPSE.
(*From an old woodcut.*)

a bow ; and a crown was given unto him : and he went forth con-quering, and to conquer " (Rev. vi. 2).

Others would see in this white horse the emblem of the Saxons and their conquering race (see chapter on the Saxon Horse), whilst still others would have it include all the white races of mankind.

Shelley represents Anarchy as mounted on a white horse :

Last came Anarchy ; he rode
On a white horse, splashed with blood.
He was pale, even to the lips,
Like Death in the Apocalypse.
(Masque of Anarchy, 8.)

The *Spectator* gives us quite a different meaning of a white horse as used symbolically in the literature of his day. He says : " In Books of Chivalry, where the Point of Honour is strained to Madness, the whole Story runs on Chastity and Courage. The Damsel is mounted on a white Palfrey, as an Emblem of her Innocence."

We wish the writer had told us also what coloured horse represented Courage. Perhaps, as with the saints we have referred to, if the hero was mounted at all, it showed he possessed this quality.

Though the Talmud has nearly lost its hold upon the modern Jewish mind as an infallible expositor of the law of Jehovah, and a large body of the Jews go so far as utterly to reject its teaching, yet reverence still remains for its venerable traditions, and the student who has patience to delve beneath the overlying rubbish of centuries may bring to light rare and fantastic treasures of Rabbinical thought and learning. Dreams and their interpretations find an important place in this book, as is only to be expected, seeing that whilst it claims to date from Sinai, it was more probably compiled by the mystic sages of Babylon, if indeed it is not attributable to an altogether later date.

According to the code of meanings found in the Talmud, to dream of a white horse whether at rest or in motion is good, but a chestnut or dark horse is only good if it is stationary. Any movement tells of evil. Moreover, this is not given as a mere opinion by the Talmudical writer, but as an authoritative statement which no orthodox child of Abraham may venture to dispute.

In British symbology the dark horse indicates uncertainty, an unknown quantity, an individual who is surrounded by mystery, etc.

The ruins of the ancient cities of Ceylon, which were discovered by an Englishman only about one hundred years ago amidst the rank jungle growth that surrounded and engulfed them, include some remarkable, exquisitely carved, semicircular granite stones which are set at the base of flights of entrance steps. These monuments are known as moonstones, though they have no connection whatever with the jewel of the same name which is also found in the island.

What interests us is that the carving on them represents four animals, always in the same order, chasing each other, and that one of these is the subject of our book.

The animals are the elephant, the horse, the lion, and the bullock, in the sequence named. The meaning of the symbolism is lost, though the carving is still as fresh as when it was completed two thousand years ago by the unknown sculptor. Many interpretations will occur to our readers. In the light of recent events we would suggest that the elephant represents science, the horse war, the lion the reversion to savagery as the result of science applied to warfare, and the ox the labour needed to enable mankind to recover its former position.

These world-tragedies are recurrent and have happened many times before, as this ruined city itself is evidence.

It has been suggested also that the four animals are representative of the four cardinal points, and this seems to be borne out by another discovery. Some rude bronze figures of men and animals very curiously fashioned were dug up in the shrines, and in each case a man with an animal lay in the direction of one of the cardinal points. North was a lion; south, a horse; east, an elephant. The bullock was missing, but was probably lost by accident or theft. It is also possible that there was some astronomical significance attached to the beasts.

On some of the moonstones another band is found of conventional floral design, within the band containing the animals; and within that again, a row of sacred geese carrying lotus flowers; whilst the centre is occupied by a conventional representation of half a lotus bloom. But these details vary somewhat on different stones.

A Chinese monk named Fa-Hien, who travelled in Ceylon and India about A.D. 400, mentions having heard that a five-storied temple in India was decorated with " elephant figures, lion shapes, horse shapes, ox shapes, and dove shapes." The last named were probably the sacred geese.

Fergusson, speaking of the temple at Halebid in South India, refers to Fa-Hien's description and says that in this temple also were animal friezes in the same order, i.e. elephant, lion, horse (this is not the same sequence as those we first noted), the ox being replaced by a conventional creature and the geese by a " bird of a species that would puzzle a naturalist."

He adds that " sometimes in modern Hindu temples only two or three animal friezes are found, but the succession is always the same."

It is certainly a strange coincidence, if nothing more, that the temples of India and the moonstones of Ceylon bear the same symbols.

We do not think the meaning we suggested in the latter case is greatly altered by the horse's place being changed with the lion's. It would now run that science (the elephant), having turned its powers to destruction (the lion), causes war (the horse) to be so devastating that a return to primitive labour (the ox) is forced on the peoples of earth, who now, in their despair, seek religion (the sacred geese). It is the history of the nations so often re-enacted, set forth in symbolical form.

The lotus blossom probably represents the spiritual privileges borne by religion, the moral of the whole allegory being that Faith always ultimately triumphs over Science.

BIBLIOGRAPHY

The Lost Cities of Ceylon, by G. E. Milton.   (John Murray, London, 1916.)
" *Fa-Hien*," by James Legge.   (1886.)
Good Words, May 1, 1870 : article on " Dreams and their Interpretation."
The Spectator, No. 99, June 23, 1711.

CHAPTER XXII

Witches, Fairies, and Horses

THE animal most intimately associated with witches and witchcraft in the mind of the average Englishman is the cat, and especially the black cat. It may therefore come as a surprise to many people to learn how closely connected with spells and enchantment the horse has always been, and how often the "wise women" transformed themselves into black and variously coloured steeds, and even forced their victims to assume equine form for the purpose of using them as mounts.

It would seem to have been one of the chief pleasures of the witch and mischievous sprite or goblin to tease and annoy mortal horses at night-time, and many are the instances which our forefathers have recorded and handed down for our instruction.

Shakespeare alludes to this widespread belief in *Romeo and Juliet* (Act I, sc. iv.) in the lines referring to the fairy queen :

> This is that very Mab
> That plats the manes of horses in the night.

It was very generally accepted as an indisputable fact at that time that not only witches, but also certain malignant sprites who lived in the woodlands or gardens, occasionally assumed the forms of women clad in white raiment, who in this guise would haunt the stables when night fell. They carried with them tapers of lighted wax, and they used the drippings from these to tangle the horses' manes into inextricable knots, to the great annoyance both of the steeds and of their grooms.

William Auvergne, who was Bishop of Paris in the thirteenth century, mentions these hags in his works, which shows how deeply rooted in antiquity the belief is, though, as we shall see, it is not dead even in this age of scepticism.

A very rare old print by Hans Burgmair has preserved a record in pictorial form. He shows us a witch entering a stable by night with a lighted torch, and practising enchantments on the sleeping groom —who is lying on his back and seems to be suffering from nightmare —preparatory to the operation of entangling the horse's mane when she has lulled his guardian into complete unconsciousness.

We may read in the *Spectator* (No. 117) that a "very old Woman had the Reputation of a Witch all over the Country" and was seriously suspected of interfering with the horses of the district. The universal verdict of the countryside was, "If a Horse sweats in the Stable, Moll White has been upon his Back."

But witches were not satisfied by merely riding earthly horses and entangling their manes. Many preferred to transform themselves into equine shape, and still others would turn their neighbours into steeds, and use them as mounts, in some cases even riding them to death.

One poor old woman who had been thus changed into equine form by witchcraft was restored to her humanity by St. Macarius sprinkling her with holy water. The saintliness of her benefactor had enabled him to recognise the woman in the mare, and so overcome the devil's plot.

Joseph Glanvill, in his *Sadducismus Triumphatus*, relates a remarkable tale of "a great army of witches" who flourished at Blocula, Sweden, in 1669, and were accused of performing on a large scale the metamorphoses of human beings into horses. This result was achieved by the witch throwing an enchanted halter over a man's head as he lay in bed, but was not without its element of danger for her, since if the newly made horse could contrive to get the halter off and slip it on to her, she became a mare and he could mount and ride her.

The last execution for witchcraft in Scotland, which took place at Dornoch in 1722, affords us another instance of equine form being the one imposed upon the victim by the witch.

In this case the witch's own daughter was said to have been turned into a pony by her black arts and she was further accused of having got the devil to shoe it ! The reputed site of the execution is in the part of the town known as Littleton, where, in one of the gardens, a stone with the date deeply cut upon it marks the place.

Another Scottish witch lived as recently as the nineteenth century. Her name was Margaret Grant, and she believed she was able to take the shapes of various animals, and asserted also that at other times evil-disposed persons had actually turned her into a pony and ridden her long distances.

A remarkable story is told at Yarrowfoot of a witch who was shod whilst in the form of a mare, and actually sold to her husband as that animal. When he removed the bridle, however, she resumed her proper form as his wife, though the horse-shoes still remained attached to her hands and feet.

The piskies or pixies of Devon and Cornwall are greatly interested by mortal horses, and though they have been described as " invisibly small," yet do they delight in riding the farmer's horses on dark nights, and in plaiting their manes, and in twisting them into inextricable knots with the seed-vessels of the burdock.

Sometimes horses that have been turned out in a field at night have been discovered in the morning in a terrified condition, panting and covered with foam—the result, according to local belief, of having been ridden by the pixies in the night.

Mr. Robert Hunt, F.R.S., narrates the two following stories of fairies' games with mortal horses in his fascinating book *Romances of the West of England*. The first is headed :

"A NATIVE PIGSEY STORY

" ' D'ye see that 'ere hoss there ? ' said a Liskeard farmer to a West-country miner.

" ' What ov it ? ' asked the miner.

" ' Well, that 'ere hoss he'n been ridden to death a'most by the pigsies again.'

" ' Pigsies ! ' said the miner ; ' thee don't b'leeve in they, do 'ee ? '

" ' 'Ees, I do ; but I specks you're a West-country bucca, ain't 'ee ? If you'd a had yourn hosses wrode to death every nite, you'd tell another tayl, I reckon. But as sure as I'se living, the pigsies do ride on 'em whenever they've a mind to.' "

Mr. Hunt's second story is called

" THE NIGHT RIDERS

" I was on a visit when a boy at a farmhouse situated near Fowey River. Well do I remember the farmer with much sorrow telling us one morning at breakfast that ' the piskie people had been riding Tom again ' ; and this he regarded as certainly leading to the destruction of a fine young horse. I was taken to the stable to see the horse. There could be no doubt that the animal was much distressed. The mane was said to be knotted into fairy stirrups ; and Mr. —— told me that he had no doubt at least twenty small people had sat upon the horse's neck. He even assured me that one of his men had seen them urging the horse to his utmost speed round and round one of his fields."

There are numerous examples of similar cases in Germany. So lately as March 1906 the *Daily Telegraph* reported a trial for witch-craft in that country as follows :

" BERLIN, *Tuesday.*—A trial for witchcraft, which has just been held in the Upper Palatinate, is attracting wide attention as a forcible illustration of the depths of ignorance and superstition in which large districts of Southern Germany are still sunk. A farm-labourer named Hirmer was employed by a woman named Koelbl to look after her horse. Hirmer, however, neglected his duties, the horse became sick, and to excuse himself, Hirmer asserted that the animal had been be-witched. Every morning he found it bathed in sweat, and with its mane and tail plaited by unearthly hands. He advised Frau Koelbl to secure the services of a neighbouring witch-doctor, a certain Hartwig. At dead of night Hartwig entered the stable, fixed a crucifix with two burning candles at the horse's head, wrote some mysterious letters on the wall with ' consecrated chalk,' drew a magic circle round him-self, opened his book, and began incantations in some unknown jargon. He shivered with the violence of his emotions, and after three-quarters of an hour revealed that the witch who had 'possessed' the horse was a certain Frau Schaumberger. At the trial the judge at first was not inclined to convict Hartwig, as he regarded the witch-doctor as perfectly sincere, but on reflection he condemned him to four weeks imprisonment as an impostor."

The judge's decision makes one ask with the poet (Tennyson):

Is it so true that second thoughts are best ?

The cumulative weight of evidence on this subject makes it difficult to relegate it to the realm of unreality. If human evidence can be accepted, an open verdict must be returned, if not a positively affirmative one.

Another instance is given in the *Occult Review* for May of the same year. Franz Hartmann, writing under the title " Witchcraft in Germany," says that his " brother-in-law, Count A. v. S——, was captain in the Bavarian cavalry (chevaux-legers), and lives at present at S., after having retired from service. Some years ago while on duty he noticed that one of his horses was sickly, and the groom reported that he found it every morning bathed in sweat, and with its mane and tail plaited in a most unaccountable way. The Count, being a total unbeliever in things unnatural, made up his mind to investigate the matter, and so he spent the night in the stable watching the horse. Everything seemed all right, but at about 2 a.m. a sudden tremor shook the horse, and in a moment its mane and tail were plaited in a most intricate manner, and the animal became covered with sweat."

A German writer, Ernst Meier, gives an instance of a witch taking the form of a horse, though he does not enlighten us as to her reason for doing so. A certain farmer who lived near Wiesensteig had four horses, but was much puzzled because he often found five animals in his stable, and could in no way account for it. At last he consulted the smith, who said, " Next time you see a fifth horse in your stable, just send for me." Before long the strange horse turned up again, and the farmer sent for the smith. He arrived bringing with him four horseshoes. " I'm sure this nag is not shod ; I'll shoe her for you," he said and at once proceeded to do so. But the cunning smith had overreached himself, for when the farmer paid him a visit next day, he discovered the smith's wife with horse-shoes nailed on her hands and feet, prancing around. The cure was an effectual one, for she never again appeared as a horse in the farmer's stable.

A similar tale of a woman being shod whilst masquerading in horse form comes from Silesia (see R. Kühnau, *Schlesiche Sagen*, No. 1380, Berlin, 1910–13).

Mr. J. G. Frazer mentions one instance of a district where the witches take their midnight rides on infernal horses instead of transformed human steeds. He says :

" In Prussia, witches and warlocks used regularly to assemble twice a year on Walpurgis Night and the Eve of St. John. . . . They generally rode on a baking-fork, but often on a black three-legged horse, and they took their departure up the chimney with the words ' Up and away and nowhere to stop.' "

The following story, which is related by Frank Hamel in his most interesting work, *Human Animals,* is chiefly remarkable because the witch who figures in it did not come as a strange horse to the stable, but apparently inhabited the bodies of several mortal horses who dwelt there. A woman at Toulon told the story in 1888, and she had been witness of the events when a child. Her father was an omnibus driver named Isidore who lived happily with his sister for years; but one day they had such a violent quarrel that they determined they must part. Isidore, who loved his sister dearly, was very troubled about it, and confided the matter to a friend. The friend told him that the cause of the quarrel was that one of his neighbours was a sorcerer and had cast a spell upon them. He added that the remedy was to give his horses a good hiding, and await the result. The person who had bewitched him would be taken ill and would bear in his or her body marks of the blows given to the horses. Isidore accepted the advice, and carried it out most thoroughly next day, feeling as though he had accomplished a praiseworthy deed. On the morrow his sister came and spoke to him as affectionately as if nothing had happened and they made up their quarrel.

Then Isidore heard that a neighbour, whom hitherto he had been fond of and never suspected of witchcraft, had been taken ill. He hurried off to see her, and found her in bed, and that she had traces of having been beaten. He had but just entered her room when she asked him why he had struck his horses so violently and what was the harm they had done to him. This was considered as a proof that the woman was a witch and that the weals on her body were caused by the beating Isidore had administered to his horses.

The rowan-tree used to be considered an infallible specific against witchcraft, and at one time farmers would have their whipstocks made of its wood (rowan-tree gads they were called), holding that this safeguarded them against having their load held up or their horses made restive by a witch. If their cart by chance got fixed, owing of course to the driver not possessing this weapon, the nearest rowan or, as it was often called, witch-wood tree was made for, and a stick cut from it with which to flog the horses, and through them the witch who was the real cause of the trouble. This was especially a Yorkshire superstition.

George Borrow has told us how he successfully used the " whisper " in controlling an intractable horse. We give his own account of this :

" I prepared to mount ; but my black entero of Andalusia would not permit me to approach his side, and whenever I made the attempt, commenced wheeling round with great rapidity. ' *C'est un mauvais signe, mon maître*,' said Antonio, who, dressed in a green jerkin, a Montero cap, and booted and spurred, stood ready to attend me, holding by the bridle the horse which I had purchased from the contrabandista. ' It is a bad sign, and in my country they would defer the journey till to-morrow.'

" ' Are there whisperers in your country ? ' I demanded ; and taking the horse by the mane, I performed the ceremony after the most approved fashion. The animal stood still, and I mounted the saddle, exclaiming—

> ' The Rommany Chal to his horse did cry,
> As he placed the bit in his horse's jaw ;
> Kosko gry ! Rommany gry !
> Muk man kistur tute knaw.' "

BIBLIOGRAPHY

Survivals in Beliefs among the Celts, by George Henderson. (James Maclehose & Sons, Glasgow, 1911.)

Human Animals, by Frank Hamel. (Wm. Rider & Son, London, 1915.)

Deutsche Sagen, Sitten und Gebräuche aus Schwaben. (Ernst Meier, Stuttgart, 1852.)

The Golden Bough, Part VII, Vol. II, p. 74, by J. G. Frazer.

Popular Romances of the West of England, edited by Robert Hunt, F.R.S. (Chatto & Windus, London, 1896.)

Abbeys, Castles, and Ancient Halls of England and Wales, by John Timbs. (Fredk. Warne & Co., London, 1869.)

British Popular Customs, Present and Past, by the Rev. T. F. Thiselton Dyer, M.A. (G. Bell & Sons, Ltd., London, 1911.)

The Bible in Spain, by George Borrow. (1842.)

CHAPTER XXIII

The Gods and Patron Saints of Horses

IT is interesting to note that St. George, the patron saint of England, is also the special protector and patron of horses, and is so recognised throughout Europe. Sacrifices to ensure the well-being and safety of their horses were until recent times offered by the Esthonians of the island of Dago on the saint's holy-day. The offerings were made under the shade of certain sacred trees, from which no one dare take so much as a fallen bough, in spite of the great scarcity of wood on the island, and consisted of an egg, a coin, and a bunch of horsehair tied by a red thread. These offerings were buried in the ground.

In Silesia a similar sacrifice for horses used to be made on St. George's Day. Mr. J. G. Frazer gives the following account of it :

" The people deem the saint very powerful in the matter of . . . horse-breeding. At the Polish village of Ostroppa, . . . a sacrifice for horses used to be offered at the little village church. It has been described by an eyewitness. Peasants on horseback streamed to the spot from all the neighbouring villages, not with the staid and solemn pace of pilgrims, but with the noise and clatter of merry-makers hastening to a revel. The sorry image of the saint, carved in wood and about an ell high, stood in the churchyard on a table covered with a white cloth. It represented him on horseback spearing a dragon. Beside it were two vessels to receive offerings of money and eggs respectively. As each farmer galloped up, he dismounted, led his horse by the bridle, knelt before the image of the saint, and prayed. After that he made his offering of money or eggs, according to his means, in the name of his horse. Then he led the beast round the church

SEA-HORSES WRECKING A BOAT.
(*By Holloway, after M. Oldfield Howey.*)

and churchyard, tethered it, and went into the church to hear mass and a sermon.   Having thus paid his devotions to the saint, every man leaped into the saddle and made for the nearest public-house as fast as his horse could lay legs to the ground."

A festival of St. George as the patron of horses used also to be held at Ertringen, in Bavaria, on April 24.   From all the surrounding country the people flocked to the chapel, riding or driving, that they might assist in the ceremony ; and the abbot and prior of the monastery of Holy Cross Vale attended in state, mounted on white steeds. One of the burghers of the town was dressed as the saint, and rode a stallion.   High mass was celebrated, after which the horses were blessed at the chapel, and finally were ridden in procession around the common lands to the village church, where the meeting broke up.

St. Stephen was also the patron of horses, and the saint's day (December 26) was a great day with our ancestors for bleeding their horses.   It was a custom among people of all ranks, and the old agricultural poet Tusser says, in his *Five Hundred Points of Husbandry* (chap. xxii. st. 16) :

> Yer, Christmas be passed, let horsse be let blood,
> For manie a purpose it dooth him much good ;
> The day of S. Steeven old fathers did use ;
> If that do mislike thee, some other day chuse.

The Danes are said to have been responsible for introducing the practice into the country.

Apropos of this matter we may appropriately quote Barnaby Googe's translation of Naogeorgus :

> Then followeth Saint Stephen's Day, whereon doth every man
> His horses jaunt and course abrode, as swiftly as he can,
> Until they doe extreemcly sweate, and then they let them blood,
> For this being done upon this day, they say doth do them good,
> And keeps them from all maladies, and sickness through the yeare,
> As if that Stephen any time took charge of horses heare.

On this day also the Pope's horses used to be doctored, and bled for the sake of the blood, which was considered a remedy in many disorders.

Yet a third patron saint of horses is St. Anthony, an Egyptian Christian, who flourished in the third and fourth centuries. The following tradition accounts for the honour accorded to him. The reigning king of Egypt persecuted the Christians, and St. Anthony remonstrated, and exhorted the monarch to leave God's people in peace. But the king tore up the saint's epistle, and, further, resolved to make him the next victim. Five days afterwards the king was out riding. His horse had always been a remarkably quiet animal, but now threw his rider to the ground, and turned upon him, biting him so severely in the thigh that he died in three days. Ever since, Anthony has been the patron of horses, and at Rome horses are blessed on this saint's day in a ceremony that is remarkable for its picturesque character.

We have already seen that Neptune is the God of Horses (*vide* " Sea-horses "). Probably what induced him thus to become their special patron was that he owed his life to one. For when at his birth his father Saturn, who devoured all the male children born to him, would have eaten him also, his mother preserved him from this fate by giving Saturn a foal to eat in his stead.

The goddess who presides over horses and stables was known to the Greeks as Hippona, which was also the name of a beautiful woman begotten by Fulvius from a mare.

BIBLIOGRAPHY

Five Hundred Points of Husbandry, by Tusser.
The Golden Bough, Part I, Vol. II, p. 336, by J. G. Frazer.
The Pantheon, representing the Fabulous Histories of the Heathen Gods and Most Illustrious Heroes, by Andrew Tooke, A.M. Thirty-fifth edition. (London, 1824.)
The Faiths of the World, by the Rev. James Gardner, M.A. (A. Fullarton & Co., London.)

CHAPTER XXIV

The Sacrificial Horse

WE have seen in earlier chapters that the horse was considered the most acceptable sacrifice that could be made either to Sun-god or Sea-god, but this by no means exhausts the subject, for many other widely separated peoples arrived, apparently independently, at the conclusion that the horse was the sacrifice most favoured by their gods. In almost every case white horses have been considered as especially sacred, not because of any superiority in size, form, or speed, but solely on account of the sanctity connected with this colour, which makes the white elephant a sacred animal in India and the white ass a venerated object in Persia.

In the chapter on the Trojan Horse we have seen that the sacrifice of horses was an important characteristic of the Grecian religion ; and if we examine the ancient creeds of the Turkish, Persian, Scandinavian, and Teutonic peoples, we find they also considered the horse to be the offering most likely to propitiate the deity (with the possible exception of a human sacrifice, which it was often used to replace), or, as in the Vedic funeral, it was killed that it might go and announce the coming of the human soul (see chapter on the Sun-horse).

To take a case in point from ancient Greece, the following charming tale may be found in Plutarch's *Lives*, of a young mare being sacrificed in place of a virgin, to ensure the favour of the gods in a critical battle.

In the year 371 B.C., the Lacedæmonians were at war with the Thebans, and so greatly did they exceed them in numbers and strength that the latter were threatened with total extermination. Pelopidas, the captain of a small but sacred band of Thebans, was called to council

with the other officers in this extremity, and strongly advised that
the enemy should be engaged in battle.   As he was highly esteemed,
it was decided to follow his counsel, but when the two armies came
in sight at Leuctra, Pelopidas was greatly troubled by a dream.   In
the field where they were camped lay buried the bodies of the daughters
of Scedasus, who had killed themselves after being raped by some
Spartans whom they had hospitably received into their house.   Their
father, being unable to obtain justice from Lacedæmon, after bitter
imprecations on the Spartans, killed himself on his daughters' tomb.
Many prophecies and oracles warned the Spartans that he would one
day be revenged.

To Pelopidas, sleeping in his tent, these young women appeared
weeping, accompanied by their father.   The latter ordered him to
sacrifice a red-haired young virgin to his daughters, if he would gain
victory in the battle.   Pelopidas and his advisers seem to have felt
many scruples as to the righteousness of the means commanded, but,
whilst they were hesitating and discussing how to act for the best,
a " she-colt " suddenly quitted the herd and ran through the camp
till she came to the place where they were assembled.

There she stood before them all.   The officers were only admiring
" her colour, which was a shining red, the stateliness of her form, the
vigour of her motions, and the sprightliness of her neighings ; but
Theocritus, the diviner, understanding the thing better, cried out
to Pelopidas, ' Here comes the victim, fortunate man that thou art !
wait for no other virgin, but sacrifice that which heaven hath sent thee.'
They then took the colt and led her to the tomb of the virgins, where,
after the usual prayers and the ceremony of crowning her, they offered
her up with joy, not forgetting to publish the vision of Pelopidas,
and the sacrifice required, to the whole army."

Needless to add, the Thebans gained a glorious victory, with
" such a rout and slaughter as had never been known before."

The Greeks annually sacrificed to Mars a horse with a docked
tail known as an " equus curtus."   As docking was not a common
practice amongst the ancients, it is evident that here it had some
special significance.   A small antique bronze model of such a horse
exists, which was possibly intended to commemorate the custom.

The ancient Persians sacrificed a horse every month to Cyrus at his famous tomb at Pasargadac. They held white horses to be specially sacred and suitable for sacrificial purposes, and when their army was on the march some of these always accompanied it. The tribute the Persians exacted from the Cilicians shows how high a value they set on white horses, probably because of the use made of them for sacrifice. It consisted of " 360 white horses, one for every day in the year," and 500 talents of silver.

It was the custom of many nations to offer sacrifice to the River-god before crossing a stream, as the water-sprites were considered very dangerous and treacherous, and likely to take offence if not propitiated when their domain was about to be encroached upon. Herodotus tells us how, when Xerxes led the Persian host, and they arrived at the River Strymon, in Thrace, the Magians sacrificed white horses, and performed certain ceremonies before entering the stream (Herodotus, VII. 113).

According to the scanty details bequeathed to us by Byzantine historians, the ancient Turks were worshippers of one supreme Being, and sacrificed to His honour horses, bulls, and sheep. They also describe how Taxander, at the ceremony of his father's funeral, ordered four Huns to be brought out of prison and slain upon the tomb along with the horses that had belonged to the dead prince.

Probably in this case the idea of the rite was less that of sacrifice, than of providing the deceased with a suitable equipage in the next world.

We have an illustration of this in the well-known story of the old Irishwoman who killed her dead husband's horse, and when remonstrated with, replied, " Do you think I would let my man go on foot in the next world ? "

Pennant tells us that in olden times the wealthy horse-owners used to sacrifice one of their steeds at a well near Abergeleu to secure a blessing on the rest.

Among Scandinavian nations in olden days the sacrifice of a horse was one of their most important religious observances, and Dithmar, Bishop of Merseburg, a chronicler of the eleventh century, says of the Danes ;

" There is a place in these parts, the capital of the country, called Lethra, in the district of Selon, where the whole people are accustomed to come together, and there to sacrifice to their gods ninety-nine men, and as many horses, together with dogs and cocks."

The God of the North, Odin (or Woden), in still earlier days was worshipped in numerous temples, and especially in the great fane at Upsala, where most solemn festivals were celebrated and sacrifices offered. The horse was the usual victim, though in times of great national emergency human offerings were made, even the king, on one occasion, being sacrificed that a famine might be averted.

The epic of the *Ramayana,* or the story of Rama's wanderings, the scenes of which are laid in Central and Southern India, dates back about twelve centuries. It relates how Dasratha, the renowned and noble King of Ayudhya, had three wives named Kausalya, Keykeyi, and Samitra, but to the deep regret of all, there was no son. It was therefore resolved to offer the Aswamedha, or horse-sacrifice, to propitiate the gods. This was done, and in course of time Rama was born to Kansalya, while to Keykeyi Bharata was born, and to Samitra twins named Lakhshmana and Satrughan. Rama became the most famous of all kings of the epic age, and the bards agree in naming his reign as the golden age of Ayudhya, and after his death his sons became the founders of mighty empires.

In the same epic a king and queen are mentioned as smelling the fat of a burning stallion to obtain a son. For further details of the Aswamedha, the reader is referred to the chapter on Sun-horses.

In the Chumbi Valley and other parts of Tibet, prayer-flags known as " dragon-horses " are mounted on tall poles planted by the wayside. These prayer-flags have in their centre the figure of a horse with the mystic " jewel " upon its back, and around it are written spells combining Indian Buddhist mysticism with Chinese myth. These are intended to invoke the aid of the Lama divinities and secure a blessing to him who offers the flag, and whose name or year of birth is usually written upon it. The five deities invoked are (1) he who conveys wisdom (Manjusri) ; (2) he who saves from hell and fears (Avalokita incarnate in the Dalai Lama) ; (3) he who saves from accidents and wounds (Vajrapani) ; (4) he who cleanses the soul from sin (Vajrasatwa) ;

and (5) he who confers long life (Amitayus). Probably this pictured horse is another instance of the substitution of a symbol for a sacrificial offering.

Certain peoples have held that trees were the abode of spirits, and consequently sacred, and in some cases even divine, and therefore to be honoured with " the king of sacrifices," the horse.

Mr. J. G. Frazer has given us an instance of this :

" In Patagonia between the Rio Negro and the Rio Colorado, there stands solitary an ancient acacia tree with a gnarled and hollow trunk. The Indians revere it as the abode of a spirit. . . . No Indian passes it without leaving something, if it be only a little horsehair which he ties to a branch. . . . But the best evidence of the sanctity of the tree are the bleached skeletons of many horses which have been killed in honour of the spirit ; for the horse is the most precious sacrifice that these Indians can offer."

Like the ancient Persians, these American Indians also sacrifice a horse when about to cross a dangerous stream, so that the spirit of the river may be friendly, not hostile towards them. It is interesting to note this unanimity in such widely divided peoples.

Among the Patagonian Indians another curious rite obtains, which is evidently of magical origin, intended to endue a human child with equine characteristics, by uniting it with the steed corporeally from its birth. The ceremony is described as follows by H. Hesketh Pritchard :

" In some cases when a child is born, a cow or mare is killed, the stomach taken out and cut open, and into this receptacle while still warm the child is laid. Upon the remainder of the animal the tribe feast. . . . A variation of the foregoing birth-ceremony is yet more savage. If a boy is born, his tribe catch a mare or a colt—if the father be rich and a ·great man among his people, the former ; if not, the latter—a lasso is placed round each leg, a couple round the neck, and a couple round the body. The tribe distribute themselves at the various ends of these lassos and take hold. The animal being thus supported cannot fall. The father of the child now advances and cuts the mare or colt open from the neck downwards, the heart, etc., is torn out, and the baby placed in the cavity. The desire is to keep the animal quivering until the child is put inside. By this means they believe that they ensure the child's becoming a fine horseman in the future." He is now as a centaur, half horse, half man.

We find a very similar rite described in the *Historical Works of Giraldus Cambrensis*, dating about the end of the twelfth century. It describes the inauguration of a king in Ireland, and evidently the object aimed at is the same as that of the Patagonian Indians. Our author writes :

" There is in the northern and most remote part of Ulster, namely at Kenil Cunil, a nation which practises a most barbarous and abominable rite in creating their King. The whole people of that country being gathered in one place, a white mare is led into the midst of them, and he who is to be inaugurated, not as a prince but as a brute, not as a king but as an outlaw, comes before the people on all-fours, confessing himself a beast with no less impudence than imprudence. The mare being immediately killed and cut in pieces and boiled, a bath is prepared for him from the broth. Sitting in this he eats of the flesh which is brought to him, the people standing round and partaking of it also. He is also required to drink of the broth in which he is bathed, not drawing it in any vessel, nor even in his hand, but lapping it with his mouth. These unrighteous rites being duly accomplished, his royal authority and dominion are ratified."

It is evident that the eating of the flesh and drinking of the broth of the sacred animal is here done sacramentally, so as to endue the man who had confessed himself mere brute and outlaw with the divine qualities typified by the white mare—indeed, to unite him with the god, and ensure the obedience and reverence of his subjects to him as the god's earthly representative.

BIBLIOGRAPHY

Origin and Influence of the Thoroughbred Horse, by Wm. Ridgeway, M.A., etc. Cambridge Biological Series.
Plutarch's *Lives*.
Herodotus, VII. 113.
Through the Heart of Patagonia, by H. Hesketh Pritchard.
Historical Works of Giraldus Cambrensis.

Mavor's Universal History, Vol. X, p. 255. (Richard Phillips, London, 1802.)

" *The Times of India* " *Illustrated Weekly*, January 10, 1917.

Lhasa and Its Mysteries, by L. Austine Waddell, LL.D.   (John Murray, London, 1905.)

British Goblins, by Wirt Sikes. (London, 1880.)

The Golden Bough, by J. G. Frazer, Part I, Vol. II, p. 16.

A Dictionary of Roman and Greek Antiquities, by Anthony Rich, B.A.   Fourth edition.
    (Longmans, Green & Co., London, 1874.)

CHAPTER XXV

Other Sacred Horses

ALTHOUGH almost every chapter of our book is more or less about sacred horses, yet there are some we want to introduce to the reader which refuse to be classified and must therefore have a chapter to themselves. As we have seen, from the earliest days of which we have any record, horses have been the objects of religious veneration.

Cyrus is reported by Herodotus (Bk. I. 189) to have ordered that the River Gyndes should be punished for having drowned one of his sacred horses; and later in the same history (Bk. VII. 55) we find an account of sacred horses preceding Xerxes himself in the crossing of the Hellespont. Ten horses of the sacred Nisæan breed, richly caparisoned and consecrated to Jupiter, swelled the pageant of his march. Behind them followed the sacred chariot of the god, drawn by eight snowy steeds, their driver walking at their rear holding the reins, for no man might mount upon this chariot. Then came the King himself in a chariot drawn by Nisæan horses. White horses were held sacred by these Persians, and the place of honour in the centre of their triumphal army was occupied by the consecrated steeds.

Many traces of animal worship have been found among the Gauls. The mare-goddess Epona had her counterpart in the male Horse-god Rudiobus, of which latter a bronze image was found near Orleans along with figures of boars and of a stag (Reinach's *Orpheus*).

The Christians of an earlier age seem to have considered the horse as a " blessed animal, since our Saviour was born in a manger." The following legend relates the honour that was paid to the horse of the Emperor Constantine the Great about A.D. 312.

Elene, the mother of the emperor, having discovered the whereabouts of the sacred nails of the holy cross, by a miracle wrought in answer to prayer, and obtained possession of them, did not know how best she might use and preserve the holy relics. The devout Cyriacus, Bishop of Jerusalem, thus advised her in her dilemma :

"O lady and queen, take these precious nails for thy son the emperor. Make of them rings for his horse's bridle. Victory shall always go with them. They shall be called holy to God, and he shall be called blessed whom that horse bears."

The queen accepted the good bishop's advice, and had a wonderfully beautiful bridle specially made, and on it fastened the holy nails. Then she sent it to her son. He received it with great reverence and ordained that April 24, which was the date when the miracle of their revelation took place, should henceforth be held in honour as Holy Cross Day.

The origin of the worship of the horse in Mexico is an interesting and amusing story.

Hernando Cortés, known as the Conqueror of Mexico, when he set out on his semi-religious, semi-military expedition in 1519 was accompanied by Franciscan friars, who persuaded the natives to destroy their idols and erect the cross in the shrines of these deities.

Now, the cross was already an ancient emblem among the Mexican Indians, and typified their God of Rain. Large crosses built of lime and stone were in existence in many parts of the continent and neighbouring islands set up in his honour, and greatly astonished these missionary explorers, who were unable to divorce the symbol from their own faith.

Among other places Cortés landed on the island of Peten, and, as he thought, his friars successfully converted the natives to his creed.

On his departure he left behind him a horse which had become disabled by an injury to its foot. The Indians, who had never seen a horse until the coming of the Spaniards, naturally associated this animal with the cross of which their conquerors had made such a point, and the cross with their own God of Storm and Sunshine. They therefore considered the horse to be a sacred creature, and when their visitors had gone made offerings of flowers to it and prepared savoury messes of poultry for its delectation.   Unfortunately this diet did not agree with the horse, and it pined away and died.

The Indians were filled with fear by this terrible omen.   They made an image of the animal in stone as a propitiation, and placing it in one of their temples, they worshipped it as a deity.

When in 1618 two Franciscan friars arrived to proselytise, they found this statue receiving the homage of the Indians as the God of Thunder and Lightning.

Every Indian village in the southern peninsula, near the island of Ceylon, has its own particular devil or devils against whom it must constantly be on the guard.   But happily it has also its guardian spirits who protect its fields and homes.   It would seem that these latter are equestrian in their tastes, for the villagers—either to propitiate them, or perhaps with the idea of giving them an advantage over the demons—provide them with horses of baked clay on which they may ride in pursuit of the foe, who have to flee on foot.

These clay horses are often life-size, but are so roughly formed that it is sometimes difficult to recognise that it is the equine shape they are intended to represent.   They are especially presented—with proper oblations—to the guardian God Ayenār, who is said to be a fearless horseman, able to ride over hedges and ditches and defeat the most active of the demon foes.   The image of this god is in human form, coloured a reddish hue, with a crown on his head, a sceptre in his hand, the *Saiva* mark on his forehead, and ornaments on his person. He is sometimes represented in a sitting attitude, sometimes on horseback.   He has two wives, Pūranī and Pudkata, who generally sit on either side of him, and at night ride around the fields with him and take an active part in driving off the demons.   This is the reason why no villager in Southern India likes to be out in the fields when darkness falls, and on no account will pass near the shrines of Ayenār at night.   He might be mistaken for an evil spirit, and slain by the god or his wives when they are patrolling the fields.

After recovery from illness, or the coming to them of any good luck, the villagers will make thank-offerings of fresh clay (or terracotta) horses to the shrine, which is generally to be found among a group of trees to the west of the village.   If cholera or pestilence, disease, blight, or other calamities attack the village, the inhabitants redouble their offerings, and endeavour to propitiate the god by the blood of swine, goats, cocks, etc., or by libations of strong liquor or cooked food, all of which are gladly received by Ayenār's priests, who are generally very poor.

It should be noted that a harvest festival is always held in honour of this god, when numerous animals are sacrificed, and his images are decorated and, mounted on the clay horses, are drawn around the village streets. This should be compared with the customs connected with the corn-horse.

BIBLIOGRAPHY

Brahmanism and Hinduism: or Religious Thought and Life in India, by Sir Monier Monier-Williams, K.C.I.E. Fourth edition. (John Murray, London, 1891.)

History of the Conquest of Mexico, by Wm. H. Prescott. (Routledge, Warne & Routledge, London, 1863.)

Origin and Influence of the Thoroughbred Horse, by Wm. Ridgeway.

Faiths of Man, II. 250, by Forlong.

Universal History, Ancient and Modern, Vol. VI, p. 153, by Wm. Mavor, LL.D. (London, 1802.)

The Golden Bough, Part I, Vol. I, p. 364, by J. G. Frazer.

Abbeys, Castles, and Ancient Halls of England and Wales, by John Timbs. (Fredk. Warne & Co., London.)

Myths of the Norsemen, by H. A. Guerber. (Geo. G. Harrap & Co., London, 1909.)

The Tale of the Great Persian War, from the Histories of Herodotus, by the Rev. George W. Cox, M.A. (Longman, Green, Longman & Roberts. London, 1861.)

CHAPTER XXVI

The Horse-loosed

WE have already given at length the myth of Hippolytus, the classical example of the horse-loosed, in our chapter on Sea-horses, but many are the heroes of ancient days who gained their freedom from the chains of this earthly " dream of life " by means of their equine friends.

And how could death come in a more ideal form to one who feels his steed to be almost as his other self ? Still in the prime and vigour of his manhood, engaged in his loved occupation of riding or driving his beautiful horse, suddenly—leaving no time for vain regrets or sad farewells—he becomes aware that the gates of the spirit-world have opened wide, and that his body no longer imprisons his soul. He has been horse-loosed ! The spectres of declining health and weary age are for ever flown. Happy, happy man !

Let us look together at some of the legendary instances in which the gods vouchsafed this gift to their worshippers. There is a curious sameness about the first three stories, so that although they come from three totally different countries it is evident that they must have had a common origin. And they are not to be taken as illustrative of the foregoing remarks, for the hero's endeavour to thwart the will of the gods rendered them anything but happy. Compliance with the divine will can alone ensure happiness. When the call is heard, go gladly.

Our first example is found in a Russian saga which describes the death of Oleg, a chieftain who usurped the kingship of Russia about the year 879. It is to be found in the Chronicle of Nestor, a monk of Kiev, who flourished some two hundred years later. The following translation is that of Mr. W. R. Morfill, M.A.

196

" And Oleg lived, having peace on all sides, residing in Kiev. And Oleg remembered his horse which he had entrusted to others to feed, himself never seeing him. For a long time ago he had asked the wizards and magicians, ' By whom is it fated that I should die ? ' And one of the magicians said to him, ' Prince, the horse which thou lovest, and upon which thou ridest, shall be the cause of thy death.' Oleg receiving this into his mind said, ' I will never ride the horse nor see him more.' And he ordered them to take care of the horse, but never to bring it to him again ; and many years passed, and he rode him no more, and he went among the Greeks. Afterwards he returned to Kiev and stayed there four years, and in the fifth he remembered his horse, by which the soothsayers had predicted that Oleg would die, and having called the oldest of his grooms, he said, ' Where is my horse which I enjoined you to feed and take care of ? ' And they said ' He is dead ! ' And Oleg laughed, and blamed the soothsayer, and said, ' The wizard spoke falsely, and it is all a lie ; the horse is dead and I am alive.' And he ordered them to saddle his steed, for he wished to see the bones of the horse. And he came to the place where the bones and the skull lay unburied. And he leapt from his steed and said with a smile, ' How can a skull be the cause of my death ? ' And he planted his foot on the skull, and out darted a snake and bit him on the foot, and from the wound he fell sick and died."

Another version of this story is immortalised in a Scandinavian saga. In this legend Oerwar Odde, the son of Grim, is warned that he will be slain by his horse. Returning home after a long absence, he found his equine friend was dead, and his body buried in a marsh. When he drew near to view the corpse, a lizard sprang from the head and killed him.

Similar tales are to be found in the folk-lore of the British Isles, and are of very early date.

One of the best known and most often retold of these tales is that which relates the adventures of Sir Robert de Shurland, who resided at Shurland, in the Isle of Sheppey, and was created a Knight Banneret by Edward I for his services at the siege of Caerlaverock, in Scotland, during the thirteenth century. The tomb of this knight is the most remarkable monument in the abbey church at Minster, and represents

Sir Robert lying, cross-legged, with his head resting on his helmet, whilst close beside him is sculptured the head of a horse emerging from the waves. On the church tower is a weather-cock, also in the form of a horse's head. The legend is that Sir Robert buried a priest alive, and then, to obtain pardon of the king—who had come near the island on board ship—he swam his horse two miles out to the king's boat to purchase his pardon, and returned with it safely, still on his gallant steed's back. He had only just regained the dry land, when an ill-favoured old hag accosted him, and prophesied that though his horse had now saved his life it would yet be the cause of his death. Thinking to thwart this threatened fate, the ungrateful knight struck off the head of his still panting steed, and taunted the witch as being a proven liar.

A year passed away, and one day, when walking on the beach, he chanced upon his horse's skull, washed on to shore by the waves. To show his contempt for the unfulfilled prophecy, he kicked the relic high into the air. But a splinter of the bone entered his foot, and mortification set up in the wound and killed him.

According to another version, the knight was hunting twelve months after dispatching his faithful steed, when the horse he was riding stumbled and threw him on to the skull of the one he had killed. The blow so bruised him that " from the contusion he contracted an inward imposthumation of which he died."

BIBLIOGRAPHY

Russia, by W. R. Morfill, M.A. (Fisher Unwin, London, 1890.)
Abbeys, Castles, and Ancient Halls of England and Wales, by John Timbs. (Fredk.

CHAPTER XXVII

The Funeral Horse

IN reviewing the position of the horse in funeral ceremonies and sacraments, we find ourselves constantly brought into contact with sacrifices and rites designed to honour the God of War. The reason for this is that owing to its military value the horse from remote antiquity has been sacred to Mars. And War stalks hand in hand with his brother Death.

To illustrate our point we will open this chapter by quoting a note from *The Pictorial Bible* :

" Herodotus informs us that the Scythians (who had no cities or enclosed towns, but tents only, aud who fought on horseback, armed with bows and arrows) sacrificed horses to the God of War as well as human victims—prisoners taken in battle. An altar to Mars is found in every district, constructed in the following manner : ' A great quantity of small wood tied up in bundles is brought together and placed upon three stadia of land, covering the whole ground both in length and breadth but not of a proportionable height. The top is quadrangular, three of the sides perpendicular, the fourth a gradual declivity of easy access. One hundred and fifty loads of faggots are annually brought to this place, because much of the wood rots every winter ; on each of these heaps an old scimitar of iron is erected which they call the image of Mars, and honour with yearly sacrifices of horses and other cattle in greater abundance than they offer to the rest of their gods.'

" The animals are first strangled, then flayed, and the flesh is boiled on a fire made of the bones. Part is offered to the god. On the death of a Scythian king the body was embalmed, and laid upon a bed, surrounded by spears, in a deep excavation ; one of his wives or concubines, a cupbearer, a groom, a waiter, a messenger, and several horses were strangled and deposited in the same receptacle, together with various utensils and cups of gold. The mouth of the pit was then covered over, and a high tumulus raised above.

" At the expiration of a year the rites were thus concluded : ' They select such servants as they judge most useful out of the rest of the king's household, which consists only of native Scythians, for the king is never served by men bought with money. These officers, fifty in number, they strangle, and with them fifty beautiful horses. After they have eviscerated the bodies, they fill them with straw and sew them up. They then lay two planks of a semi-circular form upon four pieces of timber (posts) placed at a convenient distance, and when they have erected a sufficient number of these frames, they set the horses upon them, first spitting them with a strong pole through the body to the neck ; one semi-circle supports the shoulders or chest of the horse, the other his flank, and the legs are suspended in the air. After this they bridle the horses, and hanging the reins at full length, upon posts erected for this purpose, mount one of the fifty young men they have strangled upon each horse, fixing him in his seat by spitting the body up the spine with a straight stick, which is received into a socket in the beam that spits the horse. They then place these horse-men round the tumulus and depart.' "

The mystic Anna Kingsford has given us the following interpretation of these strange funeral rites, in her wonderful work entitled *Clothed with the Sun*. At least we think the reader will agree with us that it is undoubtedly to them that she refers, though she does not give chapter and verse. She says :

" For in the mystery of Ares the Man of War, they sacrificed and ate human flesh and the flesh of horses which also war together with men. For this circle is outside the kingdom of the fourfold circles and belongeth to the beasts of prey. And his star is red, as with the blood of the slain. But the orgies of Ares, the Ram-headed, no man celebrated save in war. . . . Yet hath Ares also his interior meaning : O Knowledge, thou art hard of access ! The Horse (which is the symbol of the intellect) dieth for thee, and the Warrior is pierced. Thou art the Man of War and of iron are the wheels of thy chariot."

These Scythians were probably a Mongolian people. At all events we learn from that explorer of mediæval times, de Plano Carpini, that very similar customs prevailed among the Mongols. There, when a man of noble birth died, he was buried in a sitting posture under a tent, and with him were buried a mare and foal and a horse saddled and bridled, so that in the spirit-world the dead man might be sure of shelter, milk to drink, and a steed to ride. Also that he might be able to propagate the race of horses in that other land. Moreover, his friends would kill yet another horse, eat its flesh, and burn its bones for the benefit of the departed's soul. Then they would stuff its skin with straw and fix it up on an arrangement of poles.

A still earlier account of a similar custom is given by the Arab traveller Ibn Batuta, who flourished in the fourteenth century. He describes the funeral of a Chinese emperor who was killed in battle. The ceremony took place at Pekin. In the same vault as the emperor, four young female slaves and six guards were entombed, and over them a hillock of earth of an immense size was raised. Then four horses were forced to run round and round this mound until they were exhausted. After this they were killed and impaled, and made to stand around the grave to guard the king and be at his service in the other world.

The Patagonian Indians celebrate the funeral of a chief in a similar way. They sacrifice four horses, stuff their skins, and prop them up upon sticks, one at each corner of the grave. The flesh is eaten. When an ordinary member of the tribe dies, his own favourite horse is killed and set up as described with its head pointing to its master's grave.

Another famous tribe of American Indians, the Comanches, in Texas, kill and bury the horses of their dead comrades, so that the departed may ride them to the Happy Hunting-grounds. The widows then surround the bodies, and with loud wailings cut and gash themselves with knives until they are exhausted by the loss of their blood. The manes and tails of the horses of the tribe are cut off as a testimony of grief. As we shall see, this last is a very widespread custom among ancient peoples so separated by geographical position, race, and ideals that it can scarcely have had a common origin, but must have arisen spontaneously as a natural method of expressing extreme sorrow.

The Thebans are said to have followed this custom on the death of Pelopidas. Alexander the Great upon the death of Hephæstion had the manes of the horses and mules shorn.

Plutarch tells us that the Greeks estimated the importance of their victory over the Persians at the battle of Platæa (479 B.C.) " not by the number of their enemies lying dead upon the field, for that was but small, but by the mourning of the barbarians, who in their grief . . . cut off their hair, and the manes of all their horses and mules."

Herodotus says the Persians mourned the death of Masistius (who perished whilst leading a charge in battle) by shaving themselves and their horses and their beasts of burden.

It is interesting to contrast these customs with those of the English people in recent times.

The black funeral horse of Victorian days was not considered properly equipped without a flowing mane and tail, the longer and heavier the better.

We may here note that in England the military funeral is the only pageant in which the horse appears without rider or driver. The charger of the dead officer is led behind his body to the grave, saddled, and with its master's boots hanging reversed, one on either side. The custom, which is of great antiquity, evidently dates back to the days when the horse was led to the tomb that it might there be slaughtered for the use of its rider in the world beyond.

An instance of this custom in the days when men's faith was the ruling power of their lives was brought to light when the tomb of Childeric, the father of Clovis, was opened. The skeleton of his war-horse was found within, and with it, the hundreds of golden ornaments which had adorned its harness in the funeral procession.

To return to more modern days. In Tudor times we find that at the funeral of Sir Philip Sidney his " horse for the field " was led by an esquire and ridden by one of his pages, who trailed after him a broken lance. This horse followed immediately after the funeral car, and behind it a second squire led his " barbed " horse, which he used on state occasions. This was covered with cloth-of-gold and ridden by a page in full dress, who carried in his hand a battle-axe reversed. What the fate of these noble creatures subsequently was, history does not relate. Were their last days spent in slavery and wretchedness, or did some grateful hand tend them to the end ? Those of olden times would not have left the answer doubtful.

We have already referred to the Victorian funeral horse. When the Duke of Wellington was buried, twelve horses drew the car. They were enveloped from head to fetlock in black velvet housings, and black ostrich plumes nodded on their heads. Behind the car walked a cream-coloured horse with crimson caparisons. This was the " horse of honour," and the touch of colour it gave must have been a welcome relief to those who watched the gloomy procession. The only led horse was the Duke's charger which he had been accustomed to ride during his last years. But this solitary steed following so pathetically the dead body of its lost master appealed to the emotions of the watching multitudes as none of the preceding pomp and ceremony had been able to do.

We have not yet abandoned this impressive custom. The *Daily Mail* of June 27, 1922, published a photograph of the charger of the late Field-Marshal Sir Henry Wilson being led behind its master's coffin in the funeral procession to St. Paul's Cathedral.

The slaying of the war-horse beside his master's tomb is beautifully pictured in Longfellow's descriptive poem of the burial of a Red Indian Chief.

> Before, a dark-haired virgin train
> Chanted the death-dirge of the slain ;
> Behind the long procession came
> Of hoary men and chiefs of fame,
> With heavy hearts, and eyes of grief,
> Leading the war-horse of their chief.
>
> Stripped of his proud and martial dress,
> Uncurbed, unreined, and riderless,
> With darting eye and nostril spread,
> And heavy and impatient tread,
> He came ; and oft that eye so proud
> Asked for his rider in the crowd.

They buried the dark chief ; they freed
Beside the grave his battle steed ;
And swift an arrow cleaved its way
To his stern heart !   One piercing neigh
Arose,—and, on the dead man's plain,
The rider grasps his steed again.

(Burial of the Minnisink.)

Among peoples of the Caucasus we find it a very generally followed custom to complete the funeral ceremonies, or to celebrate the anniversary of the death of great chiefs and warriors, by games in which horse-racing plays the most prominent part, and where the prizes of victory are often horses, on some occasions hundreds of them being awarded among the successful competitors.   The horse of the deceased often figures largely in these celebrations.

In some parts of this territory it was the custom down to modern times to cut off the ears of the dead man's favourite steed to signify mourning for his departed master, but this cruel amplification of the custom of removing mane and tail for the same reason is happily now discontinued.

The two great Irish fairs of Carman and Tailtin, where horse-racing was so prominent a feature, are supposed to have been originally festivals in honour of the dead, even as were the Olympic Games.

Equestrian games in honour of the dead are described by Virgil, and Tacitus mentions that Prince Germanicus, " joining with the legions in equestrian games, performed a funeral ceremony in honour of his father."

After the death of Patroclus during the siege of Troy, Achilles thus addressed his Myrmidons : " My faithful comrades, we will not yet loose our steeds from harness, but with the horses and chariots let us bewail Patroclus ; for so do we honour our dead.   When we have indulged sad lamentations, we will unyoke our fair-maned steeds, and share the evening meal."   Hereupon Achilles led the Myrmidons in a solemn dirge, and they drove their chariots three times around the corpse of Patroclus.

Later, when the funeral games in honour of Patroclus were held, Achilles, as he laid down prizes for the chariot-race about to be run.

said that his grief at the loss of his friend did not allow him to partici-
pate as he would have done had they been in honour of one less dear
to him, but associating his horses in his grief, he continues sadly .
" But verily I will abide, I and my whole-hoofed horses, so glorious
a charioteer have they lost, and one so kind, who on their manes full
often poured smooth oil when he had washed them in clear water.
For him they stand and mourn, and their manes are trailing on the
ground, and there stand they with sorrow at their hearts."

Among northern nations the horse is closely associated with death
and funeral rites.

The Goddess of Death —Hel or Hela— rode a three-legged white
horse when she left the dismal region of Nifl-heim under the earth
to ride aboveground among mortals.

This goddess, according to the Eddaic poems, was the daughter of
Loki, and a giantess.

As Dr. Grimm has pointed out, in the Danish legends Hel is represented as riding to foretell the coming of sickness and pestilence ; or,
according to an older version, to collect and carry off the dead, whom
the gods had allotted to her. Later versions represent her as riding
in a chariot, instead of driving. Originally she was not a destroyer,
and the farther we retrace the monuments of Northern mythology,
the more refined, benign, and divine does the character of our equestrian
goddess appear. This office of a friendly messenger became gradually
converted into one of a cruel and severe nature. Christianity admitted
no goddess of death, but taught its converts to transfer her name to
their place of hideous torture. Tennyson asks .

> Is it so true that second thoughts are best ?
> Why not first thoughts, or third, which are a riper first ?

Let us return to the older conception of the mother-goddess on her
snowy three-legged steed, who has come as a friend, to release us from
sorrow and pain. Then Death and Hell will hold no terror for us.

When Hermod the Swift would visit Hela, he rode upon Odin's
beautiful steed Sleipnir, but her kingdom was so far from human habitation that even so he travelled during nine days and nights before
he reached the River Giöll, which formed the boundary to Niflheim.

The bridge that crossed this river was made of glass, and hung on but a single hair, but over it the spirits of the dead had all to pass. They generally either rode or drove, on the horses or in the waggons which had been burned with their bodies on the funeral pyre for this very purpose.

When Hermod rode over this bridge on his mission to obtain the release of Balder the Beautiful (i.e. the sun, according to the theory which would see solar myths in all ancient religious legends) from the realms of death, Sleipnir's tread shook the structure more than when a whole army of mortal spirits passed, and Mödgud, the horrid skeleton who made each spirit pay a toll of blood ere he let him pass, inquired :

> Who art thou on thy black and fiery horse,
> Under whose hoofs the bridge o'er Giöll's stream
> Rumbles and shakes ?   Tell me thy race and home.
> But yestermorn five troops of dead passed by
> Nor shook the bridge so much as thou alone.

Hermod told his quest and was informed that Balder had ridden over the bridge ahead of him, so he hurried on :

> Until he met a stretching wall
> Barring his way, and in the wall a grate.
> Then he dismounted, and drew tight the girths,
> On the smooth ice, of Sleipnir, Odin's horse,
> And made him leap the gate and came within.
> (Matthew Arnold, *Balder Dead.*)

Hermod was successful in obtaining the release of Balder, on the condition that all things wept for the god.

All things did weep for the loss of the Beautiful One except one old crone, who asked, " What have the gods done for me, that I should weep for Balder ?   Let Hel keep her dead." So the god's fate was sealed, and his throne was placed in the shadowy regions of Hel, and mourning virgins spread the eternal pall that was to give hollow honour to the god of light in the kingdom of darkness.

Macedonian folk-lore follows the widespread tradition in asserting that Death owns a steed.   In it the King of Terrors is often represented as mounted on the back of a fiery horse, and one of their best-known ballads ('O Χάρος καὶ αἱ ψυχαί) describes Charos, the gatekeeper of the subterranean realms, as mounted on horseback, driving troops of young souls in numbers before him, and carrying on his saddle-bow a load of the souls of infants. As his dread figure pursues its way, the earth quakes under the feet of his horse, and the mountains are darkened by the shadow of his coming.

BIBLIOGRAPHY

Schoolcraft's *Indian Tribes of the United States*, Vol. II, p. 133.
Native Races of the Pacific States, by H. Bancroft, Vol. I, p. 523.
The Great Persian War, Herodotus, IX. 20–24.
The Pictorial Bible.
Clothed with the Sun, by Anna Bonus Kingsford, pp. 77, 78.
Voyages d Ibn Batoutah, by Defremery & Sanguinetti, Vol. IV, p. 300 sq.
Animals at Work and Play, by C. J. Cornish.
The Golden Bough, by J. G. Frazer, Part I, Vol. I, p. 364.
Historia Mongalorum, by de Plano Carpini (Paris, 1838).
Annals, Tacitus, Book II. 7.
Æneid, Virgil, XI. 188.
The Story of the Trojan War, Anon.   (James Blackwood & Co., London, 1874.)
Macedonian Folk-lore, by G. F. Abbott, B.A.   (Cambridge University Press, 1903.)
The Art Journal, 1856, p. 365 sq.   (Published by Virtue & Co., London.)
Saxons in England, Vol. I, p. 368.

CHAPTER XXVIII

The Horse and Metempsychosis

OUR subject, the horse, brings us into contact at one point with the doctrine of metempsychosis, or transmigration of souls, and our old friend the *Spectator* has much to say on the matter, retailing the views of Simonides, and adding matter of his own for the instruction of his readers. We quote the passages that bear on the horse :

"Simonides, a Poet famous in his Generation, is, I think, Author of the oldest Satyr that is now extant ; and as some say of the first that was ever written. This Poet flourished about 400 years after the Siege of Troy. . . .

"The subject of this Satyr is Woman. He describes the Sex in their several Characters, which he derives to them from a fanciful Supposition raised upon the Doctrine of Præ-existence. He tells us that the Gods formed the Souls of Women out of those seeds and Principles which compose several kinds of Animals and Elements ; and that their good or bad Dispositions arise in them according as such and such Seeds and Principles predominate in their constitutions. I have translated the Author very faithfully. . . .

"'In the beginning God made the Souls of Womenkind out of different materials, and in a separate State from their Bodies.'"

Here follows a list of how women of different characteristics are derived from animals Simonides names, but as we are only studying the horse we will omit what is irrelevant. He proceeds :

"'The Mare with a flowing Mane, which was never broke to any servile Toil and Labour; composed an Eighth Species of Women. Those are they who have little Regard for their Husbands, who pass away their time in Dressing, Bathing, and Perfuming ; who throw their hair into the nicest Curls, and trick it up with the fairest Flowers and Garlands. A Woman of this Species is a very pretty Thing for a Stranger to look upon, but very detrimental to the Owner, unless it be a King or Prince who takes a Fancy to such a Toy.' "

The *Spectator* evidently quite agrees with Simonides here, for he says : " The Poet has shown a great Penetration in this Diversity of Female Characters." Indeed, so pleased is our friend with his poet's penetration, that he decides to emulate him by trying to trace the spiritual descent of men through brutes, but quickly settles that the male soul is so much more complex that no single animal can be named as its progenitor ! He continues :

" Instead therefore of pursuing the Thought of Simonides, I shall observe that as he has exposed the vicious Part of Women from the Doctrine of Præ-existence, some of the ancient Philosophers have, in a Manner, satyrised the vicious Part of the Human Species, in general, from a Notion of the Soul's Post-existence, if I may so call it ; and that as Simonides describes Brutes entering into the Composition of Women, others have represented human Souls as entering into Brutes. This is commonly termed the Doctrine of Transmigration which supposes that human Souls, upon their leaving the Body, become the Souls of such kinds of Brutes as they most resemble in their Manners ; or to give an Account of it, as Mr. Dryden has described it in his Translation of Pythagoras his Speech in the 15th book of Ovid, where that Philosopher disswades his Hearers from eating Flesh :

Thus all Things are but alter'd, nothing dies,
And here and there the unbody'd Spirit flies :
By Time, or Force, or Sickness, dispossess'd
And lodges where it lights in Bird or Beast,
Or hunts without till ready limbs it find,
And actuates those according to their Kind :
From Tenement to Tenement is toss'd :
The Soul is still the same, the Figure only lost.
Then let not Piety be put to Flight,
To please the taste of Glutton-Appetite ;
But suffer inmate Souls secure to dwell,
Lest from their Seats your Parents you expell :

With rabid Hunger feed upon your Kind,
Or from a Beast dislodge a Brother's Mind."

The above quotation well sums up the general position. To return to the particular :

In Addison's translation of Ovid's *Metamorphoses*, we find the description most vividly given of Ocyrrhoe's transformation into a mare.   This heroine was the daughter of Chiron the Centaur.   When she saw the infant Æsculapius she was seized by prophetic rapture in which she betrayed the secrets of Jove.   For this offence she was metamorphosed by the angry god.   Here is the poem describing her sensations :

" My voice," says she, " is gone, my language fails ;
Through every limb my kindred shape prevails.

．　　　．　　　．　　　．　　　．

What new desires are these ?   I long to pace
O'er flowery meadows, and to feed on grass.
I hasten to a brute, a maid no more ;
But why, alas ! am I transformed all o'er ?
My sire doth half a human shape retain
And in his upper part preserves the Man."
Her Tongue no more distinct complaints affords
But in shrill accent and mis-shapen words
Pours forth such hideous wailings as declare
The human form confounded in the Mare :
Till by degrees accomplished in the Beast
She neighed outright and all the Steed exprest.
Her stooping body on her hands is borne,
Her hands are turned to hoofs, and shod in horn,
Her yellow tresses ruffle in a mane,
And in a flowing tail she frisks her train.
The Mare was finished in her voice and look
And a new name from her new figure took.
                    (Ovid's *Metamorphoses*, Book II.)

Perhaps Shelley was thinking of poor Ocyrrhoe's fate when he wrote those beautiful lines :

Was there a human spirit in the steed
That thus with his proud voice, ere night was gone,
He broke our linkèd rest ? or do indeed
All living things a common nature own,

And thought erect an universal throne,
Where many shapes one tribute ever bear ?
And Earth, their mutual mother, does she groan
To see her sons contend ?   And makes she bare
Her breast, that all in peace its drainless stores may share ?
(Shelley, *The Revolt of Isalm*, X. 1.)

In this spirit we must examine the curious old legend of the Seven Foals, from J. Moe. It is perhaps in many points unique ; though it may be classified with the numerous tales in which a human soul is represented as being imprisoned in animal form, so widely diffused in ancient folk-lore.

The story tells how Cinderlad succeeded in the task he undertook of following the king's colts all through their diurnal wanderings, and correctly reporting to the king what formed their food and drink, after his elder brothers, who first undertook the mission, had ignominiously failed. The food of the foals proved to be, not moss and water as Cinderlad's brothers, deceived by an old woman who lured them from their task, had reported to the king, but consecrated bread and wine, administered in a church by the priest at the altar. When Cinderlad had made this discovery, and the foals had returned to their stable once more, he was instructed by his charges to cut off their heads and lay these beside their tails. No sooner had he done so, than the foals—who were in reality the enchanted sons of the king—resumed their proper forms and appeared as princes again. Needless to say the faithful Cinderlad was handsomely rewarded.

In these materialistic days we have almost lost the power of recognising the soul through its covering of form, and are far too apt to judge the psyche from its outermost garment, the body.

Our forefathers were more discerning, as the legends they have handed down to us prove. Looking on the animals surrounding them, they perceived that their forms sometimes concealed a human soul, and that often of no mean quality, even, it might be, the offspring of a royal race. Wistfully it awaited the moment when love should recognise its existence, and break the spell which held it so painfully in thrall. Surely here is the inner meaning of the legend of the Seven Foals, It was not moss and water, as the materialist would have it.

that sustained those brave spirits to bear the burden of their lowly form.   All unknown to the human beings around them, God Himself was their food and drink.   And, after partaking of the sacred repast, right gladly they bore the destruction of the imprisoning body by the sharp sword of pain, foreseeing with the eye of faith that death was the gateway to that fuller life which was their birthright as sons of the King.

CHAPTER XXIX

The Horse in Creation Myths

THE creation of the horse in India is attributed to Vishnu, who infused a portion of his essence into the body of an immense tortoise to aid in making or recovering certain important things which had been lost during the Deluge.

One of these was the " high-eared " horse (Uččaih-sravas), the supposed prototype of the equine race.

Indian myth generally seems to speak of the horse as a fully developed self-conscious creature, with powers (e.g. of speech) which it certainly does not now normally possess, existing long anterior to the creation of man. The following curious legend of its reception of the Creator's new beings is told by the Mundas, a primitive aboriginal tribe of Chota Nagpur.

Singbonga, the Sun-god, fashioned two figures of clay, one of them intended to become a man and the other a woman. But before he could endow his work with life, the horse, with prophetic vision of the sufferings mankind was destined to inflict upon his race in the future, trampled the new creation beneath its hoofs. In those days the horse was winged, so that his movements were much speedier than they are now. Singbonga, finding his work thus destroyed, took precautions before commencing afresh. He first created a spider, and then fashioned another pair of clay figures.

The spider was entrusted with the protecting of these against the horse. It accomplished its mission by weaving its web around them so that the horse could not get at them any more. Then the Sun-god gave them life and they became the first human beings.

A variant of this myth substitutes the dog for the spider and represents him as keeping the horse at bay with his bark.

A similar myth of the creation is found among the Korkus, an aboriginal tribe of the Central Provinces of India.

According to this version Mahadeo (i.e. Siva) at the request of Rawan, the demon King of Ceylon, undertook to people the uninhabited mountain ranges of Vindhyan and Satpura, and to this end he fashioned two clay images in the likeness of a man and woman. But he had no sooner done this than two fiery horses, sent by Indra, rose from the ground and trampled his images to dust. For two days the creator persisted in his efforts, but every time the horses foiled his attempt and destroyed his work. At last the god created a dog to aid him, and this animal kept at bay the fiery steeds of Indra. So the deity was able to complete his work, and the man and woman he formed became the ancestors of the Korku tribe.

Colonel D. C. Phillott writes as follows :

" According to Hindu legends, the horse was created a winged animal, one that could fly and run, and no man or god could snare it. Indra wanted horses for his chariots, and requested the sage Salihotra to deprive the horses of their wings. Accordingly Salihotra, by means of *yoga*, a supernatural power, derived from his austerities, accomplished Indra's wish. The horses, now deprived of the ability to visit far-off jungles in search of medicinal herbs, approached Salihotra and entreated him to write a book on the treatment of their diseases. Salihotra consented, and composed the greatest work on veterinary science known to the Hindus. This work was called *Salihotra* after him ; gradually this Sanscrit word came to mean veterinary science in general and also a horse. To-day every regiment of native cavalry has its salotris."

The student should refer to the chapter on Wind-horses, where another creation myth will be found.

BIBLIOGRAPHY

Brahmanism and Hinduism : or Religious Thought and Life in India, as based on the Veda and other sacred Books of the Hindus, by Sir Monier Monier-Williams, K.C.I.E. (John Murray, London, 1891.)

Journal of the Bihar and Orissa Research Society, Vol. II, p. 281. (Bankipore, 1916.)

The Tribes and Castes of the Central Provinces of India, by R. V. Russell. (London, 1916.)

The Faras-Nama-e Rangin, or The Book of the Horse, by Col. D. C. Phillott. (London, 1911.)

CHAPTER XXX

The Moral and Legal Responsibility of the Horse

IN ancient times the doubt of animals' moral responsibility had scarcely arisen, and solemn, judicial trials of offending beasts were quite common in the Middle Ages. Even insects were considered to be conscious of the distinction between right and wrong, and amenable to justice. The whole proceedings of their trial, sentence, and execution were conducted with the strictest formalities of the law, and this not only by ancient and barbarous peoples, but by the Christian Church, which denied that sub-human races were possessed of a soul.

So late as 1668 a treatise was published by Gaspard Bailly, a lawyer at Chambéry, on legal proceedings against animals, giving the forms of indictments and modes of pleading. This probably originated with the Jewish law propounded in Exodus xxi. 28, where it is laid down : " If an ox gore a man or a woman, that they die : then the ox shall be surely stoned, and his flesh shall not be eaten ; but the owner of the ox shall be quit. . . . According to this judgment shall it be done unto him."

It used to be the law in England that if a horse should strike his keeper so as to kill him, the horse was to be a deodand; that is, that he was to be forfeited to the king to be applied to pious uses, and his value distributed in alms by the king's high almoner. It was not until 1846 that this law was abolished, probably because its pious object had been lost sight of, and the deodand had come to be regarded as a private perquisite of the monarch, though the derivation of its name, *Deo dandum*, " a thing to be given to God," must have raised a perpetual protest. It will be seen at once what a great advance public feeling had achieved when this charitable ordinance was substituted for the barbarous law of the Jew.

But history repeats herself and progress is not uniform. Revolution rather than evolution often appears to be the law, and things have a strong tendency to return to their starting-point even after travelling far in another direction. The examples we are now about to give of the trial and execution of horses took place but yesterday, and the horses were condemned for possessing a political opinion contrary to that of the courts which tried them, and not on moral or religious grounds.

The following paragraph is taken from the *Daily Express* of December 27, 1919 :

" ROSTOFF-ON-DON (SOUTH RUSSIA).—The Bolsheviks shot the famous Russian trotter Krepysh, of Afanasyeff's stables at the railway station in Simbirsk. During its trotting career it won prizes to the amount of £35,000. It was shot for being a ' bourgeois ' horse.
                                                        RUSSIAN LIBERATION COMMITTEE."

Our next instance is also an example of Bolshevik justice, and is taken from the *Daily Express* of July 13, 1920 :

COURT-MARTIAL ON A RACEHORSE
Shot for Dealings with the Old Regime
Daily Express Correspondent, Paris. *Monday, July 12.*

" According to *Paris Sport*, several very valuable bloodstock horses have been rescued from the Bolsheviks. The animals were removed by the British authorities after General Deniken's defeat, and are now at Constantinople, where they are being held as security against Russia's debt to Great Britain. . . . A son of Sunstar was in Russia at the time of the Bolshevist outbreak, and having learned that this horse won a cup offered by the late Czar, the Bolsheviks had the horse tried by court-martial and shot it, after sentencing the horse to death for ' having had dealings with the old regime.' "

To parallel this instance of Russian justice in olden law-courts, we must return to the reign of good Queen Bess. In those days flourished Marocco, the famous dancing horse of Bankes's, which was immortalised by Shakespeare, Jonson, Donne, Hall, Taylor, Sir Kenelm Digby, and Sir Walter Raleigh. A contemporary tract has been found with a rude woodcut of the unfortunate juggler and his famous horse. One of Marocco's exploits was the ascent of St. Paul's steeple, which Dekker tells us caused delight to "a number of asses who brayed below." After amazing London by his wonderful performances, when the novelty of them had begun to wear off, Bankes took the intelligent animal to give exhibitions on the Continent (about the year 1589), going first to Paris and then to Rome. But it had been far better had they remained at home, for at Orleans the too-intelligent horse was, together with his master, accused of magic, and with him found guilty and executed at Rome. Jonson, recording this, says of them, "Being beyond the sea burned for one witch." The earliest notice of Marocco's popularity is to be found in a manuscript copy of one of Dr. Donne's satires, dated 1593, and preserved in the Harleian manuscripts, No. 5110.

Shakespeare alludes to Marocco in *Love's Labour's Lost*, I. 2, where we find the passage : "How easy it is to put 'years' to the word 'three,' and study three years in two words, the dancing horse will tell you."

Sir Walter Raleigh, in his *History of the World*, writing of "the divers kindes of unlawful magicke," says :

"And certainly if Bankes had lived in elder times he would have shamed all the inchanters of the world, for whosoever was most famous among them could never master or instruct any beast as he did his horse."

Sir Kenelm Digby writes :

"He that should tell an Indian, what feates Banks his horse would do ; how he would restore a glove to the due owner, after his master had whispered that man's name in his eare ; how he would tell the just number of pence in any piece of silver coyne barely shewed him by his master, would make him, I believe, admire more at this learned beast, then we do at their docile elephantes, upon the relations we have of them. Whereas every one of us knoweth by what means his painefull tutor brought him to do all his trickes ; and they are no whitte more extraordinary, then a fawkener's manning of a hawke, and trayning her to kill partridges and to fly at the retrieve."

Marocco was " a middle size bay English gelding " and his master was a Scotchman, a servant to the Earl of Essex and a vintner in Cheapside. He thought so highly of his horse that he had him shod with silver.[1]

Needless to say, Marocco was not the only victim of the justice of those days. As late as the year 1697 an unfortunate mare was burned to death by a decree of the Parliament of Aix, and at an earlier date many examples might be found. For instance, in 1389 a horse which was tried at Dijon, on information given by the magistrate of Montbar, was condemned to death because it had killed a man.

It has often been debated whether animals can, and occasionally do, commit suicide. The following instance of what appears to be such an attempt on the part of a horse is taken from the *Daily Express* of July 18, 1922 :

HORSE TIRED OF LIFE

" Major " makes Two Attempts at Suicide

(*Daily Express* Correspondent, New York.)

" ' Major,' a black horse in the stables of the Grand Union Tea Company at Kerboukson, New York State, has tried twice within a week to commit suicide. Everybody in the town is certain that it was attempted suicide and not accident.

" The horse on the first occasion got out of the stables during the night and wandered on the railway. Crossing a trestle bridge, he tried to jump over, but was caught by his hind legs and hung dangling in the air.

" Mr. J. E. Martin, manager of the company branch there, was aroused by groans coming from the trestle and, accompanied by the rest of the town, found ' Major.' It took two hours to release him and

---

[1] The performances of Marocco have found a parallel in recent times in the horses of Elberfeld, which were trained to do mathematical calculations, and excited great interest in psychical and scientific circles. An interesting account of these will be found in *The Unknown Guest*, by Maurice Maeterlinck.

get him back in his stall, for there was a 15-feet drop into a creek which had to be made before he could be placed on four legs again.

"The second attempt was made a few days later. 'Major' was found in his stall with his halter twisted about his throat, half dead. Those who saw 'Major' hanging declare from his position that it was voluntary and not accidental.

"A blood-vessel in his neck was broken this time, but after a veterinary had treated him for several days he again got on his feet and seems well enough now."

Without knowing "Major" personally it is impossible to attempt an explanation of his determination to take his own life. But those who have studied animals closely and sympathetically may have noted how in the cases of beasts that have been much in human society, a great, yearning sadness appears in their eyes, as the soul within the imprisoning form becomes more and more conscious of the limitations imposed on it by the animal body. If it have the necessary courage and intelligence, we need not wonder that it decides to burst the bonds that bind it.

It is not often that animals attempt such violent methods as those chosen by "Major," but everyone knows of some instance of an animal in great sorrow starving itself to death.

BIBLIOGRAPHY

A Treatise of Bodies, by Sir Kenelm Digby, p. 321, ed. 1644.
History of the World, by Sir Walter Raleigh.
Folk-lore in the Old Testament, by Sir James George Frazer.
Abbeys, Castles, and Ancient Halls of England and Wales, by John Timbs. (Fredk. Warne & Co. London.)

CHAPTER XXXI

Lucky and Unlucky Coloration of Horses

ALTHOUGH it has been said that " a good horse is never a bad colour," yet to own a piebald is supposed to be very unlucky, and we find an example of this superstition recorded in the *Daily Express* of February 24, 1922, which well illustrates how hardly such beliefs die. Even in this age of motors and materialism, the lower classes, at least, acknowledge their sway. Here is the paragraph :

HORSE OF ILL-OMEN

Do Piebalds Bring Bad Luck ?

" ' I intended to have the horse killed because I believe that piebalds bring me bad luck,' said Samuel Phillips, who appeared at Hythe Police Court yesterday on a charge of working an unfit horse. It was stated that the horse had been destroyed since the summons was issued. The hearing was adjourned."

As a corrective to this idea we advise our reader to turn to the legend of Sharatz (i.e. piebald), which will be found in the chapter on Fairy Horses.

The Sieur de Solleysell, however, tells us there is a reason why piebalds are " reputed defective," which is " that the phlegme which is betokened by the White Hair, doth too much predomine, and make them weaker than otherwise they would be."

The same authority tells us that the white horse " is Watry and Phlegmatick, and consequently dull and soft." But he leaves us in the dark as to the sort of luck attached to this colour.

According to a Yorkshire superstition, to meet a white horse when leaving home is bad, and he who would avert the omen must spit on the ground ; but we have shown in our chapter on Charm and Incantation that the white horse confers peculiar powers on its owner.

The Hungarians hold a firm belief that a man who is mounted upon a black horse is more successful in war than when upon a horse of any other colour ; and the Spaniards also think black horses specially fortunate, and have an ancient proverb to the effect that those are happy who possess a coal-black horse with no white upon him ("Morsille sin sennal muchos lo quieren, y pocos lo han ").

In France, on the other hand, black horses are regarded as unlucky, and especially so if they are without white markings.

From *Notes and Queries* we learn that there is a certain amount of good or bad luck attached to horses which have one or more white feet or legs.

It is very lucky to be the owner of a horse with the forelegs having equal white stockings ; but if one foreleg and one hindleg on the same side are white, it is unlucky. It is also unlucky if only one leg of the four is white stocking'd ; but if opposite legs, as off fore and near hind, are white, it is very lucky. Most people know the old rhyme about buying white-footed horses :

> One, buy me,
> Two, try me,
> Three, shy me,
> Four, fly me.

In Devonshire the following amplified version is found :

> If you have a horse with four white legs,
> Keep him not a day ;
> If you have a horse with three white legs,
> Send him far away ;
> If you have a horse with two white legs,
> Sell him to a friend ;
> If you have a horse with one white leg,
> Keep him to his end.

But according to the author of *The Compleat Horseman*, from whom we now quote, the matter is by no means so easily settled.

"A horse which hath his far-hind foot White, although he have other good qualities, and may be esteemed good by some actions he may discover to us, yet it is rarely a good mark, and such a horse is also lookt upon to be unluckie in a day of Battle ; but if he have either a Star, Ratch or Blaze, which is a kind of White face, they will diminish somewhat of his badness and being so unfortunate ; such Horses are called in French *Chevaux Arzels,* and the Spanish proverb saith *Cavallo Arzel, guardaze del* ; I have known very skilful people, who would not have bought a Horse at a great rate which had this mark of a White far hind foot, although he had been never so good ; but for my part, I would not slip such a good opportunity, even although I should be obliged to make use of him in the Warrs; if a Man be so superstitious as to believe such a Horse misfortunate in Warr, let him then in God's name keep him for time of peace ; for if the Horse had otherways all the good qualities required in a fine Horse, and that he were not of too extraordinary a rate, I would buy him without much considering his being *Arzel,* or having a White far hind foot. . . . To have only the near hind foot White, is a good mark, and if the Horse have also with it a Star in his Forehead, it is the best of all Marks, and is very rarely known to fail, for me I never knew many bad Horses with this Mark. In *Germany* they have such an esteem for it, that it will make them heighten considerably a Horses price, and if with this Mark he also raise his feet well, that is, have a good movement with his Legs when Trotting, it will double his price in a publick Faire. . . . To have only the two Fore-feet White is a bad Mark, but not very common ; I have known but few Horses which had this Mark, neither were they very much worth, and they are also lookt upon to be unluckie : if the Horse had with this Mark one of his hind-feet White, and had likewise a Star in his Fore-head, this would in some measure diminish the badness of his Mark, but not wholly. Such Horses as have too much White upon their Face, are said to have moist Brains, and consequently to be subject to many infirmities, especially those which proceed from a cold and moist cause. . . . A Horse which hath two White hind feet is well marked.

should be ranked amongst those which are good, and should be esteemed fortunate, especially if he have also a Star in his forehead. . . . Those Horses which have three White Feet, with a Star in their forehead, are by the Italians called *Kingly Horses*, but for what reason I know not, for I don't see that they are better than others. But perhaps they call them Kingly, because horses which are kept in Kings Stables work little, and that a horse which hath three White feet, being proper but for a moderate Labour or exercise, is therefore only fit for a King. . . .

"A Horse which hath only two feet of a side White is called *Tramled* or *Traversed* because of the resemblance those White feet have to the hoses of a half Tramel ; it is a bad mark, and besides that such horses are subject to fall and stumble, they are also lookt upon not to be good. Again a horse which is Cross-White-Footed, that is, which hath only his near fore-foot and far hind-foot White, is called *Cross Tramled* or *Cross Traversed* because of the same resemblance of the hoses of a half Tramel . . . ; this mark is worse than *Arzel*, . . . and although the horse have a Star with it, yet he is not much the better for it. A Horse which hath his far fore-foot and near hind-foot White is Cross Tramled or Cross Traversed as well as the preceding, because of his White feet not being both upon one side, but Cross-ways, and it is a mark not much better than the former, although many people look upon it to be a very good one, especially if the horse have a Star with it ; but I have observed the contrary. . . . The Star in the forehead diminishes indeed a little of the badness of the mark, but doth not rectifie it wholly. . . . It is a received Maxim, that the higher the White of any Horses feet ascends upon the legs, he is so much the worse, because he thereby resembles so much the more the Pye-balds, of which there are few to be found good, and people also say of such horses that their stockings are pulled too high. . . .

"A Star alone in the fore-head is lookt upon to be a very good Mark. . . . Horses which are all over of one colour, are called in France, *Zains*. The Darker colour a *Zain* horse be of, he is so much the worse and of less value, and people say of them all, that they are either Devils or Daws, that is, either very good or very bad."

Our author also informs us that the old French word *chanfrain* is used " to signifie that the Star in the fore-head extends downwards almost to the nose, without however being either so broad above as to touch the Eye-Brows, or extending so much downward as to go to the very tip of the nose ; such Horses are also called White-faced, and the mark is passably good : but if the White either touch the Eye-Brows, or extending so much downwards as to go to the very tip of the Nose, then it will be bad ; people commonly say of such a Horse, that his Star is a drinking, or that he drinketh out of his White, which last is but a bad expression."

What but misfortune could befall the steed whose star was so badly employed ? Let him who would purchase a horse beware, for our friend assures us " the whole foundation and certainty of observation which people draw " from these varied markings " proceeds only from experience which is our sole guide in this matter, . . . so that the grounds of Law and Equity with which many people are so mightily taken, and in a manner infatuate, have not a more sure foundation than these observations."

BIBLIOGRAPHY

The Compleat Horseman : discovering the Surest Marks of the Beauty, Goodness, Faults, and Imperfections of Horses, . . . By the Sieur de Solleysell, Querry to the present *French* King for his Great Horses, and one of the Royal Academy of *Paris.* . . . Made *English* from the Eighth Edition of the Original. London, . . . MDCXCVI.

Notes and Queries, Fifth Series, Vol. VII, p. 64.

M. Oldfield Howey.

CHAPTER XXXII

Centaurs, Hyppogryphs, and Unicorns

ACCORDING to the poets of ancient Greece, there lived in Thessaly a race of beings, half man, half horse in form, called centaurs. They were said to have derived from a union of Ixion and Nephele (a Cloud), or according to other authorities to be the offspring of Centaurus, the son of Apollo, and Stilbia, the daughter of Peneus. They were rude and savage beings typifying the destructive and uncontrollable forces of nature, but Chiron, the wise instructor of Achilles, and Pholus, the friend of Hercules, were beneficent centaurs.

Originally the centaur was represented in art as a complete man to whose body were attached behind the barrel and hind-quarters of a horse ; but later this ungraceful form was abandoned, and was universally replaced by one in which the human body to the waist took the place of the head and neck of the horse. Examples of the earlier type still survive on archaic painted vases, and in a few small vases, terra-cottas, etcetera, and also among the reliefs from the temple of Assos and in certain wall-paintings.

The cause of the famous battle between the centaurs and the Lapithæ was a dispute which arose at the marriage of Hippodamia

(Horse-tamer) and Pirithous, ruler of the Lapithæ, the descendants of Lapithes, son of Apollo. The centaurs attempted to carry off the bride and other women from the wedding-feast, and Theseus aided the Lapithæ in chastising them for this outrage. Combats between Lapithæ and centaurs were a favourite subject with Greek artists and were pictured in the metopes of the Parthenon, part of which

BATTLE BETWEEN CENTAURS AND LAPITHÆ.
From an old woodcut, Augsburg, 1681.

are now in the British Museum, and were also represented on the Phigaleian frieze, which is likewise in the British Museum.

The most celebrated of the centaurs was Chiron, whose accomplishments included astronomy, music, hunting, medicine, surgery, botany, and justice.

He lived, whilst on earth, in a grotto at the foot of Mount Pelion, which his reputation for knowledge made the most famous school in Greece. Achilles and Hercules were among his pupils. The Argonauts visited him and Orpheus sang before him. He was known as the "Divine Beast." After his death he was placed by Jupiter among the stars. There he is known as Sagittarius, the Archer. The constellation bearing his name is situated in the southern zodiac below Aquila, between Scorpius and Capricornus, and is, especially in the latitudes of the southern United States, a prominent object in the heavens on summer evenings. The symbol of the constellation ♐ shows the Archer's arrow and part of his bow.

A FEMALE CENTAUR.
From a bronze relief of Greek workmanship discovered at Pompeii.

In the *Destruction of Troy* there is an account of "a marvellous beast that was called Sagittary," whose characteristics are circumstantially related by Lydgate:

CHIRON TEACHING THE YOUNG ACHILLES TO PLAY UPON THE LYRE.

From a painting discovered during the excavations at Herculaneum. The engraving is taken from *Grecian Stories*, by Maria Hack. (Published by Harvey & Darton, London, 1819.)

And with him Guido saith that he had
A wonder archer of sight mervaylous
Of form and shape in manner monstrous:
For like mine auctour as I rehearse can,
Fro the navel upward he was man,
And lower down like a horse yshaped:
And thilke part that after man was maked
Of skin was black and rough as any bear,
Cover'd with hair fro cold him for to wear.
Passing foul and horrible of sight,
Whose eyes twain were sparkling as bright
As is a furnace with his red leven,
Or the lightning that falleth from the heaven;
Dreadful of look, and red as fire of cheer,
And, as I read, he was a good archer;
And with his bow both at even and morrow
Upon Greeks he wrought much sorrow.

Shakespeare refers to this monster in the play *Troilus and Cressida*, where

Agamemnon is represented as saying : " The dreadful Sagittary appals our numbers."

The southern constellation known as " the Centaur " is situated under Virgo and Libra, and must not be confounded with Sagittarius. It is evidently connected with Lupus (the Wolf) and Ara (the Altar). Ptolemy's *Catalogue* makes it plain that he considered the Centaur to be holding the Wolf (or Wild Beast) in one hand, whilst in the other he grasped the Bacchic Thyrsus. From the close proximity of Ara, it is plain that a sacrifice is alluded to. According to Grotius (notes on Aratus), the Thyrsus used to be pictured with a hare hanging from it. Centaurs are among the terrors seen by Dante in his *Vision of Hell*, and Gustave Doré's beautiful pictures of them have made their form acceptable and almost familiar to our eyes. According to Dante, Chiron's mission is far from being a heavenly one, for it is to guard the lake of boiling blood in the seventh circle of Hell, wherein are confined those who have been guilty of crimes of violence. He is assisted by a troop of centaurs armed with bows and arrows with which they shoot at those who try to escape from their terrible doom.

Another famous Italian poet, Torquator Tasso, in his heroic poem *Jerusalem Delivered*, names the centaurs as being among the Gods of Hell summoned in council by Pluto (Bk. IV., l. 33).

It is indeed difficult to imagine that a being so noble and beautiful as Chiron could occupy himself in the terrible task assigned to him by Dante and other Christian poets, but all the centaurs of ancient legend were not equally good and wise, as we have already noted. Shakespeare thus refers to these beings :

> Come, come, be every one officious
> To make this banquet, which I wish may prove
> More stern and bloody than the Centaur's feast.
> (*Titus Andronicus*, V. 2.)

Virgil in the *Æneid* also mentions the centaurs as being inhabitants of Hell, but when Æneas would have slain these and other monsters and rushed upon them with his sword, his guide warned him that they were only shadows.

Dante informs us that Virgil was his guide through Hell, and after they had together viewed the centaurs carrying out their awful mission, Virgil prevailed upon Chiron to grant them Nessus to conduct them safely across the ford. Nessus is properly assigned this task, for Sophocles says of this centaur :

> He in his arms across Evenus' stream
> Deep-flowing, bore the passengers for hire,
> Without or sail or billow-cleaving oar.

Dante says :

>   Chiron thus
> To Nessus spake : " Return and be their guide.
> And if you chance to cross another troop,
> Command them keep aloof."   Onward we moved,
> The faithful escort by our side, along
> The border of the crimson-seething flood,
> Whence from those steeped within, loud shrieks arose.

Dante vividly describes the awful scene before them when first they arrive at the centaur-guarded river of blood :

> I beheld an ample fosse, that in a bow was bent,
> As circling all the plain. . . .
>   . . . Between it and the ramparts base,
> On trail ran Centaurs, with keen arrows armed,
> As to the chase they on the earth were wont.
>   At seeing us descend they each one stood ;
> And issuing from the troop, three sped with bows
> And missile weapons chosen first ; of whom
> One cried from far : " Say, to what pain ye come
> Condemned, who down this steep have journeyed. Speak
> From whence ye stand, or else the bow I draw ! "
>   To whom my guide : " Our answer shall be made
> To Chiron, there, when nearer him we come.
> Ill was thy mind, thus ever quick and rash."
> Then me he touched, and spake : " Nessus is this,
> Who for the fair Deianira died,
> And wrought himself revenge for his own fate.
> He in the midst, that on his breast looks down,
> Is the great Chiron who Achilles nursed ;

That other, Pholus, prone to wrath." Around
The fosse these go by thousands, aiming shafts
At whatsoever spirit dares emerge
From out the blood more than his guilt allows.

(*Hell*, Canto XII, ll. 49–72.)

The story of Nessus, unlike that of Chiron, reveals a cruel and treacherous nature not out of harmony with the hellish work on which Dante found him engaged. We have already noted his earthly occupation had been the carrying of passengers over the River Evenus. One day when the river was particularly turbulent and swollen by violent rains, Hercules, with his newly-made and hardly-won bride Deianeira, was pondering how he might safely convey himself and her to the farther side. As he stood hesitating, unable to see how to overcome the difficulty, Nessus trotted up to him and offered to take Deianeira across the stream on his back, if she would but entrust herself to his care and consent to mount. Hercules, all unsuspecting of treachery, at once accepted the offer and assisted his bride into place. He himself then struggled through the torrent in their wake, holding aloft his bow and arrows. But no sooner had Nessus reached the opposite bank than he started to gallop off with his fair rider, hoping to escape before Hercules could assist her. A loud cry from Deianeira attracted her bridegroom's attention, and a second later the centaur lay dying, pierced by a poisoned arrow at his heart. With his last breath he professed himself repentant, and told Deianeira to take as a parting gift his robe, but slightly stained with the blood that gushed from the poisoned wound. He said it had magical power, and if her husband's love for her ever waned, and she could induce him to put on the robe, it would return with all its first fervour.

Deianeira gratefully accepted the gift, but for many years had no occasion to use it. Those who were in trouble often came from afar to seek the aid of Hercules, the fame of his strength and goodness having travelled over the world, and the missions he undertook to help those in distress often took him away from his wife for long periods. On one occasion he had been absent even longer than usual and Deianeira had become terribly anxious. Then she heard that he was returning accompanied by his old love Iole and a numerous train.

> Then I,
> Mingling despair with love, rapt in deep joy
> That he was come, plunged in the depths of hell
> That she came too, bethought me of the robe
> The Centaur gave me, and the words he spake,
> Forgetting the deep hatred in his eyes,
> And all but love, and sent a messenger
> Bidding him wear it for the sacrifice
> To the Immortals, knowing not at all
> Whom fate decreed the victim.
>
> (Sir Lewis Morris.)

After this terrible tragedy poor Deianeira strangled herself, hoping to join her beloved on the other side ; but even there she found herself separated from him by her error and condemned to existence in Hades. Jupiter had caught from the altar the noble soul of Hercules, and had borne him to Olympus to dwell for ever with the gods.

Sir Lewis Morris ends the wonderful and sympathetic poem from which we have just quoted on a note of hope.   Deianeira says :

> " I am forgiven, I know,
> Who loved so much, and one day, if Zeus will,
> I shall go free from hence, and join my Lord,
> And be with him again."

Perhaps the nearest approach to a centaur in British mythology is provided by King Mark, or March of Cornwall (*marc* = " horse " ; *marach* = " rider ").   This hero is said to have had horse's ears and was a Celtic Midas, though his Phrygian counterpart had asses' ears. He is found in Gælic as well as British myth as a deity of the underworld.

The Irish " morc " also has horse's ears, and seems to be a sort of centaur, sharing the qualities of man and horse.   He was originally a king of the Fomors.

The mythical king of early Ireland, Labraid Loṅgsech, was another horse-eared man.

Farther afield the centaur loses in grace and beauty, and becomes more demoniacal in form and character.   One of the monstrous deities of the later Indian Buddhists is an example.   This god is known as " the Horse-necked Tamdin," and together with his spouse—a fury with a pig's face known as " the Thunderbolt Sow "—was given the task of defending Buddhism against its enemies.

The Hyppogryph, or Hippogriff (there are various spellings of the name, which is derived from two Greek words—*hippos*, " a horse," and *gryphos*, " a griffin "), was a fabulous winged creature, its forequarters resembling a griffin, but its barrel and hindparts being those of a horse. It symbolises love, and was probably invented in imitation of Pegasus by the romancers of the Middle Ages so as to give their heroes a means of transportation through the air.

Thus Milton alludes to it :

> He caught him up, and, without wing
> Of hippogrif, bore through the air sublime.
> (Paradise Regained, IV. 542.)

And Scott refers to it, saying : " It reminded me of the Magician Atlantes on his hippogriff " (*Redgauntlet*, letter iv.).

Wieland sings :

> Saddle the Hippogriffs, ye Muses nine,
> And straight we'll ride to the land of old Romance.

Heraldry has made us all familiar with the graceful outline of the Unicorn or Monoceros, the beautiful salient supporter of the royal arms of Britain. This delightful, compound creature has the head, neck, and body of the horse, the legs of the stag, the tail of the lion, and a long twisted horn upon its forehead. Its origin may be traced to the accounts of such an animal bequeathed to us by certain ancient writers whom we now uncharitably think were not remarkable for their veracity.

Ctesias, writing about 400 B.C., thus describes these animals :

" The *Onoi agrioi* are as large as horses, and even larger, with white bodies, red heads, blue eyes, and have each on their foreheads a horn a cubit and a half long, the base of which is white, the upper part red, the middle part black. Drinking cups are formed of these horns ; and those who drink out of them are said to be subject neither to spasm nor epilepsy, nor to the effects of poison."

This curative effect of the unicorn's horn is referred to by Purchas.

He says : " The roots of Mandioca had almost killed them all, but by a peece of Vnicorne's horne they were preserued " (*Pilgrimage*, p. 841).

Pliny, writing A.D. 70, varies slightly from the above in his description of this creature.   He says :

" The Orsœan Indians hunt a very fierce animal, called the monoceros, which has the body of a horse, the head of a stag, the feet of an elephant and the tail of a wild boar ; it utters a deep lowing noise, and has a single horn, two cubits long, projecting from the middle of its forehead."

And Ælian, a Roman citizen, who wrote about the middle part of the third century of the Christian era *On the Peculiarities of Animals*, gives us a similar account.   He writes :

" The monoceros is as big as a full-grown horse, with a mane and yellow woolly hair, of greatest swiftness, with feet like the elephant, and the tail of a wild boar.   It has a black horn growing between the eyebrows, which is not smooth, but with natural twistings, and is very sharp at the point.   It utters loud, harsh sounds.   It lives peaceably with other animals, but quarrels with those of its own kind, the males even destroying the females, excepting at breeding-time, at which season the animals are gregarious ; but at other times they live in solitude in wild regions."

Sir John Mandeville, in a narrative of his travels written about 1360 and dedicated to Edward III, also mentions the unicorn, though alas ! his reputation for truthfulness is not all it might be.   So many and great marvels does he describe that those who read them doubt. He writes : " In that Contre ben manye white Olifantes with outen nombre, and of Unycornes, and of Lyouns of many maneres, and many of suche Bestes that I have told before, and of many other hydouse Bestes withouten nombre."

Where the unicorn is referred to in the Bible, it is said to be a mistranslation of the Hebrew word " re'ēm," which in the Revised Version is translated " wild ox," so I have not quoted from this source.

BIBLIOGRAPHY

The Vision of Hell, by Dante Alighieri, translated by the Rev. Henry Francis Cary, M.A. (Cassell, London, Paris & New York.)

Metamorphoses, L. ix, Ovid.

Trachiniæ, 570, Sophocles.

The Works of Sir Lewis Morris. (Osgood, McIlvaine & Co., London, 1896.)

Lhasa and its Mysteries, by L. Austine Waddell, LL.D., C.B., etc. (John Murray, London, 1905.)

Studies in the Arthurian Legend, by John Rhys. (Oxford, 1901.)

The National Encyclopædia, by Writers of Eminence. (Wm. Mackenzie, London.)

Purchas his Pilgrimage, or Relations of the World, and the Religions observed in all Ages and Places discovered, from the Creation unto this Present. (Folio, 1613.)

Travels, by Sir John de Mandeville. (Wynkyn de Worde, Westminster, 1499.)

INDEX